NEVER BE SILENT

PUBLISHING & IMPERIALISM IN KENYA
1884 - 1963

SHIRAZ DURRANI

Vita Books, P.O. Box 2908, London N17 6YY, UK

**Never Be Silent
Publishing and Imperialism in Kenya
1884 - 1963**

PUBLISHERS
Vita Books, P.O. Box 2908, London N17 6YY, UK
books@vitabooks.info

www.vitabooks.info

COPYRIGHT
Shiraz Durrani © 2006

creative
commons
COMMONS DEED

This is an Open Access publication distributed under the terms of the
Creative Commons Attribution License
(http://creativecommons.org/licenses/by/2.0),
which permits unrestricted use, distribution, and reproduction in any
medium, provided the original work is properly cited.

Mau Mau Research Centre,
PO Box 138-28 107th Avenue
South Richmond Hill Station, Jamaica, NY 11419, USA

ISBN
978-1-869886-05-9

FIRST EDITION
2006

DESIGN & LAYOUT
Lakhvir Singh
www.scorpiusink.com

Typset in Baskerville

PRINTERS
Zand Graphics Ltd, PO Box 32843 00600, Nairobi. Kenya

VITA BOOKS DISTRIBUTORS

Eastern and Southern Africa
Zand Graphics Ltd, PO Box 32843 00600, Nairobi • Tel 0722 344900 • Email zand.graphics@gmail.com

Vita Books/MMRC in Kenya
P.O. Box 79711, Nairobi, Kenya.

Europe
Africa Book Centre / Global Book Marketing, 38 King Street, London, WC2E 8JT

USA
Mau Mau Research Centre, 138-28 107th Avenue, Jamaica, NY 11435 USA

WE WILL NEVER BE SILENT [1]

On January 7th we were surrounded at Bahati
by the colonial army.

We will never be silent
until we get land to cultivate
and freedom in this country of ours, Kenya.

Home Guards were the first to go and close the gates
and Johnnies entered while the police surrounded the location.
You, traitors! You dislike your children,
caring only for your stomachs;
You are the enemies of our people.

We will never be silent
until we get land to cultivate
and freedom in this country of ours, Kenya.

---

[1] Mau Mau liberation song, quoted in Mathu (1974), pp. 23-24.

POVERTY CAN BE STOPPED

"The poor are the Mau Mau. Poverty can be stopped, but not by bombs and weapons from the imperialists. Only the revolutionary justice of the struggles of the poor can end poverty for Kenyans."

KIMAATHI WA WACHIURI
in a letter he wrote from his headquarters in Nyandarua in 1955 to the Nairobi newspaper Habari za Dunia

contents

INTRODUCTION
A VOICE OF SILENCE - NGUGI WA THIONG'O i
HISTORICAL PERSPECTIVE - MARIKA SHERWOOD iv
BREAKING THE CULTURE OF SILENCE - SHIRAZ DURRANI vii
A NOTE ON TERMINOLOGY x

CHAPTER ONE
A HISTORY OF PUBLISHING . . . A HISTORY OF STRUGGLES 13

CHAPTER TWO
1884 - 1922: RESISTANCE OF NATIONALITIES 22
SETTLER AND COLONIAL GOVERNMENT PUBLICATIONS 29
CHURCH PUBLICATIONS 31
SOUTH ASIAN PUBLICATIONS 34
AFRICAN PUBLICATIONS 44

CHAPTER THREE
1922 - 1948: CONSOLIDATION OF WORKING CLASS 51
NATIONALIST AND WORKING CLASS POLITICS 53
SETTLER PUBLICATIONS 55
CHURCH PUBLICATIONS 60
COLONIAL GOVERNMENT PUBLICATIONS 61
SOUTH ASIAN PUBLICATIONS 62
AFRICAN PUBLICATIONS 67
TRADE UNION MOVEMENT LEADS THE WAY 74

CHAPTER FOUR
KISWAHILI RESISTANCE PUBLISHING AT THE COAST 85
EARLY KISWAHILI EPICS 85
KISWAHILI BOOK PRODUCTION 88
KISWAHILI AS A LANGUAGE OF RESISTANCE 89

CHAPTER FIVE
1948-1963: MAU MAU REVOLUTIONARY STRUGGLE 97
A HIDDEN HISTORY 98

LEGAL ASPECTS OF PUBLISHING	103
THE ESTABLISHMENT OF LIBERATED TERRITORIES	119
COLONIAL GOVERNMENT PUBLICATIONS	126
SETTLER PUBLICATIONS	129
SOUTH ASIAN PUBLISHING	139
THE MAU MAU COMMUNICATION STRATEGY	153
ORAL COMMUNICATIONS	157
REVOLUTIONARY PUBLISHING	176
PREPARATION FOR ARMED PHASE	189
SOME PRESS PROFILES	200
PAMPHLETS, HANDBILLS AND LETTERS	212
ESTABLISHMENT OF A PEOPLE'S PRESS	216

CHAPTER SIX
OVERSEAS SUPPORT FOR KENYA LIBERATION — 222

UK	223
CANADA	228
USSR	229
EGYPT	230
IRELAND	230
INDIA	231
USA	231
TRINIDAD	232

CHAPTER SEVEN
INDEPENDENCE AND NEO-COLONIALISM — 233

"THE STRUGGLE FOR KENYA'S FUTURE"	235

CHAPTER EIGHT
CONCLUSION: NEVER BE SILENT — 239

BIBLIOGRAPHY — 241

APPENDIX A: SELECTED LISTS — 252

NEWSPAPERS	252
PUBLISHERS	262
INFORMATION ACTIVISTS	264
KENYAN NEWSPAPERS AVAILABLE IN THE BRITISH LIBRARY	264

APPENDIX B: BANNED IMPORTS, A SELECTED LIST — 267

INDEX — 269

YOU CANNOT UNEDUCATE
THE PERSON

Once social change begins, it cannot be reversed. You cannot uneducate the person who has learned to read. You cannot humiliate the person who feels pride. You cannot oppress the people who are not afraid anymore.

- CESAR CHAVEZ [2]

[2] Cesar Chavez founded United Farm Workers of America, AFL-CIO in 1962. Quoted by Dana Lubow in a posting to owner-PLGNet-L@listproc.sjsu.edu on 2 April 2005. Details about the United Farm Workers of America are available from www.ufw.org [accessed 3 April, 2005]

INTRODUCTION

A voice of silence

NGUGI WA THIONG'O

Information is power in war and peace. But information, particularly in the struggle between the dominated and the dominating, is never neutral. The dominating try to control the sources, agents and contents of information. They want the dominated to view the world through the filters of the dominating. What they choose to package, how they package it, and even how, when and where they choose to spread the packaged information are all geared to realising their strategic and tactical ends of dominating. But the dominated do not just absorb the information as packaged. They will read between and behind the lines. But more important they will also try to collect and package information which will counter that of their enemies. For in order for them to struggle with a measure of success they must arm their minds with the correct data of what is really going on around them. The packaged information of the dominating aims at creating confusion or silence among the dominated. The packaged information of the dominated aims at providing clarity and voice to their struggle. It gives voice to silence. Never be Silent in word, mind and spirit becomes their motto, law and order. Information is therefore a site of intense struggle and nowhere is this better illustrated than in a colonial situation.

All this, and more, is very well captured in Durrani's narrative of publishing in Kenya from the times of the Berlin Conference of 1884 to the Lancaster House Conference of 1963. And what a tremendous exemplary effort it is covering as it does the entire colonial period of Kenyan history from the earliest information bulletins of the colonial settler state to the Mau Mau publishing efforts in the fifties and sixties! Information in the print and oral media was vital to the resistance struggles of the Kenyan people and contributed in a large measure to their very successes. And that is why the British and the colonial state spent so much energy not only in producing counter-propaganda but also used the legal system to ban the information emanating from those on the side of the Kenya people's struggle. In a sense Durrani's narrative documents the monumental failure on the part of the colonial machine and independence of the country in 1963 is a proof of that failure or in another sense a proof of the success of the information strategies and tactics of the Kenyan anti-colonial struggle.

That is why it is impossible to read this fascinating drama without realising the enormity of the ideological crimes perpetrated by the successive post-colonial KANU regimes against the Kenyan people. These regimes have literally tried to take the colonial measures and practices a stage further. Where, for instance, in pre-independence Kenya there were several newspapers and magazines in African languages, these regimes ensured that for more than twenty-five years, there were hardly any meaningful newspapers or magazines in African languages. Where, in colonial Kenya, there were radio stations catering to the various regions in their dominant languages, the post-colonial regimes ensured that such did not exist. Where, in colonial times, there were thriving trade unions, civic societies, cultural groups, the post-colonial regimes ensured that in the new Kenya there would not be any space for free trade union and cultural activities. But they should also have learnt well from the drama outlined in Durrani's narrative: that no amount of state anti-people propaganda can actually eliminate the correct information arising from a people's own experience of reality. If people are getting low wages, or are being tortured, or subjected to genocide, no amounts of information trying to convince them of the contrary can actually succeed; that in the end people will struggle to create their own information systems to meet the needs of the struggle. So that although the narrative ends with the year of independence in 1963, it has a lot to teach Kenyans in their current struggles for national liberation and social revolution.

This book is a wealth of resource data and should be of interest to historians, political scientists, cultural workers, and all those engaged in active struggle. It is information. It is drama. It is history. It is also a salute to the spirit of struggle.

CONSPIRACY OF SILENCE

Our plea to break the conspiracy of silence about the Kenya Land and Freedom Army struggle includes also a plea for a more serious study of the history of Kenya since the Second World War and more particularly since 1952. [3]

THE STORY OF MAU MAU

The story of Mau Mau should be studied carefully for the lessons that can be learnt from such a bitter failure. Political independence without genuine decolonisation and socialism yields continued misery and oppression for the peasant-worker masses. Karigo's prayer [See Muchai, 1973] – "I only pray that after independence our children will not be forced to fight again" – as with those of other peasants and workers caught up in the web of neo-colonial accommodation after long years of struggle, will not be answered. His and their children *will* be forced to fight again.
BARNETT (1972)

---

[3] The plea is made by B.M. Kaggia, Fred Kubai, J. Murumbi, and Achieng Oneko. See Barnett, Donald and Njama, Karari (1966). Preface. p.ii.

Historical Perspective

MARIKA SHERWOOD

A fundamental requirement for the struggle for equality and freedom is for like-minded people to recognise and then to be able to communicate with each other. Another requirement is to inform the opposition and if possible a wider audience of your critique, your perspective and your aims and demands. One way to fulfil these requirements is through the printed word.

One of the problems faced by colonial rulers was how to disseminate information. They had to convince the subject population to accept their overlords and point out the futility of resistance. But, if they encouraged the teaching of spoken and written English, the 'natives' would be able to read not only material reinforcing British superiority and right to rule, but also what would be considered 'subversive' literature.

Literacy education thus had to be accompanied by very strict controls. The imperialists could not risk the free availability of criticism. Nor could they possibly condone the publication of histories of struggle against imperialism, or the entrenchment of such struggles into the histories and traditions of those they occupied.

What this book does is set out the history of publishing in the very complex colony of Kenya. How was it complex? It was the home of diverse African peoples speaking different languages and with different cultures and social structures. As the Africans could not be coerced to do the work, or were deemed too unskilled, from 1896 the British colonial masters imported workers from India to build the Kenya-Uganda railway. With a healthier climate than that of West Africa, Kenya was a settler colony: by 1921 there were some 10,000 European residents. The intention of many settlers was to farm the good – the best – Kenyan lands. This meant the forcible displacement of Africans. Naturally they resisted.

Publication thus became crucial both for control purposes and for communication. The first in the control league was the Universities' Mission to Central Africa, who began publication in 1887. While Christianity was used to subjugate, it has to be admitted that some missionaries also transcribed previously unwritten languages and collected some oral histories and myths, of course to use for their own purposes. Some of these ubiquitous and diverse missionaries were also landowners, while spreading a creed which encompassed the acceptance of a man always depicted as a European as the son of the all-powerful Christian God of the rulers of Kenya.

The first settler publication, *The Weekly Mail*, began to appear in 1899; it and its peers and successors, were devoted to settler interests. The first national paper to oppose racial differentiation and to publish commercial and government information was started by an Indian, A.M. Jeevanjee, clearly a man trying to survive as a 'middle-class' Indian, who was probably as far removed from the Indian workers as from Africans and Whites. The first paper in Kiswahili, *Wahindi*, which 'reflected the growing links between the progressive Asian and African peoples', was closed down and its publisher, Chatrabh Bhat had to move to Dar es Salaam to continue publishing. 1919 saw the publication of the first bilingual (Gujarati-English) paper, the *East African Chronicle*, published by Manilal Desai in 1919. Desai was president of the East African Indian National Congress so we should not be surprised to learn the he published the articles and pamphlets of Harry Thuku, the African nationalist leader.

This excellently researched book traces the history of publication chronologically, as indicated above, and gives the full political context of each period. There is thorough discussion of government reactions and suppressions as well as of the relationships between African and Indian political activists. The 'Mau-Mau' period is dealt with very fully and greatly enhances the understandings one gained from the autobiographies of the freedom fighters as well as from the diverse histories of that freedom movement. There is also an excellent section on the overseas support for the

Land and Freedom Army and a list of banned publications.

Reading this well-documented history of the struggles in Kenya for free expression should make us reflect on the applicability of those struggles to the so-called civilised world today. Is it possible to exercise the same degree of censorship? Is it still possible to jail those who raise their voices? Or do we employ different techniques today to achieve the same ends? Why does the premier of Italy feel the need to control the sources of information in his country? What is the influence exerted by Rupert Murdoch on the media in the USA and the UK and why have these governments acceded to this level of control? How much of what we read in the papers, or hear on the radio or TV can we believe?

As a historian I must mention another crucial aspect of the politics of publication. For events beyond the range of oral history and the vigilance of intelligence services (whose reports are frequently withheld from the public), we have to rely on newspapers for stories – the histories – of struggles and resistance to injustices, to oppression, to inequalities. We historians will write the histories from reading these articles and pamphlets as well as from the material released by government. If those who want to recruit support, or at least present a countervailing perspective on issues, which is surely a hallmark of democracy, cannot publish freely, the histories we write will be biased and incomplete. We will be presenting a history of the rulers, not of the ruled. This is wholly unacceptable in a democracy.

Shiraz Durrani's book warns us of these dangers by demonstrating how the power of the state was employed in Kenya and the urgent need then – as now – for freedom of communication and association.

Marika Sherwood is Senior Research Fellow, Institute of Commonwealth Studies, University of London; Editor, *Black & Asian Studies Association* Newsletter

Breaking the culture of silence

SHIRAZ DURRANI

The idea of writing this book was born when a group of progressive librarians at the University of Nairobi were searching for relevance in the information field in Kenya by organising a workshop at the Kabete Campus of the University of Nairobi in 1979. I decided to look at the history of mass communication and publishing to see what lessons could be learnt from those experiences. I presented a short version of my paper at the workshop. The fuller version was too big for inclusion in the proceedings of the Workshop which carried another paper I wrote.[4]

But the subject matter of the paper on publishing became an obsession with me the more I read. The fascinating struggles in the information field that unfolded with each new angle explored began to reflect the totality of anti-imperialist struggles in Kenya. I needed to devote more time to the research into publishing. I planned to take sabbatical leave in 1985 to research at the Kenya Archives as well as the Colonial Office files. But the research seemed to take a life of its own and in a curious turn of events became "political" and led to my exile to Britain in 1984.

In the early 1980s, the underground opposition to the KANU-Moi regime penetrated every field of activity. It was led by December Twelve Movement which published its own underground newspaper - *Pambana* - and which circulated widely throughout the country. The students at the University of Nairobi joined hands with the underground resistance. They lost no opportunity to attack the regime in every possible way. One of the ways was to publish progressive material on the history of resistance and the progressive anti-imperialist stand of the Kenyan people of all nationalities. A new generation was growing up, they argued, without the awareness of the real history of struggle that created the current society. They approached me in early 1994 for help in some aspects of their publication, *The University Platform*. They also wanted me to write articles on the history of Kenya from

---

[4] "Agri-Vet information: production, organisation, storage and retrieval". University of Nairobi Library Magazine (Nairobi). 2 (23-37) 1979.

a working class point of view. I provided three articles, two from my research on the history of publishing: one on Pio Gama Pinto and the other on Kimaathi.[5] The third was an article I had written as part of the publicity of the progressive play *Kinjikitile – Maji Maji* which was directed by Naila Durrani and staged to full houses at the Education Theatre by the Takhto Arts of Nairobi in conjunction with the University Library's Sehemu ya Utungaji ("creative wing") which I had set up with a group of progressive library workers.

All three articles proved popular and I decided to give them wider circulation. 1984 was in many ways a crucial year: following the 1982 coup, the KANU regime savagely attacked the forces of democracy. The subsequent killing, arrests and exile of thousands of people, whose only "crime" was opposition to the Moi dictatorship, meant that 1984 saw the nation recovering from the ravages of much government-led savagery. The publication of the articles in the national press, I decided, would give a message to those active in the struggle that, in spite of the jailing and exiling of many activists, progressive forces were still active in Kenya. It was necessary for the dispersed groups to come together once again and continue their struggle. The underground opposition forces were regrouping and finding their feet once again and different groups were using different methods to re-establish connections with each other.

It was in this national context that my article on Pio Gama Pinto was published in *The Standard* of September 17-18th, 1984.[6] The following week, *The Standard* was scheduled to publish a three-part follow-up article by me on Kimaathi, to be followed in future by a series of articles on Makhan Singh. But it was at the publication of the first set of articles on Pinto that the regime struck and unleashed a series of events that forced me to seek political asylum in Britain. However, in the brief space of time between the publication of the articles and the Special Branch starting to take "special interest" in me, a large number of activists, including many from Mau Mau days, started sending messages of support. Their main message was that they wished to continue and consolidate the process of recording the true history

---

[5] This is the spelling used throughout the book.
[6] Durrani, S. (1984 a and b).

of Kenya and to apply the lessons of history to current struggle.

The questions that the Special Branch fired at me during interviews at the Nyayo House give an indication of how hurt the regime was at my research into the history of publishing and the anti-imperialist struggle in Kenya: Why are you writing about Pinto and Kimaathi, and not about Kenyatta? Even historians are not allowed to do research into Mau Mau. Why are you, a mere librarian, doing this research? Do you not know that people at the highest level in the Government are offended by your article on Pinto? Are you a communist? Why do you write about workers and peasants? What do you understand by workers - even Moi is a worker, why are you not writing about him? Do you think that you will escape the wrath of the Government machinery just because you are "an Indian"? And on and on.

It is a matter of utmost satisfaction to me that in the years that I have been in exile in Britain, I have continued work on the struggles in the information field in the context of the national struggle for liberation. This has included a number of articles published in various journals on the politics of information. Among other publications is *Kimaathi, Mau Mau's First Prime Minister of Kenya*[7].

It also gives me personal satisfaction that the very reason for my exile from Kenya has enabled me to complete the documentation of an important aspect of Kenya's history - something that the KANU-Moi regime found so unpalatable. It is also a matter of pride to me that I completed the project while still remaining a "mere librarian". The work of the underground movement contributed in no small measure to the events that led to the overthrow of KANU-Moi in December 2002. The new social climate in early 2003 has enabled a new debate about the whole colonial and post colonial history of anti-imperialism not only in Kenya, but in Britain as well. This book, I hope, will throw light on some aspects of the history which had been suppressed by successive KANU regimes.

Shiraz Durrani is Senior Lecturer, Information Management, Department of Applied Social Sciences, London Metropolitan University. 10 April, 2005

[7] Durrani, S (1986)

A note on terminology

PROGRESSIVE PEOPLE, POLICIES ETC
The Cambridge Dictionaries online[8] define the term "progressive" thus:
- Thinking or behaving in a new or modern way;
- Progressive ideas or systems encourage change in society or in the way things are done: "She worked for women's rights, labor reforms, and other progressive causes".

The term "progressive" is used in this book to indicate those who favour change and development from the "status quo" that represents colonialism and imperialism in Kenya. It refers to those who actively oppose colonialism and imperialism as well as the negative aspects of capitalism e.g. inequality in wealth and property distribution, landlessness for the majority, availability of education, housing, jobs to some classes only, poor wages, unsuitable working conditions, opposition to unionisation, degradation of work/skills in order to achieve more for less (piece work etc), discouragement of collectivism, encouragement of dependence on employer rather than self reliance, etc.

Colonialism sought to "divide and rule" Kenyan people on the basis of their race and colour and discouraged people from looking at class as the real divisive social force.

Those who sought to defeat colonialism and imperialism are referred to in this book as "progressive" and are seen in opposition to those who favoured the continuation of colonialism and neo-colonialism and its culture, practices and values which favour a minority at the expense of the majority.

As used in this book, the concept "progressive" overcomes the artificial social barriers created by imperialism. It sees people on the basis of whether they are for, or against, social change. It is used to indicate those who wanted to unite people of all races and colour on the basis of their commitment to principles of social and economic justice and human rights.

[8] http://dictionary.cambridge.org/define.asp?dict=L&key=HW*4515

SOUTH ASIAN PEOPLE / COMMUNITIES
People who originated from South Asia have been variously described in Kenya over the years as Indians, Asian Africans, and Asians etc. The term "South Asian" is used in this book to indicate those who came to Kenya from India, Pakistan, Bangladesh, or Sri Lanka. No judgement is passed on their nationality or what passports they hold.

SPELLINGS
The spellings of proper names used consistently in the text are those preferred by the author. However, these may vary from the usage in some sources quoted. When quoting material which uses this different form, the original spellings are retained. For example, the preferred spelling of "Kimaathi" is used in the text throughout, but "Kimathi" is retained if source material uses this form. The same applies to names like "Ahmed" which have a number of variations.

CHAPTER ONE
A History of Publishing
... A History of Struggles

The version of history of colonialism and imperialism which the colonial powers want people to know is the one told by those who represent the interests of the colonisers. The power relations in the world today ensure that the victim's side of history remains hidden and almost forgotten – except by the victims themselves. This is as true of the struggles in Kenya, Algeria and Vietnam in the last century as it is for the current struggle of the people of Iraq against the 21st century invaders of their land. Thus in Iraq today:

> Western state terrorism is erased, and a tenet of western journalism is to excuse or minimise "our" culpability, however atrocious. Our dead are counted; theirs are not. Our victims are worthy; theirs are not.[9]

What is happing in manipulating news and history in Iraq today was the same that happened in earlier colonial wars. Pilger looks back in time to a similar distortion of reality in the Kenyan context:

> This is an old story; there have been many Iraqs, or what Blair calls "historic struggles" waged against "insurgents and terrorists". Take Kenya in the 1950s. The approved version is still cherished in the west - first popularised in the press, then in fiction and movies; and like Iraq, it is a lie. "The task to which we have set our minds," declared the governor of Kenya in 1955, "is to civilise a great mass of human beings who are in a very primitive moral and social

[9] Pilger (2004)

state." The slaughter of thousands of nationalists, who were never called nationalists, was British government policy. The myth of the Kenyan uprising was that the Mau Mau brought "demonic terror" to the heroic white settlers. In fact, the Mau Mau killed just 32 Europeans, compared with the estimated 10,000 Kenyans killed by the British, who ran concentration camps where the conditions were so harsh that 402 inmates died in just one month. Torture, flogging and abuse of women and children were commonplace. "The special prisons," wrote the imperial historian V G Kiernan, "were probably as bad as any similar Nazi or Japanese establishments." None of this was reported. The "demonic terror" was all one way: black against white. The racist message was unmistakable.[10]

Many historical records of the Mau Mau period of resistance to British colonialism had been destroyed by the departing colonial power. What was not destroyed was carted away to London to be permanently hidden from a world not told the truth. Elkins refers to the destruction of colonial files:

> The British government has carefully withheld documents detailing the horrors of their counter-insurgency operations; and, accounts are legion detailing the burning of files in Nairobi prior to the lowering of the Union Jack... In the course of the author's research, several informants described the destruction of files prior to Britain's decolonisation from Kenya. The majority of those describing such purges recalled the files and documents being destroyed in large fires, some on the streets of Nairobi... In the Kenya National Archives today the files from entire ministries are missing in nearly the entirety. Many of these ministries, like the Ministry for Internal Security and Defence, were directly responsible for some of the civilian counterinsurgency operations. In addition, several different ministries maintained files on each of the thousands of detainees held during Mau Mau. With the

[10] Pilger, (2004)

exception of a handful of files, these too are missing from the official record.[11]

Elkins goes on to record the reason why the post-independence governments of Kenyatta and Moi were equally keen as the departing colonial authorities to suppress the history of the Mau Mau period:

> Kenya is still reeling from the brutal destruction of Mau Mau partly because the Kenyatta and Moi regimes, as well as the country's former British colonizers, have deliberately suppressed the history of this period. Unlike South Africa, Kenya never had a truth commission, or public trials, or even recognition that human rights abuses took place during the Mau Mau Emergency.
>
> That there was never an opportunity for a public purging and uncensored debate over the meaning of the Mau Mau past is hardly a surprise. Unlike South Africa, there was no negotiated settlement in the wake of Mau Mau. In so far as one existed, the African loyalists – many of whom manned the detention camps and patrolled the Emergency villages – and the retreating colonial government colluded in silencing the Mau Mau majority.
>
> Jomo Kenyatta, the alleged master-mind of Mau Mau, was no "leader of darkness and death". In fact, the Kikuyu demigod was a conservative at heart whose agenda moved further to the right during the post-Emergency period. He embraced loyalists into his government, and through his decree of "forgive and forget" he was complicit in washing their blood-stained hands. Colonial Secretary Ian Macleod emerged as Kenyatta's counterpart in Whitehall. Though privately rebuking a few of the British officers directing Emergency crimes, he deliberately "decided to draw a veil over the past" and thereby thwart any incriminating investigations into the human rights violations that underscored his government's drive to defeat Mau Mau.

[11] Elkins (2000)

Many within the independent Kenyan government had reason to contribute to the purge as they, too, had bloodied their hands during the suppression of Mau Mau. The official record is seductive, and so too is the decidedly cultivated story of colonial benevolence and African progress at the end of Empire in Kenya.

The distortion of many positive aspects of anti-imperialist struggles is not the only reason why Mau Mau has not been accorded its rightful place in the history of Africa. The development of people's war as a method of struggle against colonialism and imperialism after the Second World War is itself played down by western historians. Jacques refers to "the development of a new kind of people's war against foreign invaders." "People's war", he says, "could not afford the latest technology, or anything like it. Instead, it depended on mobilising popular support". Jacques raises some important issues which also point to the way in which the achievement of Mau Mau should be assessed:

> As empires crumbled - the Japanese, British, French, Dutch and later Portuguese - people's war became the weapon of choice of many independence movements, from south-east Asia to North Africa. In the face of overwhelming military power, it delivered self-rule to hundreds of millions of people.
> What lies at the core of people's war is the desire of people to rule themselves rather than be governed by foreign countries, often from thousands of miles away, that are possessed of utterly alien values and their own self-serving priorities. This is a principle that the west has found extremely difficult to learn.
>
> The Vietnamese proved, with extraordinary courage and intelligence that people's war could triumph against the most formidable and frightening odds.[12]

It is this desire, on the part of the people of Kenya, to rule themselves that

---
[12] Jacques (2004)

gave amazing power to the Mau Mau movement. In many ways, this was among the first examples in Africa of the new kind of people's war against colonial Europe. The Algerian war against French colonialism is in the same league.

This book sees the history of Kenyan struggle for liberation from the victim's point of view. This is done from the very heart of the process where distortion of history happens – in the mass media where current events are turned into pages of history. The struggle is seen through the contemporary news reports as recorded by antagonists sitting on the opposite sides of the on-going battles.

Endre Sik mentions the one-sided recording of the history which this book seeks to redress:

> For nearly ten years, the British Government found it better to keep silent on the Mau Mau affair. Until 1960, hardly anything had been made public in official documents. A large number of books, pamphlets and articles on the Mau Mau affair appeared from the pen of "private individuals" – mostly British settlers in Kenya. Some of these persons were themselves active participants in the heinous acts committed by the police and the colonial authorities.[13]

The history of publishing in Kenya is a history of struggles, reflecting the main contradiction in the society. The two aspects of this struggle are represented by two social classes: one aspect is that of Kenyan workers, peasants and other working people and their class allies who included progressive African and South Asian intellectuals and professionals. The other aspect is that of the British colonial administration, settlers and Christian missionaries, backed by forces of international finance at one level and by the African and South Asian petty-bourgeoisie at another.

This basic social contradiction was reflected in all aspects of Kenyan life, including the information field. The publishing field saw a fierce battle over

---
[13] Sik (1974), p.41

news, information, ideas and ideologies for the ultimate control over national resources. The importance of publishing has to be understood in the context of the ever-present class struggle and the struggle for national liberation. The colonial power sought to impose its values, its world outlook, and its point of view on the colonised people as a way of ensuring effective control over Kenyan resources - both natural and human. The colonial mass media and the education system were mobilised to "prove" that there was only one culture, one world outlook, and one "correct" way of life - that represented by colonialism and imperialism. It sought to universalise its own values as being the only ones valid and possible in the colonies. This was to be achieved by controlling the process of social communication and by controlling the content of information going to the people. The education system, religion, the radio, newspapers, libraries, publishing - all were used to control the content of information flow and to provide a one-sided, colonial world view.

The British colonial forces, however, did not have a monopoly in influencing Kenyan people. The resistance movements in different historical stages used different methods not only to negate information and views from a colonial and neo-colonial point of view but also to provide an alternative, people's point of view. For example, in the course of the struggle for independence, the organised forces of Kenyan workers and peasants started their own independent schools, teacher training colleges, publishing houses and religious organisations. In 1952, the colonial authorities banned 400 independent schools, with 62,000 pupils. These schools were "supported voluntarily by Africans out of their meagre earnings"[14]. They built a powerful anti-imperialist content in their well developed orature. It is doubtful if formal independence could have been won if these social means of communications had not been developed, controlled and used as weapons in the struggle for liberation by the people.

Another factor which contributed to the success of the Kenyan communication practices was the fact that the *content* of resistance publishing addressed people's material *needs*. It was because of this that it was so readily

---

[14] "The burning shame of Kenya". World News and Views (London) Vol. 33, N0. 48. 5 December, 1953, p. 576

accepted by the people who rejected colonial publications. In addition, the resistance publishing was in an accessible, appropriate *form* and *language*.

Thus the history of publishing in Kenya is a history of struggle between the two contending forces, each bringing into the battle all the weapons it could muster. But the struggle in the publishing field was only one aspect of the struggle for total liberation. Publishing and social communication do not take place in isolation. They are influenced by, and in turn, influence the economic, social, cultural and political struggles taking place in the society at a particular time.

Publishing in Kenya has developed in the course of the struggle between the two antagonistic power bases that have dominated the history of the country. Each side in this social contradiction influenced, and was in turn influenced by, the other. Each side in the struggle represented its own class interests. This book examines how this contradiction in publishing developed hand in hand with, and as an important aspect of, the overall anti-imperialist struggle. It will look at this larger contradiction in the society in its three particular historical stages and examine how these influenced the publishing scene in Kenya – how, during each period listed below, liberation publishing developed in contradiction to colonial publishing:

- 1886 -1922: Resistance of nationalities.
- 1922 -1948: Working class struggles.
- 1948 -1963: Mau Mau and the struggle for national and social liberation.

The book examines the publishing activities of three broad groups: the colonial group (made up of colonial administration, missionaries, settlers, and their local allies); the African peasant and working class; and South Asian Kenyans. Colonial policy had divided the country into these three segments and each needs to be seen in the context of its own particular setting and experiences, which influenced its actions. For example, in the period as a whole, there runs an almost continuous force of progressive South Asian Kenyan editors, publishers, printers and political activists who influenced the outcome in the information, as well as in the larger political field out of all proportion to their numbers in the total population. Although they are variously referred to as Indians or Asians, the term "South Asians" is the term used in this book to refer to the people who came from India, Pakistan, Bangladesh and Sri Lanka. Many of them allied with progressive African struggle and helped to blur the strict colour approach of colonialism. Colonial interests sought to hide the sharp class contradictions it had developed in Kenya by focusing on issues of race: economic realities had to be hidden behind social differences in order to prevent the unity of all exploited people.

The overall contradiction in the Kenyan society during the whole colonial period has been summed up by Makhan Singh (1969):

> There was now a fierce struggle between two great forces. On the one hand were the British rulers, helped by settlers and other employers. They were determined to perpetuate for ever their complete domination over the African people and exploit the human and natural resources of Kenya for the benefit of imperialism and colonial interests. On the other hand were the African and other freedom-loving people. They were bent upon resisting, attacking and defeating the imperialist colonial rule and its consequences - land robbery, forced labour, low wages, long working hours, compulsory registration system, racial segregation, colour bar, oppressive laws and such other practices. The basic contradiction was the main driving force throughout the colonial period in Kenya and has influenced the historical development in Kenya.[15]

This book aims to document this struggle in the information and publishing fields against the background of Kenyan anti-imperialist history.

---

[15] Singh, Makhan (1969) pp. xi-xii

> ## UHURU FOR THE MASSES
> The sacrifices of the hundreds of thousands of Kenya's freedom fighters must be honoured by the effective implementation of the policy - a democratic, African, socialist state in which the people have the right to be free from economic exploitation and the right to social equality. Kenya's uhuru must not be transformed into freedom to exploit, or freedom to be hungry and live in ignorance. Uhuru must be uhuru for the masses - uhuru from exploitation, from ignorance, disease and poverty."
> *Pinto (1963)*

CHAPTER TWO

1884 - 1922: Resistance of Nationalities

The imperialist powers met in Berlin in 1884-85 to divide Africa among themselves in order to control African labour and resources. As Sicherman says, they met to "regulate the 'scramble' for Africa by the European powers"[16]. It was during this division of Africa that British control over Kenya was recognised by the other imperialist powers. The "division" of East African people and land was done in a casual fashion by rival European powers:

> After lengthy discussions the first Anglo-German agreement was signed by Germany and Britain in late 1886. Barghash's lands were reduced to Zanzibar, Pemba, Mafia, Lamu, and a ten mile (16km) wide coastal strip stretching around 1200km (750 miles) from the Tana River, near Lamu, to the Rovuma River, near Cape Delgado. The rest of the mainland, east of Lake Victoria and Lake Tanganyika, was divided between Britain and Germany. Britain took the northern portion, between the Tana and Umba Rivers, which became British East Africa, later Kenya. Germany took the southern portion, between the Umba and Rovuma Rivers.[17]

Following this division, the Imperial British East Africa Company was given a royal charter in 1888 to administer the area allocated to Britain. In 1890, an Anglo-German treaty allocated the interior of Kenya as well as all of Uganda to Britain. The East African Protectorate, which replaced the Imperial British East Africa Company, was created in 1895.

---
[16] Sicherman (1990) p.45
[17] "The scramble for Africa; an exploration in anthropology for a new millennium". http://www.zanzibararchives.com/vault.htm

All the Kenyan nationalities resisted British control by waging struggles on many fronts. For example, forces under Waiyaki wa Hinga attacked and burnt the British station in Dagoretti in 1890; the Wakamba people refused to sell food to the British mission in Machakos in protest against theft, rape, and destruction of their property. Similarly, the Nandi, the Maasai, the Giriama, and the Somali people formed resistance organisations against British colonialism. The British response to the resistance of the people of Kenya to its rule was to wage an open warfare which included killing, confiscation and burning of property, including land, cattle, sheep and goats which formed the basis of peasant survival. As Sicherman (1990) says "the history of the next twenty-five years (from the punitive "expedition" against the Taita in 1890) is littered with many such expeditions, described ironically by McGregor Ross as 'such swift thunderbolts of retribution' that the victims 'put up with peace'."

Beauttah explains the struggle of the Kenyan people against British colonialism:

> Our people fought those foreign savage invaders for more than 25 years before they were able to completely occupy our country. The brunt of this war was borne heavily by the peasant masses who, in unequal and incomparably heroic struggle, carried on the fight with courage and steel-like determination to keep our country free from those savage invaders.[18]

Britain decided to build the Kenya-Uganda Railway in 1895 in order to exploit better the resources in the interior. The building and running of the railway needed labour and Britain turned to India which had been colonised earlier. Thus began the settlement in Kenya of people from South Asia. Between 1896 and 1901, about 32,000 workers were brought from India to work on the railways. Of these, 6,724 decided to remain in Kenya after the expiry of their labour contracts.

About 2,500 workers died during the construction of the railway - four for

---

[18] Beauttah, James, quoted in Kinyatti (forthcoming)

each mile of track laid. Much of the track ran through the inhospitable territory of what is now the Tsavo Game Park, and some of the workers were killed by man-eating lions.[19]

> ## A DATE CHECK[20]
>
> 1886   The European colonial powers divide Africa between them at a conference in Berlin. Germany and Britain are the main players in the game of control with East Africa. The Sultan of Oman is still granted a strip on the Coastline.
>
> 1888   Imperial British East Africa starts "economic development" in their possessions (today's Kenya and Uganda).
>
> 1895   Britain's protectorate is formed and officially named British East Africa.
>
> 1898   Construction of a railway from Mombasa to Lake Victoria is progressing fast, but delayed in Tsavo. Two lions kill and eat 135 Indian and African railway workers.
>
> 1898   The railway reaches half way through Kenya. The city of Nairobi is founded a few years later.
>
> 1901   The railway from Mombasa to Kisumu is completed with its 965 km. European and Indian settlers now arrive in great numbers to East Africa. White settlers are favoured from the beginning and given influence on the management of the colony. The African

---
[19] Evans, Ruth (2000)
[20] Crawfurd homepage: http://crawfurd.dk/africa/kenya_timeline.htm. Accessed 28 June, 2004

> inhabitants of the "White highlands" are forced into "native reserves". In the following years several local uprisings are stopped by British soldiers. As in the other African colonies some tribes are favoured by the British. This makes the foundation for jealousy, hatred and ethnic clashes for generations ahead.
>
> 1905 First experiments with growing coffee in Kenya are made by British settlers. Today Kenya is the African country exporting most coffee.
>
> 1907 The British colonial administration moves from Mombasa to Nairobi.

The period up to 1922 was a period of great historical significance as it created the economic basis for the struggle between the people of Kenya and the settlers. Cone and Lipscomb provide some details:

> The railway, the harbour at Mombasa, the settler agricultural economy in the Highlands and in the surrounding African areas, the European farmers, the Indian traders and workers, the capital city of Nairobi, and the location of the various African peoples in Kenya today were established during this period. Much of the pattern on which Kenya was to develop was also established, such as the working relations between the early settlers and the African labourers, the role of the Indian in Kenya, and the future policy of the British administration in terms of the African people.[21]

The economic interests of each group (Africans, South Asians, and the settlers) were thus set. It is instructive to see what these interests were as the publishing activities of each group were dependent upon these economic interests. The period 1886-1922 can best be considered as one of resistance

[21] Cone and Lipscomb (1972) p.27

of nationalities and the beginning of worker struggles. This reflected the particularity of the contradictions in Kenya in this period of early colonialism.

When colonialism first came to Kenya, the social organisation of the people reflected their economic life which was organised to satisfy the basic material needs. The majority of people were dependent on land, water and other resources for their survival: they were peasants, pastoralists, and fisher people. Some were active in other fields such as small industries and crafts, manufacture of items like agricultural tools, household material, housing and clothing material. Their social and political organisations reflected their basic economic activities which were closely dependent on land.

The people of the country belonged to various nationalities, such as the Somalis, the Gikuyu, and the Giriama. Their major social activities were also centred on their nationalities. Their anti-colonial activities, of necessity, were also organised along nationality lines. So, also, their communication and publishing activities. It was their economic means of survival - land - which colonialism attacked and in defence of which they organised resistance. The full exploration of the history of resistance of Kenyan people against British colonialism is beyond the scope of this book.

Another group attacked by colonialism included those involved in small scale manufacturing and those working in local industries. This included the blacksmiths, the craftspeople, and the building and woodwork experts. Colonialism flooded local market with cheap imports which attacked the very survival of local experts and thus destroyed the foundation of an independent local industrial base.

As colonialism consolidated itself, it established its own industries to make use of cheap Kenyan labour and resources. At the same time it found a large market for products from factories established as a result of the industrial revolution. It began to establish capitalist relations in earnest. This resulted in the creation of a powerful proletariat which began to organise against colonialism. This worker-led activity was in its initial stage during the first historical period we are examining here. And yet their communication activities were already taking shape for a more organised attack in the following phase.

It is ironic that the very group of people – South Asian working class - brought in by Britain to consolidate its rule in Kenya was the very class that brought in anti-imperialist ideologies and experiences from South Asia. This class, working closely with progressive African workers, developed working class organisations and activities which helped to create a united anti-colonial movement in Kenya.

Right from the beginning, the workers had started organising themselves and undertaking various anti-colonial and anti-capitalist activities, such as strikes. They were supported in their struggles by peasants whose main struggle was for the recovery of their land and resources. This united front of workers and peasants was the source of strength of the Kenyan people's struggle against colonialism which sought to divide Kenyan people along racial or ethnic lines in order to weaken them. Their aim was to prevent the South Asian workers and progressive intellectuals, many of whom had brought with them a tradition of resistance, from uniting with their fellow African workers. As the following sections show, this attempt failed as there developed a strong bond among the working class of all nationalities. This is the background against which the following historical periods and their communication practices need to be seen.

The 1921 population census showed that the settler population had reached almost 10,000. Cone and Lipscomb explain what attracted the settlers to Kenya:

> Many of the Europeans who had visited Kenya, including travellers, missionaries, and others, had all been impressed by the good soil, adequate rainfall and healthy climate, and most important for settlement the apparent amount of unoccupied

land... Also new areas for raw materials and markets for British industries might be established.[22]

The Society to promote European immigration into East Africa was formed in 1902. Beginning in 1903, "Europeans - particularly British from South Africa dissatisfied with results of Boer War - pour into Protectorate".[23] By 1905, 700 of the 954 Europeans in Kenya were South Africans and until just before World War I, the Highlands were "essentially a South African colony".[24]

Thus land was the important reason that attracted the settlers to Kenya. But internal factors within Britain gave an added impetus that saw the British Government actively encourage settlement in Kenya after the First World War:

> By 1918, the British Government was haunted by the possible spectre of massive unemployment [in Britain] when millions of men were released from the [armed] forces and while factories that had been geared to war production were getting back into peacetime production and struggling to regain lost markets. Any scheme that was likely to absorb some of the potential unemployed was welcome and the British East Africa Settlement Scheme received full approval.[25]

The economic interest of the settlers is thus clear - the use of land and resources of Kenya for their personal and their home country's use. This economic aspect was the principal contradiction throughout the colonial period. As Cone and Lipscomb (1972) say, "The controversy over land in Kenya was continuous from the conception and implementation of European settlement to the day of the handing over the political power to an African Government in 1963." In fact, it remains a central issue in Kenya even today. At the same time, resistance to British rule also dates from the time that colonialism entered Kenya. Not only was there massive peasant resistance, workers joined in as well. Thus the first strike by Africans took

---
[22] Ibid.,.p. 32
[23] Sicherman (1990) p.49
[24] Sorrenson (1968), quoted in Sicherman (1990), p.50
[25] Cone and Lipscomb (1972) pp. 55-56

place in December 1902 in Mombasa when about fifty police constables refused to work. Their strike lasted several days. (1969) provides a comprehensive record of the resistance of the working class in the early colonial days.

Sicherman, quoting various sources, recalls the taking over of land of Kenyan people under the Soldier Settler Scheme:

> 1919: Government announces Soldier Settler Scheme, which takes land from African areas and allots it on 999-year leaseholds as reward to British veterans of World War I. Some 2,000,000 acres, much of it taken from Nandi reserves without compensation, are involved, most of it given free if settlers make "satisfactory improvements".[26]

SLOW-BURNING ANGER

Colonialism brought Europe undreamed of wealth. Rubber, ivory, copper, gold, cotton, cocoa, tobacco: all flowed out of Africa, leaving behind a newly-impoverished peasant workforce. The new economy demanded a system of migrant labour that destroyed for ever the unity of traditional communities. The violent consequences of this rapid disruption, coupled with the paternalistic attitudes that justified white rule, began a slow-burning anger among Africans.[27]

SETTLER AND COLONIAL GOVERNMENT PUBLICATIONS

[26] Sicherman (1990) p. 59
[27] Brittain (1999)

Among the earliest settler publication was the *Weekly Mail* which was published by Charles Palmer in 1899. It was printed at Ndia Kuu and was edited by Olive Grey (Patel, 1997). Grey also wrote a novel entitled *the phenomenal rise of the rat* which was perhaps the earliest fiction to be published in Kenya. The settler interest in land and agriculture is reflected in the predominance of these subjects in early settler newspapers and other publications. These included:

- *East African Natural History Society and National Museum. Journal* (1910)
- *East African Quarterly* (1904) [Published by East African Agricultural and Horticultural Society, it covered topics in agriculture, commerce, and geography].
- *Reveille* (1915) (Superseded by *Farmers Journal*).
- *Plateau News: The Voice of the Settlers on the Uasin Gishu and Trans Nzoia.* Eldoret. (1919).
- *Leader of British East Africa and Uganda Mail*: One of the first settler publication, it started publication in Mombasa in 1899 in Mombasa. It moved to Nairobi in 1908.
- *Limuru, British East Africa; Brightest Gem in British Empire.* The title of this monograph, published by the Leader Press in 1916 and illustrated by the Swift Press, indicated the content of settler publications of the time: it aimed to encourage British settlement in Limuru and in Kenya.

Other settler publications included:
- *Observer* (Malindi) (1901-2)
- *Fort Ternan Times* (1905)
- *Nairobi News; Planter's Paper* (1905) - its policy was "If any partisanship were indulged in, it should be for the benefit of the white settlers collectively".
- *Times of East Africa* (1905- 1907?)
- *Nairobi Star* (1905)
- *Advertiser of East Africa* (1907-1910) – appointed official advertiser for the Nairobi Municipality. Founder and editor: D. S. Garvie; started by the East African Standard to achieve newspaper monopoly.
- *Advertiser* (1909)

- *Globe-Trotter* (1906-1909)

The settlers were not the only ones interested in publishing material on agriculture and land issues. The colonial government also published such material, in addition to Gazette of British East Africa (Mombasa, 1899):

- *Agricultural Journal of British East Africa* (1908-1904) [Published by the Agricultural Department, East African Protectorate].
- *Kenya. Agriculture Department. Bulletin* (1914-1922)
- *Kenya. Agriculture Department. Leaflet* (1905-1907)
- *Kenya. Agriculture Department. Meteorological Records - Reports* (1904-)

CHURCH PUBLICATIONS

While officially spreading the word of God to African people, "all missionaries strongly supported the [colonial] government's action in alienating Gikuyuland and had no doubts about their right or that of the settlers to acquire Gikuyuland" (Pugliese, 1995). Their primary economic interest is reflected in their taking up land in common with other settlers. Pugliese examines church ownership of land, showing the shared economic interests between the settlers and missionaries:

> The missionary occupation of Gikuyuland coincided with that of the settlers and the missionaries took up land alongside settlers, under the same land regulations, adopting the same methods of cultivation.[28]

Church publications started as early as 1887 as recorded by Ndegwa:

> The first printing press in Kenya was in a (Christian) Mission. Already, Dr. Steere in Zanzibar had installed a printing press in the U.M.C.A. (Universities Mission to Central Africa) Mission house in

[28] Pugliese (1995) p.20

1875 and was printing Swahili vocabularies... In 1887, the Church Missionary Society reported that a Mr. Dodd had been engaged to manage the new printing press (in Freretown near Mombasa). And so, Kenya had entered into the world of book production.[29]

Ndegwa (1973) provides some useful information about early Kenyan publications. Church publications started at the beginning of the century indicating that the Church recognised early the importance of having written material to disseminate its message. In addition, they also realised the importance of publishing in Kenyan nationality languages to ensure that their message would reach the intended audience. Missionaries collected people's stories, songs and proverbs in their nationality languages. "With the help of Gikuyu converts, the early missionaries transcribed, translated and collected traditional folktales, proverbs and songs in the course of spreading the Gospel" (Pugliese, 1995).

It is an interesting fact that many Kenyans who "assisted" the European missionaries came later to be politically active, for example Matthew Njoroge Kabetu who helped H. W. Leakey and his daughter to translate the Bible into Gikuyu. Kabetu became the first secretary of the Kikuyu Association in 1920 and wrote two Gikuyu publications, including the 1947 publication *Kirira kia Ugikuyu (Gikuyu Beliefs)*, published in Nairobi by the Eagle Press.

As mentioned earlier, the Church had major interest in agriculture as well. In fact, the first coffee in Kenya was planted by the Catholic Fathers of St. Austin's Mission in Nairobi and St. Augustine's Mission at Kikuyu. Among the earliest Church publication was a quarterly *Taveta Chronicle*, published by Rev. Albert Stegal of the Church Missionary Society as early as 1895 and ran until 1901. Another Church publication was the *Kikuyu News* (1908-1957), an English monthly published by the Church of Scotland Mission in Kikuyu. It was initially printed in Scotland. Church publications included:

- *Lenga Juu* ["Aim High"](1911) Church Missionary Society (CMS),

[29] Ndegwa (n.d.).

Mombasa
- *Mombasa Diocesan Gazette* (1922)
- *Mombasa Diocesan Magazine* (1903)
- *Wathioma Mokinyu* [Great Friend] (1916-) [Published by Consolata Catholic Mission Press, Nyeri] [In Gikuyu].

Pugliese (1995) mentions other European Church writers and publishers and shows that they depended on Kenyan writers to provide raw material and important information from Kenyan languages. These Kenyan pioneers remain unacknowledged in the publications they helped to write as well as in Kenyan history. Some facts mentioned by Pugliese:

- Arthur Ruffell Barlow can be considered "perhaps [one of] the greatest early scholars in the Gikuyu language". He started to work on Gikuyu-English dictionary in 1904. It was published in 1914. Barlow was the main translator of the first edition of the New Testament in Gikuyu "with the help of his secretary, Ruben Muriuki Kihuha". Pugliese notes that Barlow, with all the political and social information he had come to understand in these early days, was recruited by the colonial government in 1953 "to help the government information service in anti-Mau Mau propaganda".[30]
- J. W. Arthur came to Kenya in 1907 and worked on the first Gikuyu translation of the New Testament for the London-based British and Foreign Bible Society which "from the earliest days of Protestant missions, assisted in translating and publishing the Scriptures in Kenya's languages".[31]
- A. W. MacGregor (of the Church Missionary Society - CMS), anon H. W. Leakey) were among the first pioneers in the study of Gikuyu. MacGregor's *English-Kikuyu vocabulary* and *A grammar of the Kikuyu language* were published in London by the Society for Promoting Christian Knowledge, as early as 1904.[32]
- The first to publish a Gikuyu grammer was A. Hemery, a HGF (Holy Ghost Fathers) missionary, who brought out his booklet, *English-Kikuyu Hand-Book*, as early as 1902.[33]

[30] Pugliese (1995), p. 22
[31] ibid, p.23
[32] Ibid, p.23
[33] Ibid,p. 34

SOUTH ASIAN PUBLICATIONS

WE ASK ONLY FOR JUSTICE
We do not ask for concessions, we scorn concessions; we do not ask for generosity, generosity is for the weak; we ask for no rewards, rewards are for slaves. We ask only for justice.
- Statement carried at the top of the first page of the first issue of *East African Chronicle*, 1919. Editor: Manilal A. Desai

South Asian publishing reflected both the contradictions facing the community: the external contradiction with the capitalist, colonial situation and the internal contradictions within South Asian communities based on economic and political differences. In essence, this was a reflection of the twin face of South Asian lives in Kenya – the particular race and class situation that they faced as members of a racial minority as well as members of a particular class. A small section had started as traders, and many prospered and expanded their businesses. Although some of them saw their interests linked with the settlers, the racial divide – a crude form of apartheid – created by colonialism prevented them from totally identifying with the white settler and colonial interests. For example, the South Asians were prohibited by colonial laws from owning land even if they could afford to buy it on open market. They concentrated their efforts in other economic activities. They thus retained an objective unity as South Asian people and saw colonialism as their enemy, aligning often with the anti-colonial movement in South Asia whose lessons they often applied in Kenya.

This is not to say that this view was shared by all people who were of South Asian origin. Many aspired to join the ranks of white petty bourgeoisie and comprador status and saw the radical South Asians, as well as African workers and peasants, as their enemies.

The other section of South Asians was workers, who initially provided skilled and unskilled labour for the railway. Yet others worked throughout the country in various industries, as well as in civil service. Included in this group were many professionals such as printers, publishers and teachers who were opposed to colonialism. They developed a strong bond of solidarity with African workers and peasants based on shared interests. This was shown in the joint strike actions right from the beginning of the century. For example, there was a railway workers strike in 1900, only a few years after the construction of the railway began. The strike started in Mombasa and quickly spread to other centres. The backbone of the strike was provided by South Asian and African workers. Again in 1914, most of the South Asian railway and Public Works Department workers and the African railway workers organised a joint strike to oppose the introduction of poll tax and for other grievances: housing, rations, medical facilities and low wages. The strike lasted more than a week and the employers were forced to meet the demands of the workers, although they got the colonial government to deport some workers' leaders, including L. W. Ritch, Mehrchand Puri and Tirath Ram.[34]

This solidarity against a common enemy moulded the thinking of workers as a class and this was to result in more co-operation in all areas, including publishing. The South Asian working class became active in the publishing field and issued material that reflected their economic interests. The first national newspaper in East Africa was started by A.M. Jeevanjee, who started The *African Standard*, *Mombasa Times* and *Uganda Argus* in Mombasa in November 1901). Zarina Patel records that "at the turn of the century, Mombasa's commerce was largely controlled by Jeevanjee". She then looks at how South Asian anti-colonial struggles influenced Jeevanjee:

> In the last quarter of the 19th century, a multitude (708) of newspapers were published in India and even though the Government had drastic and sweeping powers of censorship and press freedom was unheard of, many of them aroused nationalistic public opinion. Through them AMJ [Jeevanjee] had learnt about democracy and civil liberties and doubtless perceived the print medium as a powerful weapon.[35]

[34] Singh, Makhan (1969), pp. 7-8
[35] Patel, Z. (1997), p. 31

Jeevanjee invited William Henry Tiller from England to edit the paper. The conflict between *The African Standard* and the colonial *Mail* is discussed further by Zarina Patel: the former stood for preventing the perpetuation of racial differences; it was the first to publish important government and commercial news, while the Mail "became more and more filled with gossip gleaned from the editor's social rounds".[36]

Jeevanjee sold the African Standard to A.G. Anderson and F. Mayer in 1905 by which time it had a "circulation five times as large as that of any East African journal and was sold at four outlets in Mombasa and one each in Nairobi, Entebbe and London."[37] The reason for selling, according to Patel (1997), was that Jeevanjee thrived on challenge and had started the paper as a way of opposing the conservative stand of the editor of Mail. With the bankruptcy and closure of Mail, Jeevanjee had "scored a bull's-eye".

Many other newspapers were started by South Asians in this period, and a tradition grew among them to publish not only in English, the colonial language, but in South Asian languages such as Gujarati, Hindi, and Punjabi as well. Many papers were also published in Kiswahili, reflecting the growing links between the progressive South Asian and African peoples. Thus for example Chatrabh Bhat started the Kiswahili language Wahindi. The colonial government found this too much of a challenge to its divide-and-rule policy and deported Bhat to Tanzania. However, Bhat continued publishing Wahindi from Dar es Salaam.[38]

Among the South Asian progressive, working class orientated publications of this period was the *East African Chronicle* (1919-1922), a bilingual (Gujarati-English) newspaper published by Manilal Ambalal Desai, President of the East African Indian National Congress. It was founded in 1919 by Desai and championed the cause of workers - both South Asians and Africans. Its content included records of struggles against British imperialism from around the world, including articles on the Sinn Fein, Gandhi, and Marcus Garvey, among others.

[36] Ibid, p. 34
[37] Ibid, p.35
[38] Kimali (1977?), p.1

Besides these international issues, the paper was directly involved in the nationalist movement of the time. Desai publicised in the *East African Chronicle* many grievances of the African people over land, labour, and wages. He printed articles and pamphlets in Kiswahili for Harry Thuku[39] at a time when no other publisher or printer was ready to do so. Desai's newspaper offices were raided by the police many times for such activities.

Desai also made available his office to Thuku and gave him clerical and financial support. An outspoken critic of colonial rule, Desai turned the offices of *East African Chronicle* into a meeting place of South Asian and African political activists. His defence of humanity encouraged many young men like Jomo Kenyatta of the Kikuyu Central Association (KAU) to do likewise. Desai inspired and helped other Africans to publish their own papers, including Harry Thuku who published Tangazo with Desai's support.

The stand taken by the *East African Chronicle* came under attack from a settler contemporary, The Leader of British East Africa, as the settlers realised that the unity of African and South Asian nationalist, progressive forces could do much damage to their economic and political monopoly. The battleground was not only the streets of Nairobi, where hundreds were massacred after the arrest of Harry Thuku, but also the columns of local newspapers. Chanan Singh explains why The Leader took up the struggle against the *East African Chronicle* so seriously:

> A European contemporary once declared: 'Its [*East African Chronicle*'s] native policy is a danger to this European settlement.' Desai and his paper came under attack specially when Mr. Harry Thuku was arrested and deported. The *East African Chronicle* was criticised by The Leader for writing another article to justify the Thuku movement. The Leader also stated: 'The recent shooting was the direct outcome of the Thuku movement, this movement was encouraged by Mr. Desai and his friends, and by no other

---
[39] Harry Thuku (1895-1970): Founded the East African Association in 1921. He "inspired the workers to organise to fight against forced labour, female and child slavery, high taxation without even a little representation, low wages and the oppressive kipande" (Sicherman, 1990, quoting Ngugi wa Thiong'o)… Arrested in 1922 and deported to a remote desert until 1931. "Broken by exile, Thuku became a moderate and then a loyalist, eventually opposing the Mau Mau. In latter life, he became a considerable landowner and farmer, much favoured by the authorities," (Sicherman, 1990, p. 180)
[40] Singh, Chanan (1974), p.129

authority.[40]

The Leader of March 20, 1922 listed nine charges against Desai and his supporters. The following three relate directly to the publishing field and to the *East African Chronicle*:

(a) The *East African Chronicle* did the printing for Harry Thuku.
(b) Harry Thuku received a measure of financial support to the extent, at least, of a credit at [*East African Chronicle*] Printing Press.
(c) The *East African Chronicle* of Saturday openly defends Thuku and condemns the action of Government in its sharp measure to prevent worse happening.

The *East African Chronicle* had to close in 1922 "owing to financial liabilities resulting from its anti-Government political line."[41]

Some other South Asian newspapers of this period were:
- *Chronicle* (1906): published by Goss.
- *Coast Guardian* (1920s) In Gujarati and English.
- *Indian Voice* (1915) Published and edited by M. A. Desai, it portrayed the on-going struggle between South w Asian workers and the settlers
- *Indian Voice of British East Africa, Uganda and Zanzibar* (1911-1913) - in Gujarati and English.

THE GHADAR MOVEMENT
CALL FOR A REVOLUTION

The word Ghadar means mutiny...it is aimed at bringing about a revolution in India in order to secure liberation from British Control. The headquarters of the Ghadar Party were established in San Francisco and the Party published their own paper known as the *Ghadar*, and founded an institution known as the Yugantar Ashram, the object of the institution being to

[41] Patel, Z. (1997), p.36

> instil patriotic feelings in young Indians and train them for a rising in India."
>
> - *Director of the Intelligence Bureau, Home Department, New Delhi 1934*
>
> To organize the Hindustanis abroad and in India for revolution was the chief aim of the Ghadar Party. *Ghadar*, and other publications of the Yugantar Ashram became tools for this organizing activity. Soon there were Ghadar Party branches in China, Malaya, Siam, Europe, the Philippines, Africa, Hongkong, Singapore, Panama, Argentina, Brazil, Iran, Afghanistan, Japan, Russia, amongst other locations. Wherever there were Hindustanis, there were Ghadar Party branches. By 1916, it is estimated that one million copies of Ghadar were published per week.[42]

The militant wing of the South Asian population was very active in this period. They set a high standard of anti-imperialist struggle against which all future struggles came to be measured. It was the legacy of these early patriots that was continued by uncompromising fighters like Makhan Singh, Pio Gama Pinto, and Ambu Patel in later years.

The South Asian activist tradition in East Africa was influenced by the international Indian revolutionary movement. Besides the anti-imperialist organisation in South Asia, there grew up a powerful international front with its headquarters in the United States of America.

This international front came to be known as the Ghadar Party (Revolutionary Party) which was active in over 22 countries, including Kenya and East Africa generally. In order to understand the powerful revolutionary effect that this movement had in Kenya, it is necessary to understand the activities of the movement as a whole, especially as its publishing activities contributed significantly to its success. It was this publishing aspect that influenced the Kenyan publishing scene as well.

[42] Punjabilok: http://www.punjabilok.com/misc/freedom/history_of_the_ghadar_movement.htm. Accessed 2 May, 2004

The Hindustan Ghadar Party was formed in 1913 in the USA by Lala Hardayal who had given up his colonial government scholarship at Oxford in 1907, saying that "no one who loved his country ought to compromise his principles and barter his rectitude for any favours from the alien and oppressive British rulers". The object of the Party was to liberate India from British rule through an armed struggle and to establish a national government on the basis of equality and justice. Every member of the Party was declared to be honour and duty bound to participate in the fight against oppression carried out anywhere in the world. But the main aim was to crush British imperialism in India.

The success of the Party in gaining a vast following throughout the world was due to its support for the struggles of the people for liberation. This policy was carried to all corners of the world by Ghadar Party publications, the main one being *Ghadar* (Revolution) which was published weekly in Urdu and Punjabi and irregularly in Hindi, and Pashtoo. It was initially cyclostyled but after the establishment of the Ghadar Press, it began to be printed. The Ghadar Press also published a large number of pamphlets, handbooks, and revolutionary songbooks. *Punjabilok* gives further information:

> Special issues of Ghadar were also printed in Nepali, Bengali, Pashto, Gujarati, as well as many other languages. The British government used every means to stop the circulation of *Ghadar* and other publications of the Yugantar Ashram, mainly to stop it from reaching India, but they were not successful. The Ghadarites always found ways and means of distributing their publications in India in spite of proscription and efforts by the British to stop the distribution of Ghadar.[43]

This publishing activity of *Ghadar* had a direct influence on Kenyan progressive publishing in terms of its language and printing policies as well as in content.

The first issue of Ghadar was dated November 1, 1913 and stated:

---
[43] Punjabilok http://www.punjabilok.com/misc/freedom/history_of_the_ghadar_movement.htm. Accessed 2 May, 2004

> The people can no longer bear the oppression and tyranny practised under British rule and are ready to fight and die for freedom..... The time will soon come when rifles and blood will take the place of pens and ink.

The message of Ghadar had an extraordinary effect on people everywhere. It circulated not only in USA and Canada but in all countries in the world where Indians were residing and working. *Ghadar* was being sent in bundles to all these countries. Josh reflects on the impact it had on people:

> The paper brought a revolutionary transformation in the minds of overseas South Asians. It transformed their lives. They became new people. It cemented their unity to such an extent that they forgot their old enmity and bickering and became close comrades, ready to sacrifice their lives for one another. It fostered human dignity and self respect among them and they began to walk with their heads held erect - something which colonialism had taken from them.[44]

Ghadar also published revolutionary poems, some of which were later published as a book of revolutionary poems entitled *Ghadar di Goonj* (Echo of Revolution). 10,000 copies of the first edition were sold. The poems also carried the line of the Ghadar Party:

> Take up the sword; kill the British and rise up for the revolution. Our house is on fire. Why don't we rise up to extinguish it? Set up secret societies and get ready for martyrdom and fight to kill or get killed. Let us awaken the whole country and fight as guerrillas. Those who help the colonial government are not children of their parents. We fought many battles for the whites. We made a mistake. All mistakes and sins will be washed away when we fight for our country."

---

[44] The facts about the Ghadhar Party in this section are from Josh (1977), especially Chapter 14: GhadarError! Bookmark not defined. - the Organ of Revolt, and Sareen (1979). "Ghadar" is the spelling used in this book

One of the Ghadar songs goes,

> My heart will leap with joy
> When you (mother earth) catch the feringhee (foreigner) by the neck.
> The tyrant wants to exterminate my name
> O my sons
> Preserve it with determination.
> Still there is time to save the house
> And preserve it for ourselves.

Lala Hardayal pointed out that the Ghadar Party policy was equality of all people, that there was no room for the rich to exploit the workers. "The rich will always rule the poor... without economic equality, fraternity is only a dream" he declared. This background of the Ghadar Party and the movement throughout the world shows how important it was in arousing anti-imperialist feeling among people around the world. It also explains why the British colonial authorities reacted so severely when they uncovered the Ghadar movement in Kenya.

Lala Hardayal wrote (*Ghadar* 14 July, 1914 "The voice of Revolution - Ghadar - has reached China, Japan, Manila, Sumatra, Java, Singapore, Egypt, Paris, South Africa, South America, East Africa and Panama." It is to this voice of *Ghadar* in East Africa that we now turn.[45] *Ghadar* regularly circulated among many in South Asian communities in East Africa. One of the leaders of the Ghadar movement in East Africa was Sitaram Acharia. In this capacity, he regularly kept contact with the revolutionary movement in Europe and circulated revolutionary and anti-imperialist material among the movement's supporters in East Africa. A British military officer recognised him as "the brains and the moving spirit of the whole of the anti-British movement in East Africa." In 1915, the British colonial authorities arrested and deported Sitaram to be detained in the Punjab in India. As we shall see later, Sitaram returned to Kenya and started publishing another anti-imperialist paper, *The Democrat*, which was again seen by the colonial

[45] Details about this period are taken from Gregory (1971)

authorities as too dangerous and consequently, in 1930, Sitaram was again arrested and detained.

In 1915, Sitaram was fortunate to be merely deported. Other workers in the Ghadar movement were given much more brutal treatment. Chandan (2004) records that "three Punjabis, Bishan Singh of Jalandar, Ganesh Das and Yog Raj Bali of Rawalpindi were sentenced to death in Mombasa in December 1915 charged, among other things, for possessing and distributing the Ghadar Party newspaper *Ghadar*. By May 1916, some were court marshalled; eight of them were imprisoned for terms ranging from six months to fourteen years. Three others were shot and two were hanged. Charges against them included "possessing seditious publications, assisting the enemy, and spreading false intelligence and alarmist reports."

In December 1915, Keshavlal Dwivedi, Chief Clerk in the High Court, was sentenced to death by hanging for having in his house two letters from Sitaram Acharia, and a collection of "seditious" newspaper clippings. L.M. Savle, another active organiser, was sentenced to death for the same "offence" as that of Dwivedi.

An important Ghadar activist in Kenya was Gopal Singh. The Ghadar Party was reorganised in India in 1915 when branches in many countries were re-established. According to Chandan, "between the two World Wars, Kenya became an underground conduit of the Ghadar/Kirti with Gopal Singh as one of its chief protagonists becoming a middleman for many revolutionaries en route to Moscow".[46] Gopal Singh with his "progressive ideas and association with freedom struggle of East Africa" was active in Sikh institutions in Kenya. The leadership of Singh Sabha in Nairobi, which included Gopal Singh, acted as "a front organisation for the secular Ghadar/Kirti Party".[47]

The significance of the Kenyan connection with the Ghadar movement was that it connected progressive forces with Marxism and experiences of the Soviet Union. This connection was strengthened by links with the

[46] Chandan (2004), p.12
[47] Chandan (2004), p. 13

Communist Party of India with many Kenyan progressive people linking with the struggle in India.

The British authorities took a very serious view of the activities of the Ghadar movement, not only in Kenya, but throughout the world. It saw the movement threatening the British Empire which Lala Hardayal had once described as the "British Vampire". As for the Ghadar activists in Kenya, it was clear that they were deeply influenced by the anti-imperialist ideology and organisational principles of the Ghadar movement. They also learnt valuable lessons on the importance of appropriate forms and contents of publications as tools in their struggle. These lessons became part of the growing experience in the communication field in the country.

AFRICAN PUBLICATIONS

Important political developments were taking place among African communities towards the end of the period we are considering. The people who had suffered most from colonial grabbing of land began to organise politically. From the earliest days of colonial intrusion in Kenya, each affected nationality took up arms to defend their territories and lives. Mwakenya summaries Kenyan people's resistance to colonialism:

> The heroic Kenyan people started resisting the imperialist forces of colonization right from the first days of occupation. The British forces were met with widespread resistance by our people during the early years of invasion of our homeland. Patriotic leaders like Me Katilili (a Giriama heroine from the Coast), Koitalel (a Kalenjin from the Rift Valley), Waiyaki (a Kikuyu from Central Kenya) and others from various nationalities, all led our grandparents in brave battles to resist the imperialist take over of our country. For more than sixty years, our people consistently continued to oppose colonial domination, a culture of enslavement, racial

discrimination, land alienation policies, pass laws, forced labour and other oppressive and exploitative colonial evils.

The history of organised resistance against colonial rule can be traced through various protests, strikes, demonstrations, confrontations, revolts, insurrections and all the overt activities organised by the workers' trade unions, welfare associations and political organisations. These groups include the East African Association, Young Kikuyu Association, African Independent Schools, Kavirondo Welfare Association, North Kavirondo Central Association, Taita Hills Association, Ukamba Members Association, Kikuyu Central Association, The Forty Group and Kenya African Union. The highest peak was reached with the armed struggle spearheaded by the Kenya Land and Freedom Army (Man Mau Movement) led by Kimathi wa Waciuri.[48]

The participation of Africans in the First World War increased their confidence in defeating colonialism through organised activities. Thus 1919 saw the formation of the Kikuyu Association by a group of people who saw no other way to fight colonialism. The Association opposed the government alienation of land as well as forced labour, tax increases, and the proposed wage cuts. In 1921 Harry Thuku and others formed a more militant organisation - East African Association - which rejected the "fundamental premises of white rule".[49] Thuku protested against the proposed reduction in African wages, land alienation, compulsory labour recruitment, increases in hut and poll taxes, and kipande[50] laws which were introduced for "controlling movements of African labourers and for locating and identifying them."[51]

The process of formation of political organisations - such as Kikuyu Central Association - continued in the following period as we will examine in the next chapter. But as Pugliese says, "from the early twenties onward, the Gikuyu increasingly began to question missionary motives and objectives..... The authority of the missions was no longer taken for granted by the mission-educated Gikuyu.... Among the group of mission-educated young men were

---

[48] Mwakenya (1987), p.10
[49] Rosberg and Nottingham (1966), p.43
[50] Kipande - "registration certificate recording work periods, wages, comments by employers, and other employment-related matters; from 1920, all adult males were required to carry the kipande under penalty of heavy fines" - Sicherman (1990), p.210
[51] Singh, Makhan (1969), p.4
[52] Pugliese (1985), p.27

most, if not all, the future Gikuyu politicians and intellectuals of the 'first generation'."[52]

Colonial laws prevented the African population from owning printing presses or newspapers. But this did not mean that they lacked effective means of communication. We shall examine later an important aspect of their communication practice - oral communication systems which were further developed during the period of Mau Mau. As far as print medium and newspapers were concerned, many innovative methods were evolved to bypass the embargo placed by colonial administration. Alliances were made with progressive South Asian workers in the press field to carry news and views that reflected the African point of view. Special features carried news of significant developments affecting the majority African population. This was the case, for instance, when Harry Thuku formed the Young Kikuyu Association in 1921. The announcement about the formation of the Association was made by Harry Thuku in a local newspaper on June 11, 1921.[53]

A number of key developments on the broader social and political level during this period influenced the communication field as well. The contradictions between European settlers and Kenyans were sharpening. During the First World War, one hundred thousand Africans working as carriers lost their lives. After the War, while the colonial Government provided free or cheap land in Kenya to white British soldiers, it took no steps to compensate Kenyan soldiers similarly returning from the war. Indeed, it increased repression by increasing taxes, reducing wages and introduced the hated *kipande* (similar to the notorious pass in South Africa) so as to consolidate the forced labour system. The government also sought to divide the African population from the South Asian communities by various policies so as to divide African and South Asian workers who were beginning to form a working class alliance.

In July 1920, the British Government declared Kenya a "Colony". Makhan Singh (1969) explains the reasons for this:

[53] Singh, Makhan (1969): 10-11 (where a part of the announcement is reproduced)

This was aimed at ensuring that the British could deal with the land and labour of African people as they thought fit. It was to guarantee that the land taken away from the African people and given to settlers would remain settlers' land and that the forced labour system prevailing in Kenya could be further tightened. Secondly a conspiracy began to be organised to make Kenya a "White Man's Country" and to establish a white settlers' government. Thus the African people were being turned from a "protected people" into a slave people.[54]

The Kenyan people resisted these moves of the British to consolidate their control over Kenya. They started organising themselves into various organisations which could lead the struggle against the British rule. These included the Kikuyu Association (1919); the Young Kikuyu Association which later changed to East African Association in order to allow all Kenyan and East African nationalities to come together in one organisation; the Piny Owacho - Young Kavirondo Association which was founded in December 1921 at a meeting at Lunda, Gem, attended by about 8,000 people.

The settlers used the press they controlled to fight the growth of such African organisations. For example, the settlers' daily, The Leader commented thus on the growth of powerful organisations among the African and South Asian peoples and the unity among them:

> According to all evidence, the natives of the country ...have been moved to make up an attempt towards political and industrial organisation. This is... further excited by the unmeasured agitation of the Indian community for equal political rights... A new situation has arisen and it would be foolish to ignore it... Those who play with the principles of political equality when no racial equality exists are playing with fire with risk of grave disaster.[55]

The Leader again reflected the settlers' alarm in January, 1922 in connection with the activities of the Kavirondo Association:

[54] Singh, Makhan (1969), p.9
[55] The Leader (July 7, 1921)

The petition (sent by the Kavirondo Association) to the Chief Native Commissioner, is therefore the more significant coming as it does on the heels of similar memorials from other native bodies...the native races not only in Kenya Colony but in other parts of Africa are aspiring to high things...

The year 1922 was an important one in the history of Kenyan people's struggle against colonial rule. A new unity among various nationalities, large and small, was being forged together with the consolidation of powerful anti-colonial organisation which gave a direction to the aspiration for freedom of the people. Makhan Singh shows the situation in the country by early 1922:

> The African people in Kenya were struggling unitedly for their rights under the leadership of the East African Association. The militancy, enthusiasm and unity of Africans of all [nationalities] were being built from the Coast to Nyanza. Co-operation between Africans, Indians and progressive Europeans was also moving forward from strength to strength.[56]

The colonial government regarded this militant situation with much concern. It clearly saw the leaders, as well as the organisations they led, as their chief enemies. The East African Association was considered its main enemy. It therefore arrested its leader, Harry Thuku, on March 14, 1922 hoping that the organisation would thereby collapse. But instead, the working class saw this as a direct attack against their economic and political interests and organised a general strike. Thousands of people took part in a demonstration in Nairobi, demanding the release of Harry Thuku. Unable to control the situation, the colonial police, helped by armed settlers, began firing on unarmed demonstrators. Over 200 people were massacred on that day[57] although the settler paper, *The Leader*, tried to minimise the seriousness of the situation by reporting that 27 were killed – yet another case of colonial news manipulation.

This massacre was to prove a turning point in the history of Kenya. It

---

[56] Singh, Makhan (1969), p.15
[57] "According to our secret count, the correct number (who had been shot) was between 210 and 230, including...Mary Nyanjiru" (James Beauttah in Spencer, 1983)

showed clearly the fact that the colonial rule was maintained by armed force and the only way to dislodge it was through armed resistance. The events leading to the arrest of Harry Thuku, and the stand taken by various publications, demonstrated the opposing sides that the press supported. An examination of the two newspapers, *The East African Chronicle* and the *Leader of British East Africa*, is instructive in seeing the opposing positions they took over the major issues of the time. The *East African Chronicle* founded in 1919 by Manilal A. Desai, spoke for the interests of the workers - both South Asian and African. Its stand came under attack from the settler contemporary, the *Leader of British East Africa*.

Ngoju sums up the anti-colonial publishing activities over the whole period:

> The precursor of vernacular newspapers published in the 1940s, in form and content, was, of course, *Muiguithania* (The Reconciler). Started by the KCA in May 1928 and with the motto "Pray and Work", its first editor was Jomo Kenyatta. In 1940 the colonial government prescribed Kikuyu Central Association and banned *Muiguithania*.
>
> However, in 1945 the weekly *Mumenyereri*[58] (The Guardian) was started by the late Henry Mworia Mwaniki. Further, the late 1940s saw a proliferation of African newspapers and magazines. These included KAU's *Sauti ya Mwafrika*, Kaggia's *Inooro ria Agikuyu*[59] (The Whetstone of the Agikuyu) John Cege's *Wiyathi* (Freedom), *Muthamaki* (The Stateman) *Hindi ya Agikuyu* (The Time of the Agikuyu), *Mwaraniria* (The Conversationalist), *Wihuge* (Stay Alert) and *Muramati* (The Caretaker). It is within that context of intense journalistic activity that Gakaara [wa Wanjau] was to start his own *Gikuyu na Mumbi* magazine as well as the monthly *Waigua Atia* (What's up?) In these, he published original articles and songs.
>
> These journalists worked closely with Asian businessmen in printing the papers and magazines, such as the Regal Printers, V.G.

[58] The full title was: 'Mumenyereri wa Maundu Mega Ma Ugikuyu' (Guardian of Kikuyu Culture and Tradition)
[59] Referred to by Kaggia as Inooro ria Gikuyu

Patel and G.L. Vidyarthi. and Vidyathi were later to go to jail for printing Mumenyereri and Sauti ya Mwafrika respectively.

In order to curb the spirit of resistance and the discourse of freedom and self-determination of these newspapers, the colonial government started its own paper Mucemanio, which lasted for only three months. Other regional news sheets were also started.[60]

Thus, by 1922, the contradictions between the settlers and the colonial administration on the one hand and the African peasants and workers as well as South Asian workers and progressive South Asian intellectuals on the other were becoming sharper. Each side had mustered its forces for the intensification of the struggle in the next period. The publishing industry became a major tool in the armoury of each side.

[60] Njogu, (n.d.)

CHAPTER THREE

1922-1948: Consolidation of Working Class

The experiences of the East African Association and the General Strike of 1922 changed the direction of events in Kenya. Makhan Singh sums up the new situation:

> Before the formation of East African Association, the policy of British rulers was that 'European interests must be paramount'. It was then the practice that nearly four million Africans in Kenya were always ignored and their representatives were never invited to any negotiations about constitutional, political and economic matters. To such meetings the representatives of about 10,000 Europeans were always invited and the representatives of about 25,000 Indians were occasionally invited. This situation, however, radically changed after the General Strike and the huge anti-government demonstration for Harry Thuku's release. In future, the roused African giant (the African people), stretching his arms, was always to be there, either in the background or indirectly or directly represented in all the constitutional, political, social or economic negotiations.[61]

The first constitutional victory won was the publication by the British Government in 1923 of the Devonshire White Paper. This changed the official policy of primacy of European interests and was a reflection of the power of Kenyan people in changing colonial policy. The new policy stated:

[61] Singh, Makhan (1969), p.18

> Primarily Kenya is an African territory and His Majesty's Government thinks it necessary definitely to record their considered opinion that the interests of the African natives must be paramount and that if and when these interests and the interests of the immigrant races should conflict the former should prevail.[62]

This victory, however, was merely on paper and the nationalists were not lulled by their "success". If anything, the new policy of the so-called "African paramountcy" was used to divide South Asian people and Africans. There was no change in the position of the settlers as a result of the Paper, nor were there any improvements in the conditions of the Africans. The period from this "victory" to 1945 saw the consolidation of the nationalist movements and the trade unions which represented proletarian power. The development of publishing will be seen as a struggle to move to the next stage of working class struggle for liberation.

The strategic importance of Kenya for Britain, against which the political events of the period need to be seen, is summed up by Sik:

> After World War II the importance of Kenya for the British imperialists was increasing. Having lost a whole series of strategic bases in the Near and Middle East (India, Egypt, Palestine), they found Kenya most fitted to be developed into a strategic base. To attain this aim they had to build roads and airfields, to develop agriculture and industry, and these projects needed – in addition to capital – the assistance of the settlers who aspired to independence and the more intense utilization of the cheap (and in part free) labour of African millions.
>
> Accordingly the post-war policy of Britain was directed towards increased economic development of the colonies, by breaking the resistance of Africans and silencing their demands, by forcing them to serve meekly the united interests of monopoly capitalists and settlers.[63]

---

[62] Ibid, p. 19, quoting from Indian in Kenya, Cmd. 1922, 1923).
[63] Sik (1974), p. 21.

NATIONALIST AND WORKING CLASS POLITICS

Thus the year 1922 marked a turning point in the history of Kenya. The small, almost imperceptible changes taking place over the years led to a qualitatively different path in the anti-imperialist struggle. The general strike of 1922 pointed to a change in direction for future struggles.

As we saw before, the earliest anti-colonial struggles were waged along the lines of nationalities and were peasant-based. These proved difficult for the colonialist to suppress and involved years of bitter fighting. It ended in success for colonialism only after the use of superior arms and after thousands of peasants had been murdered, their land burnt, houses destroyed, and livestock seized and killed. The lessons of this stage of battle were not lost on the people of Kenya. It became obvious that a much stronger base of people's organisation would be needed to defeat the enemy whose military hardware was built with resources brought together from around the colonised world. Beauttah looks at the transition to a new form of struggle:

> ...our people's resistance to the foreign occupiers ...dialectically took on new forms - especially in the urban centres where our people were more in contact with the fascist colonialists, suffered from daily racism and economic exploitation more directly. The period from say between 1920 and 1945 saw the development of African political organisations ...We tried to use democratic methods to regain our independence and freedom, but this did not work. In fact it was misinterpreted by our enemy as weakness on our part. Eventually we realised that independence can be won only through armed struggle. It was at this juncture we collectively decided to fight the British colonialists and their running dogs with fire and blood. We formed Mau Mau as an armed liberation movement[64].

[64] Quoted in Maina wa Kinyatti (2000), 6.

This period was mainly one of democratic methods of struggle. There gradually developed a new consciousness and new organisations based on concepts of Kenyan nationhood, with the aim of total national independence. This was given added strength by those who travelled to other parts of the world as soldiers during the Second World War and who were exposed to experiences of other wars of liberation and to ideas of liberation and struggle.

This nationalist phase was a definite advance over the earlier phase of struggle. But even here, weaknesses began to be seen, especially in the tactics to be used in the anti-imperialist struggle. Colonialism and capitalism had created a petty bourgeois class which sided with imperialism in the long run. Some former progressive people changed their politics when their economic base changed on acquiring land or other sources of wealth. They sought to become the new dominant class. Their tactic was that of accommodating colonialism, and in fact looked to colonialism as their protection against the people. Imperialism actively promoted this trend as it provided an easy base for neo-colonialism.

But this petty bourgeois trend did not have the field to itself. The development of capitalist relations of production and the exploitation of Kenyan labour had raised the class consciousness of Kenyan working people. Led by workers, this class clearly saw its historic mission to end not only colonialism but class exploitation itself. This was to lead to militant working class organisation, closely allied to peasant struggles for land, which saw that only armed struggle would dislodge imperialism from Kenya.

Thus the period as a whole saw struggles at two levels: the people's struggle against colonialism at one level, and the class struggle on the other. They often worked together, but were in conflict with each other at other times. Colonialism exploited and magnified their differences. These different struggles and their various aspects are evident in the publications of this period.

The section below examines the publishing activities of the three groups within their ethnic and class affiliations in the context of the overall political situation.

SETTLER PUBLICATIONS

As far as the settler publications were concerned, the major ones that had been established earlier continued to be published in this period as well (e.g. *The East African Standard*). New ones were also started. Some of these new ones reflected the conflict of interests within the settler community: on one level was the contradiction between those who supported the continuation of colonial rule and those who wanted some form of independence for settlers from colonial rule. On another level was the contradiction between the old, established, rich settlers and the new settlers who were comparatively poor, had less land or were employed in the service sector. These contradictions within the settler community were clearly reflected in their respective publications.

Among the newspapers that represented the rich settlers and the colonial interests was *The East African Standard*, founded by A. M. Jeevanjee in 1902. It was acquired by C. B. Anderson and R. M. Mayer in 1905. It moved to Nairobi after taking over The Nairobi Advertiser and was renamed *The East African Standard*. The Mombasa Times continued publishing in Mombasa. In 1923, The Standard absorbed *The Leader of British East Africa* which had represented the settler interests so well.

Other new papers were:
- *East African Weekly* 1931-1932
- *East African Weekly Times* 1932-1934
- *Kenya Notes and News* 1929-1936
- *Kenya Weekly News* 1928-1969: "An outstanding settler newspaper; gradually lost its leadership and advertising with changes in White

Highlands after independence".[65]

* *The Kenya Critic* (incorporating the Outlaw): One of the papers which championed the cause of the "poor" settlers. It was started by J. K. Robertson who at various times worked for the *East African Standard*, the Leader of British East Africa, the Outlaw, and the Mombasa Times. He also started the Coast Guardian in 1933. Robertson started publishing the Kenya Critic in May 1922. Zwanenberg (1971) looks at the content of Kenya Critic:

> Robertson's writings show that he was absorbed by the white section of the population...and was only concerned with "Africans" or "Indians" on some major issues of the time. In the main, the paper reflected the social-political milieu of the Europeans. As a result, on many of the issues of the day concerning Africans or Indians, Robertson had nothing to say. Nevertheless the paper's importance lies in the fact that Robertson supported the interests of the "small man", that is the European with limited means of raising capital. His radical background led him to view the social world in terms of class struggle. [He championed the cause of] the white man of limited means. He saw this group as a social class whose interests diverged from the interests of the very wealthy Europeans which were prominent in politics in the 1920s and 1930s and so identified a class struggle within the European sector.[66]

The following quotation from one of the issues of Kenya Critic shows the internal contradictions within the settler community. It also gives a picture of the reality of land grabbing in Kenya:

> Land was secured in the early days for next to nothing (sometimes for the bare survey fees). Many of these gentlemen have hung on to their holdings, doing nothing whatever to them and waiting for the windfall they anticipated when prices boomed and their land automatically increased in value by the labour and incentive of others.[67]

[65] Kaplan (1976).
[66] Zwanenberg (1971), pp. 142-43.
[67] Kenya Critic (19 Aug, 1922) quoted in Zwanenberg (1971), p. 147.

It is ironic that Robertson did not see the plight of the African workers and peasants (the "others") whose efforts created the wealth of the rich settlers.

The settler publishing activity did not restrict itself to addressing the needs of the settler community. It sought to mould the mind of the Africans as well. Thus it ventured into the field of publishing for African readership in African languages. On the outbreak of the Second World War, the colonial government and the settlers decided to start a new newspaper, this time in Kiswahili in order to reach the people directly. They realised the importance of communicating in the language of the people in order to ensure that their message reached the intended readership - a lesson which the missionaries had learnt much earlier. Thus was born Baraza in 1939 and published until December, 1979. Francis Khamisi, the Editor of *Baraza*, recalls how the paper started:

> ... (There was) considerable fear and uncertainty among the various British-ruled states, namely Kenya, Uganda and Tanzania. In these countries, the only news media, besides English newspapers were the BBC broadcasts which were monitored (i.e. relayed) from the Cable & Wireless station, Nairobi 710.
>
> When the war broke out in September 1939, the colonial government had to face the problem of maintaining morale among the African soldiers. In order to do so effectively, two things had to be done urgently. First, broadcasts in the vernacular languages had to be started at once (and also) Swahili broadcasts. Second, a regulated, properly tailored news service had to be started and provision made for its delivery to the frontlines and wherever African soldiers were posted.[68]

Since *Baraza* served the interests of the colonial government and the settlers, it was not accepted by Africans. The history of *Baraza* is a history of how it survived in the face of a hostile readership which rejected its content. The

[68] Khamisi (1977), p. xii.

first reason why *Baraza* survived was the financial support it got from the colonial government and the settlers. This was of major importance, as shown by the fact that when Francis Khamisi started other Kiswahili publications, *Mwalimu* and *Pori* they could not survive for financial reasons. *The Weekly Review* explained reasons why Baraza survived:

> *Baraza* was started in 1939 by the *East African Standard* Ltd... at the instigation of the colonial government to bring news of the Second World War to non-English speakers. The government gave a three year guarantee to make good any loss. Besides the war news, *Baraza* gave its readers local news, specially the proceedings of the then native councils, court proceedings, and some smattering of international news. If *Baraza* flourished, not every other Swahili paper could. Owned by the settlers - with a majority of the shares held by Claude Anderson and his family - *Baraza* managed rather well in getting advertising. Even when it could not, it survived from funds raised by its sister paper, *The East African Standard*.[69]

Another reason why *Baraza* survived was that the colonial government banned all nationality language papers, giving *Baraza* a monopoly of news reporting. As Khamisi (1977) says:

> When the war was still on, most of the vernacular newspapers were banned, together with all political parties and associations. Therefore it could be argued that, at the stage of the development, the role of *Baraza* was more or less to act as an agent of Government policy.

Baraza attacked the two wings of the Kenyan movement for national independence - the national political parties and the trade union movement. The first attack was against the nationalist movement. Kaggia recalls the stand taken by the paper, and explains the reasons why the resistance movement was able to survive:

> The Kikuyu were now going wild with political passion and

---

[69] Weekly Review (1980), Baraza: the end of an era in Kenya. 11 January, 1980, p.24).

excitement. They were prepared to read cyclostyled sheets rather than the well printed, conservative *Baraza*. Due to its militant nature and outspokenness, my paper [*Inoorio ria Rika*] quickly became popular. And its success encouraged other editors to start papers. Within a short time, KAU's news was very well reported, and people didn't need *Baraza* or any other foreign-owned newspapers. We boldly attacked these newspapers, as we could do without them. *Baraza* responded by strongly attacking KAU. In the middle of 1952 KAU replied by passing a resolution to boycott Baraza. This resolution was passed in KAU meetings throughout the country. The sales of *Baraza* quickly started to fall, and we enjoyed seeing the *Baraza* vans return thousands of copies to the publishers every week. These bundles became bigger and bigger and *Baraza* was only saved by the declaration of the State of Emergency. Otherwise it would have been forced to close down within a few months.[70]

Baraza also attacked the working class and the trade unions. Soon after the formation of East African Trade Unions Congress (EATUC) in August 1949, the Central Council of the EATUC adopted the following statement:

> A campaign of slander and hatred has been launched against the East African Trade Union Congress, the central organisation of trade unions. This campaign is led by the two leading newspapers of the white settlers and employers. These papers are the English daily *East African Standard* and the Swahili weekly *Baraza* (17 and 20 August 1949 respectively). From the very beginning the employers and the white settlers have not liked even the idea of trade unions in this country. Now when the trade unions have come into existence in spite of their opposition the same people neither like their existence nor their uniting in the East African Trade Unions Congress. It is this unity that stinks in their nostrils and of which they are afraid. In order to weaken the same unity they are now trying to confuse and poison the minds of the people by telling the biggest possible lies. But the Central Council feels that they would

---
[70] Kaggia (1975), p.84-85.

not succeed in their nefarious purpose as they did not succeed in preventing the formation of trade unions.

The whole purpose of the slander campaign is exposed when *Baraza* makes slanderous attacks on Chege Kibachia, the beloved leader of the East African working class. His action was taken solely on behalf of the East African workers, whose cause was dearer to him than his own liberty. *Baraza* calls such a leader of the workers a "scoundrel" in the editorial mentioned above.

But this attack upon Chege Kibachia makes another thing clear. The enemies of the workers are afraid of the power of the trade unions. Therefore they slander and abuse working class leaders. Yesterday they attacked Chege Kibachia. Today they are attacking the present Indian and African leaders of the movement. Today the excuse is "communism". Tomorrow some other excuse would be found or invented."[71]

The colonial government and the settlers thus used newspapers under their control to consolidate their rule in Kenya. It is ironic that *Baraza* and *East African Standard* campaigned against the East African Trade Unions Congress, because among its aims was freedom of press and communication: "To secure and maintain for the workers (i) freedom of speech; (ii) freedom of press". Demands of the Union included the "provision of recreation centres, playgrounds, libraries, reading rooms and rest rooms for workers - and their families and children".[72]

CHURCH PUBLICATIONS

Christian Missions continued to publish new newspapers during this period. Among these were:
- *Books for Africa* (All Africa Conference of Churches) 1931-63

[71] Quoted in Singh, Makhan (1969),pp. 221-225..
[72] ibid, pp. 204-205

- *Catholic Times of East Africa* 1937-
- *Kenya Church News* 1929-52
- *Kenya Church Review; Quarterly Review for the European Parishes in the Diocesan of Mombasa* 1929-
- *Rafiki Yetu* 1929-

In addition, Christian Missions entered the publishing field by establishing a large printing press, called Ndia Kuu Press, run by the Christian Missionary Service [CMS]. The need for a local press became evident when the Second World War prevented the importation of books from England. The aims of Ndia Kuu Press included the stimulation of local production with increased African participation. In 1946-47 Ndia Kuu Press produced a total of 350,000 books in eight different languages. In 1947 however, the publishing activities of CMS stopped.

In January 1955, the Church Missionary Society published a special bulletin, "Kenya -Time for Action".

COLONIAL GOVERNMENT PUBLICATIONS

New colonial government publications reflected the new contradictions in Kenya during this period. It responded to people's struggles by expanding the armed forces - the army, the police and with it courts of colonial law. New publications of this period reflected this increased armed presence. All the following were published by the East African Command Headquarters:
- *Askari* 1943 (In Kiswahili)
- *Jambo* 1942-45 (monthly, in Kiswahili)
- *Off Parade* 1943-
- *Weekly News Review*

SOUTH ASIAN PUBLICATIONS

> ### DIRECT CHALLENGES TO THE COLONIAL GOVERNMENT
>
> In the struggle for the freedom of the press, Asian African journalists and publishers also played a critical part. These included Haroun Ahamed, Editor, *The Colonial Times*, D.K. Sharda, Sitaram Achariar (*The Democrat*). N.S. Thakur, and four generations of the Vidyarthi family. Achariar also printed the Gikuyu newspaper *Muigwithania*, (1928) the Kikuyu Central Association (KCA) paper edited by Achieng Oneko. Among others that the Vidyarthis published were *Sauti ya Mwafrika*, the Kenya African Union (KAU) newspaper, Henry Githigira's *Habari za Dunia*, Henry Mworia's *Mumenyereri*, and Francis Khamisi's *Mwalimu*. The printing of all these papers for the forty years between 1920 and 1963 were direct challenges to the colonial government which sought to suppress the African voice against colonialism and for freedom.
>
> - "Roots of the Kenyan Struggle For Independence". Global Literacy Project. http://www.glpinc.org/Classroom%20Activities/Kenya%20Articles/Struggle%20for%20Independence.htm (accessed: 27 May, 2004)

The South Asian publishing reflected the economic and political struggles of the South Asian community in Kenya during this period. There is a gradual qualitative change from the beginning of the period (1922) to the end (1948) as the progressive sections of the South Asian community joined hands with the progressive sections of the African community. This co-operation took place in the context of economic and political struggles. Before World War II, many South Asian newspapers supported South Asian interests against the white settlers; after the war more of them began to support the nationalist cause as well.

NEVER BE SILENT

Among South Asian newspapers of the period was The Democrat (1922-30). This was a weekly, published in Nairobi (and Mombasa for a time). It was anti-colonial in outlook and stood for democratic rights for all. It was started by Sitaram Acharia with assistance of Narayan Shrinivas Thakur and Manilal A. Desai. It was outstanding in its stand and fight for the rights of the South Asian community, but supported the rights of all. Articles were directed towards equal opportunities and attacked arrogant superiority of one race over South Asians and Africans. The colonial government decided that this paper should not be allowed to communicate to the African reading population. Sitaram Acharia was arrested and detained in 1930 for his political and publishing activities.

Another Indian newspaper was *Kenya Daily Mail* (1926-63). It was published in Gujarati and English in Mombasa by Jaganath Bhavanishankar Pandya and A. Z. Patel. *Kenya Daily Mail* represented the voice of those who wished to see developments along constitutional lines. It published interviews with African leaders who were overseas.

Colonial Times (1932-62, continued in 1962 as *African Times*), on the other hand, was a radical paper. It was edited and published by G. L. Vidyarthi and Chanan Singh was responsible for editorial policy for 15 years.

Many South Asian newspaper owners and editors, including G. L. Vidyarthi were often to get into trouble with colonial law for their publishing activities and for championing the cause of the oppressed. Many served terms in prison for championing political and press freedoms. Some of these are listed in Appendix A. A few cases throw light on such events:

Vidyarthi had been fined Shs. 2,000 in 1945 when the *Colonial Times* condemned the provision of land to white soldiers in the fertile highlands while African ex-soldiers were left to survive as best as they could in the "native reserves". Vidyarthi faced the harsh colonial laws again in February, 1946. Vidyarthi and W.L. Sohan were sentenced to 4 months' hard labour for publishing, on July 28, 1945, a letter by Mr. Sohan in which the colonial conditions in Kenya were described as similar to those prevailing in the Nazi concentration camp of Belsen in Germany. Again, Stephen Ruhenda, the editor of *Habari za Dunia* and G. L. Vidyarthi, the proprietor, were imprisoned for 24 months in 1947 for criticising discriminatory provisions for the welfare of African soldiers returning from war.

Haroon Ahmed, the editor of *Daily Chronicle*, was also jailed for six months for expressing sympathy with the Mombasa Dockworkers' Strike in 1947. Women also joined in the anti colonial struggle. For example Basant Kaur was one of the four sentenced to a fine or one month in prison in June 1950 for being a partner in a firm which printed 'seditious material' in *Hindi ya Gikuyu* whose editors, K. C. Kamau and Victor Murage were also fined, and sentenced to imprisonment. The others sentenced were V.G. Patel, Amar Singh, and Temal Singh. V. G. Patel who was also publishing and printing the *Daily Chronicle* was brought to court again in 1951 on charges of 'sedition' and 'criminal libel'.

Other Indian publications of this period were the *Goan Voice* and *Fairplay*, both founded by A.C.L. de Souza. Both became voices of radical South Asians who rejected compromising with colonialism.

As African nationalist, and especially working class, movements gathered momentum after 1935, progressive South Asian publishing activities began to merge with these struggles. Increasingly, the South Asian publishing came to be divided along clear class lines. There were other South Asians who contributed much to develop the anti-colonial struggle but whose importance has often been overlooked by colonial and post-colonial historians. These were the men in the newspaper business: printers, publishers, and editors whose machines produced the African papers. It would be difficult to overstate the significance of these publications. All these papers helped build a political awareness that had not existed before. No European printers would publish them and, at least for several years after the Second World War, no African could afford to publish them on their own. It was left to the South Asians, men like V.G. Patel who went to jail for producing Mumenyereri, to support such progressive publications. L. Vidyarthi who printed *Sauti ya Mwafrika*, *Habari*, Awori's paper and the *Colonial Times*, and D. K. Sharda who edited the *Daily Chronicle*, had the commitment and courage to print these new African papers.[73]

Another prominent activist was Pranlal Sheth who was born in Kenya in 1924, and educated at the Nairobi Indian High School. Bhikhu Parekh records his contribution to the Kenyan struggle:

> Pranlal Purshotam Sheth began his career as a journalist, first as a sub-editor of the weekly *Colonial Times* and then as editor of *The Daily Chronicle*. He was also active in the trade-union movement, and played a leading part in founding the East African Trades Union Congress.
>
> In the aftermath of Mau Mau, the colonial government severely curbed press freedom and clamped down on trade-union activity. Since Sheth's paper campaigned for Kenyan independence, whose likely consequences frightened some sections of Asian businessmen, the latter began to withdraw advertisement from it.
>
> Seeing no future in journalism, Pranlal decided to train as a lawyer. He came to England, where he was enrolled at Lincoln's Inn and called to the Bar in 1962. He returned to Kenya that year, and started practice as an advocate in Kisumu, while also remaining active as a trade unionist.
>
> He participated in the negotiations for Kenyan independence, and was a much-respected adviser to the Kenyan delegation at the Lancaster House conference. He was particularly close to Oginga Odinga, one of the important nationalist leaders.
>
> When Kenyatta became the President and Oginga Odinga the Vice-President of independent Kenya in 1963, Sheth's services

---
[73] Spencer, (1983), pp. 78-79..

were greatly in demand. He served on public bodies such as the Central Agricultural Board, the Economic Planning and Development Council, the Commission on the Future of Broadcasting Services, and the Sugar Advisory Board. He also chaired the Commission of Inquiry into Tribal Riots in western Kenya, and produced a well thought-out report whose recommendations were implemented by the Kenyatta government.

As the relations between the President and the Vice-President turned sour, Sheth's position in public life became precarious; his life was even in danger. He was deprived of his Kenyan citizenship by a presidential order, allowed no legal redress, and put on a plane to India in 1966. Thanks to the help of well-placed British friends, he was able some months later to come to England, where he was joined by his wife, Indumati, and young family.[74]

DISSENT AND POLITICAL ACTIVITY

In fact, the Asian African community had long been involved in dissent and political activity against oppression in Kenya. As Kenyan history shows, there are figures such as A.M. Jeevanjee and M.A. Desai, who continuously and successfully challenged and controlled settler ambitions for their self-rule in Kenya on the apartheid model of South Africa. Makhan Singh and Pio Gama Pinto spent years in detention in the struggle for Kenya's freedom. Pio Pinto, over the 35 years since his assassination, remains a major influence and national role model for Kenyans. Joseph Murumbi was the voice in exile of a silenced Kenya during the Emergency, and later Foreign Minister and second Vice-President.

- "Roots of the Kenyan Struggle For Independence". Global Literacy Project.
http://www.glpinc.org/Classroom20Activities/Kenya20Articles/Struggle20for20Independence.htm (accessed: 27 May, 2004)

---

[74] Parekh (2003).

AFRICAN PUBLICATIONS

The period from 1922 to 1948 was characterised by two simultaneous movements for national liberation representing the two-lines among the people for solving political, economic and social problems facing Kenya: one was the nationalist movement and the other was the working class struggle. The nationalist line wanted to see an end to colonialism but felt that change would come peacefully by the colonial power responding to their pleas for handing over power. Some of those who followed the nationalist line merely wanted to replace the colonial master with their own leadership. In effect, the nationalist line represented the interest of the petty-bourgeoisie. This later became the line of the comprador class which came together under the Kenya African National Union (KANU) after independence.

The working class, in contrast, represented the proletarian line which sought not merely to replace the colonial ruling class by a local one, but sought real development by changing the system itself so as to remove exploitation of one class by another. They realised that no meaningful change would come except through an armed struggle. This movement later developed into the Mau Mau movement for national liberation. The two lines representing opposing class perspectives often worked together but in course of time the worker movement became more dominant and ultimately led the nation towards independence. However, as a result of colonial manipulation, it was the petty bourgeoisie who got power at independence through colonial manipulation.

In line with the general political situation, the publishing scene also saw this two line development. Each of these reflected the organisation, the consciousness and the interests of the nationalist and worker movements. While at the beginning of the period, the nationalist movement was more advanced, the leadership had been taken over by the working class movement by the end of the period.

The nationalist movement gave birth to various national organisations, initially covering the whole country. The colonial government feared the strength of this united movement and so placed restrictions which banned country-wide organisations. Only nationality-based ("tribal") organisations were allowed legal existence. Thus each nationality organisation could be active only in its own nationality area – a form of "majimboism" (regionalism) later taken up by the Kenya African Democratic Union (KADU) under Ronald Ngala and Daniel arap Moi. As there are over 40 nationalities in Kenya, the divisive effects of such rules are obvious. The people continued their resistance by forming their own nationality-based organisations, as they saw strong organisations as an essential requirement in their fight against British colonialism. Some of these nationality-based organisations were:

- East African Association (changed in 1921 from Young Kikuyu Association)
- Kavirondo Association (1921) - a militant organisation fighting for the political and economic interests of African people.
- Kikuyu Central Association (1924).
- Ukamba Members Association (1938) - formed to stop the Government from forcing the people to sell cattle against their will.
- North Kavirondo Central Association (1938) - formed to defend land rights of the people, especially in the Kakamega area.
- Taita Hills Association (1937) - formed to struggle for the return of the land which had been stolen by European settlers.
- Kenya African Union (Kenya African Study Union before 1946)
- Kipsigis Central Association - banned by the colonial government in 1948.
- Somali Youth League - declared illegal and its leaders deported to Lokitaung in the Turkana District in 1948.
- Luo Thrift and Trading Corporation - 1947.

It was the activities of these nationality-based organisations which mobilised the Kenyan people for independence. The colonial government had found the all-Kenyan organisations too powerful and allowed only nationality movements. But it failed in stopping the march to independence - the nationality organisations strengthened their links with peasants and workers and worked closely with each other in what became, in effect, a nation-wide movement made of various nationality organisations. The colonial administration tried to control them by banning some of them, for example the Somali Youth League. But it was too late to stop the march of history.

These nationalist movements realised that they would need to organise a proper communication systems in order to mobilise, keep in touch with, and to educate, their supporters. They needed printing presses to run their own newspapers. Thus the Kikuyu Central Association, which worked very closely with the North Kavirondo Central Association, the Taita Hills Association and the Ukamba Members Association, started publishing the monthly Muigwithania (Giluyu) in 1928. It was printed for the KCA by Sitaram Acharia (who was then publishing the Democrat) and his Manager and Assistant Editor, Narayan Shrinivas Thakur. It was in Gikuyu and was initially edited by Jomo Kenyatta. It was banned by the colonial government after the outbreak of World War II. *Muigwithania* was successful in mobilising the people behind the national political and economic demands:

> Its articles and news showed that it was not only the voice of the people, but also their guide and leader. Month after month it published complaints of the people about taxes, forced labour, low wages and horrible treatment given by settlers to their labourers and squatters. Often it exposed the oppressive doings of Government officials (including some bad chiefs) and anti-people actions of some missionaries. Occasionally the articles were written in parables. By this method the people were able to understand what action was expected of them, but the Government was unable to take any legal action against the paper. Sometimes *Muigwithania* printed national progressive songs which aroused the people to action.
>
> In one of the issues of *Muigwithania* published during this period,

Kenyatta quoted Biblical passages about strangers having come, taking our land and making us slaves. He was then called by the Provincial Commissioner and was instructed to declare in the next issue that such passages should not be deemed to have political implications. *Muigwithania* did not take any such action.[75]

Other early nationalist publications included *Sauti ya Mwafrika*, the official organ of Kenya African Union (KAU). It started publication in 1945, but ceased between 1949 and 1951 when it was revived with Fred Kubai as Editor. Chege Kibachia who founded the African Workers Federation in 1947 and led the Mombasa general strike, was was one of the two assistant editors of *Sauti ya Mwafrika*. J.D. Kali edited it in 1952.

Mwalimu was another well known publication of that time. It was published by Francis Khamisi and started publication in 1945. It was suppressed by the colonial government when it declared a State of Emergency in 1952. The anti-imperialist stand of the paper was shown by an article appearing on April 1, 1947:

> ABOLITION OF SLAVERY
> The true facts why the British abolished the slave trade is for foreigners' advantage, so that they may get profits in their present trades. It was found much better to let the African stay in his own land and be used to work in such places as cocoa plantations, coffee, tea, sisal, and wheat. It was discovered that if he is used in that service he will produce more profit than selling him to far-off countries.[76]

Other publications of this period included:
- *Mwaraniria* (also known as *Dunia*) (Gikuyu) 1946-53
- *Luo Magazine* (Dholuo) 1937
- *Mumenyereri* 1945-52
- *Nyanza Times*

---

[75] Singh, Makhan (1969), pp. 34-35.
[76] Mwalimu (April 1, 1947), quoted in Kenya, Colony (1960), p. 199.

In 1946, Achieng Oneko started publishing *Ramogi* (in Dholuo) which was very critical of the colonial government. It played an important role in making the people link their local issues to national politics.

An important event which affected publishing was the formation in 1947 of Luo Thrift and Trading Corporation. The Corporation purchased a printing press and began to publish not only its own papers, but those of many other organisations as well, giving African publishing a great boost. In addition, many Kenyans were trained in printing and technical work. Odinga recalls this extremely active publishing period:

> Our second undertaking was to launch a press to propagate our aims and objects. Orinda Okun and James Omoga had started the *Nyanza Times* but printing costs were crippling them so it was agreed that we would purchase a press and publish the paper...
>
> By the end of our first year, in 1947, we had purchased and established a press in Nairobi, an old flatbed machine on which we printed *Ramogi*. Soon other African editors were knocking on our doors. We printed the Kikuyu *Mumenyereri* edited by Mworia and Agikikuyu; *Mwiathi* in Kikamba; *Mulinavosi* in Maragoli; *Radioposta* in Swahili, published by W. W. Awori; and *Mwalimu* published by Francis Khamisi. The level of politics differed in these papers but some were quite outspokenly critical of the government; I wondered sometimes whether the government knew what was in these papers. The most radical, hard-hitting paper was *Uhuru wa Afrika*, run by Paul Ngei, the young fiery and impressive Kamba leader.
>
> We made no profit from printing these African weekly papers, but this was our contribution to the cause of African independence. We took a decision to employ only Africans and from our devoted Zablon Oti our young employees learnt printing techniques and the management of the business. One of our first apprentices who later

became the manager of the press in Kisumu, was Atinga Odima.[77]

The other major printing press was that owned by Henry Mworia. This press was used to print *Mumenyereri* and very many pamphlets in various Kenyan languages. Mworia (1994) gives details of his publishing activities in this period, including the publishing of various pamphlets.

James Beauttah also started two newspapers in this period:

> I started newspapers, the first in Mombasa in 1931 for distribution among the coastal Kikuyu. It did not come out on a regular basis and only four issues were produced. In 1937 I started a real newspaper called *Muthithu* which means "treasure". If it had not been for G. L. Vidyarthi of the *Colonial Times*, I could never have produced this paper. We could not afford a printing press and he did all our composing and printing for us. I shall always be grateful to him for what he did. He did not get any financial reward; he just wanted Africans to have a chance to speak out.[78]

Bodil Frederiksen provides some details of Henry, Judith and Ruth Mworia's work in the publication of Mumenyereri:

> Henry Mworia left Kenya in mid-1952 to buy an automatic printing press in England. Henry was a successful newspaper- and businessman. He planned to stay in Europe for six months. After the declaration of the Emergency, friends in London advised him that it would be unwise to return to Kenya.
>
> - Henry's second wife, Judith Nyamurwa, who continued bringing out *Mumenyereri* after her husband had left, was arrested and detained for two years when the authorities could not get at Mworia
> - Mworia's first book, *Tungika, atia iiya witu?* ("What should we do for our sake?") came out in 1945.

[77] Odinga, Oginga (1968, pp. 79, 82-83.
[78] James Beauttah quoted by Spencer (1983), p. 79.

- Judith co-authored a book with Henry on child care and modern living, drawing on her training as a teacher and her own experience as a mother. Ruth Mworia assisted him in getting together the material for his pamphlet *Our Mother the Soil. Knowledge our Father*; she wrote stories for the paper, allegorical tales with a moral.
- Both wives (Judith and Ruth) helped with production, packing and distribution of *Mumenyereri*. When the printing machine broke down, Mworia rented a duplicator and continued producing the paper - 2000 copies twice a week, against heavy odds. Ruth describes this period in their life like this: "We used to duplicate in Eastleigh. First we did it in my mother's place, but there was a kind of strike in Majengo, people were not allowed to strike, they were beaten, arrested. We knew that if they came and found it they would take it away. We moved and did it in Kangemi [with] a friend of my husband called Mugo. He used to type on the stencil; my job was to pin it together . . . .We would do it all night without sleeping. In the morning the newspaper was ready. The people would buy so much. They used to fight for it, they used to wait in the street." For the first time, the paper made a profit, which whetted Mworia's appetite for new technologies, and for being independent of printers who took 50% of his income from the newspaper. When he had enough money he bought a second-hand printing press from an Indian and established his workshop and office in a rented space in central Nairobi".
- The authorities watched *Mumenyereri* and the other African newspapers closely. The paper's report on a strike at the Uplands Bacon Factory in 1947, where two strikers were shot dead by African police officers, led to court proceedings. The reporter who wrote the story was sent to prison for six months, Mworia and the printer, Mr. Patel, were fined.
- Mworia deliberately continued "sailing as close to the wind as possible", and sought to shake African trust in the colonial masters. In 1950 the paper brought a letter warning Africans

against believing what they were being told in government pamphlets and publications: "Whenever you see a European give you anything free, remember that there is something he is trying to get out of you." An editorial stressed the need for African newspapers: "There is no reason why the African Press should publish articles just to suit Europeans while the Europeans do not publish theirs to suit the Africans." The editor ended by quoting one of his favourite proverbs: "Chase a man with the truth and he will go away for good. But if you chase a man with a stick, he will turn back to you with a stick."

- Mworia died unknown in his London exile in 1997. He was the writer of a number of published and unpublished books and pamphlets, and a retired railway guard on the London Underground.[79]

It can be seen that there was a qualitative leap in the publishing activities of the liberation forces in this period. Modern methods of communication were now used to connect with larger numbers of people and the content also reflected the reality of the need for greater efforts to dislodge colonialism.

TRADE UNION MOVEMENT LEADS THE WAY

The working class in Kenya has brought about fundamental change in the political and economic fields. While every progressive social class has been struggling for change, it was the working class that ensured major qualitative changes and influenced other classes in the process.

Kenyan workers began struggling for their economic and political rights as soon as foreign capital came to Kenyan for its resources and labour. The first mass campaigns against colonialism were organised by peasants and were

[79] Frederiksen (2000).

nationality-based. Although they scored valuable victories, they were defeated by a better armed colonial force. The lessons of these struggles were not lost on the growing working class who soon took leadership in the anti-colonial movements.

The working class began to set up their own organisations - trade unions - and used the strike weapon to achieve their goals. The first strike was organised in the year 1900. The colonial administration tried to divide the working class by preventing the formation of non-racial trade unions. Early trade unions included the Indian Trade Union (Mombasa and Nairobi, 1914), Workers Federation of British East Africa (for European workers) which was formed in 1919 with Lee Mellor as the President, and the Indian Employees Association formed in 1919 under Hassanali Amershi's Presidency.

The first African workers' movements had to take the form of Associations, for example the Kenya African Civil Servants Association, the Railway African Staff Association, and the various local government staff associations - all formed after the First World War Other early trade unions included:

- Railway Artisan Union (1922) – formed by Sudh Singh (Makhan Singh's father) as a way of uniting Asian and African workers.[80]
- Trade Union Committee of Mombasa (1931)
- Workers' Protective Society of Kenya (1931)

Workers in Mombasa organised the Trade Union Committee of Mombasa in 1931 at a mass meeting of artisans, masons, and workers, while in Nairobi, the railway artisans formed the Kenya Indian Labour Trade Union in 1934. But by April 1935, it was decided to make the Union non-racial and to change the name to the Labour Trade Union of Kenya. This was a significant development for the working class in Kenya as it brought together workers of all races. It was also to prove an important development for publishing in Kenya.

[80] Chandan (2004), p. 16.

In the early period of worker organisations, their newspapers and publishing as a whole helped to give publicity to worker meetings and news about strikes. They informed workers throughout the country about worker actions in one town or in one industry.

The formation of workers' organisations was an event of great significance. But this could not have been achieved without an effective communications strategy which ensured that all workers were informed and involved in the work of such an organisation. It was necessary to publicise their activities and to gain more support from other workers. This was initially done by the use of established friendly newspapers. An example of this was the use of newspapers to report the aims of the Trade Union Committee of Mombasa. These reports were carried by *Fairplay* which was edited by Dr. A.C.L. de Souza. *Fairplay* reported the speech of R. M. Shah, the President of the Trade Union Committee, giving particular emphasis to his reference to "the position of the artisan and labour class in this country and their various grievances arising out of the social injustices being done to them."[81]

Fairplay also carried reports from another meeting which was attended by about a thousand people. It asked the Government to ensure that "in fixing the common electorate and the qualification of the voters it should include the people of the artisan, labour, workman and mason class."[82] Such reports encouraged workers in other parts of the country to take a more active part in the struggle, and also helped to build worker solidarity. This in turn led to the formation of more worker organisations.

In the same way, the formation of the new non-racial Labour Trade Union of Kenya[83] was followed by communication from the Union which was published in the *Colonial Times*:

> Various speakers spoke upon the conditions of workers in Kenya... the Union was the only body in East Africa that could struggle for the demands of the workers... the main objects [of the Union] were to organise workers in Kenya, defend their rights and struggle for

---

[81] *Fairplay* February 14, 1931, quoted in Singh, Makhan (1969), pp. 41-42.
[82] *Colonial Times* April 27, 1935, quoted in Singh, Makhan (1969), p. 42.
[83] The name was changed in March 1937 to the Labour Trade Union of East Africa "to meet the demands for membership from Uganda and Tanganyika workers" - Singh, Makhan (1969), p.59.
[84] *Colonial Times*, April 27, 1935, quoted in Singh, Makhan (1969), p.49.

anything in their interests.[84]

One of the first acts of the Union was to purchase a typewriter and a rotary cyclostyle machine. Thus began a new phase in Kenyan publishing. Previously, publishing was beyond the reach of most nationals, particularly the working class, as a consequence of the exorbitant charges for printing. The costs were high not only because the machinery had to be imported from Britain, but the charges were kept high to discourage Kenyan publishing. Most presses were owned by colonial interests and the few controlled by Kenyans could not meet the needs of all.

Thus the decision of the Union to use cheap cyclostyling was significant as it brought relevant technology within its reach. In addition, the Union developed the use of handbills which could be produced cheaply and distributed easily without colonial censorship, formal or informal. These handbills contained information of relevance to workers about their rights, and also about union matters and activities. In addition, they carried news items of interest to workers, since not many newspapers catered for the needs of workers. The Union produced its handbills in the main worker languages such as Kiswahili, Gikuyu, Gujarati, Hindi, and Punjabi, as well as English. These handbills then provided relevant content to activists who used the well-established oral channels of communication to pass on the messages to people throughout the country. The easy availability of relevant news, in a form and language that made it easily accessible, played an important part in raising class consciousness of Kenyan workers and helped to strengthen their organisations.

A whole new set of worker activities developed around the production and distribution of these handbills. Such activities, in turn, strengthened the organisation capability of the resistance movement.

One of the early activities of the Union was to struggle for an eight hour working day. This was the decision of the Second Annual General Meeting of the Labour Trade Union of Kenya, held from 6-13 September, 1936.

Makhan Singh explains some of the ways in which mass publicity was given to this important decision and examines the contents of one of the Kiswahili handbills:

> The decision [to campaign for an eight hour working day] was further popularised through handbills, meetings in residential areas, works discussion and public announcements (preceded by ringing of a large bell) in the main thoroughfares of Nairobi. After about ten days of this campaign, daily mass meetings began to be held in Ramgarhia Plot, Campos Ribeiro Avenue, Nairobi. The campaign created a new spirit among workers. A Union announcement issued during the campaign stated:
>
> > *Hii ni kuwapa habari ya kuwa tangu mwezi wa 1st Oktoba, 1936, mfanyaji-wa-kazi wowote asifanzi kazi zaidi ya saa nane, na wala asipunguziwe mshahara wake. Na iwapo mfanyaji-wa-kazi ameondolewa kazini kutofanza kazi zaidi ya saa nane siku moja haikubaliwi kunadikwa mtu mengine pahali pake, isipokuwa ni kwa yule aliyeondolewa na kuandika tena.*
> > *Jambo maujudi kitakiwalo ni ya kuwa tangu 1st Oktoba saa kufanza kazi saa nane, na kazi kufungwa papo hapo. Iwapo kazi yatakikana kwa haraka zaidi ya hizo saa nane lazima kulipwa kwa hizo saa zaidi.*
> >
> > ENGLISH TRANSLATION
> > With effect from 1st October, 1936, no worker should work for more than eight hours a day and there should be no reduction of wages. If any worker is dismissed for not having worked for more than eight hours a day, no one else should take up the job, and efforts should be made to get the worker reinstated.
> > The method to make the campaign a success is

that from 1st October onwards all work should be stopped at the completion of eight hours. If in urgent cases work is to be done for more than eight hours, overtime should be paid.

Makhan Singh notes that:
> The effect of the success was felt all over Kenya and in Uganda and Tanganyika too. The membership of the Union went up to more than 1,000. The campaign clearly demonstrated how the unity and solidarity of workers could be built up for a common cause. The success created a tremendous enthusiasm and encouragement amongst members of the Union and other workers for the coming struggle for increase in wages and recognition of the Union.[85]

Such handbills became a regular way for the Union to announce its meetings, to organise workers for strikes, and to educate workers on their rights. Examples of some other handbills are given below:

A handbill was issued to invite workers to a meeting on Sunday September 6, 1936. It was printed by the Khalsa Press, Nairobi and was issued in several languages. The following is a translation from the Gujarati one. The handbill invited workers to the meeting which would discuss 12 points, some of which were:

- Do not work for low salary, work 8 hours a day, and be paid monthly, not by hours.
- Railway and PWD [Public Works Department] workers are temporary, and should be made permanent.
- Congratulate press workers for establishing their own Union.
- Reduce school fees.
- Compensation should be paid by Government on injury at work.
- Appeal to all Kenyan workers to unite.[86]

The handbill calling workers for a meeting on October 18, 1936 stated:

[85] Singh, Makhan (1969), p. 55.
[86] This handbill, and the ones mentioned later, are available in the Makhan SinghError! Bookmark not defined. Archives, Institute of African Studies, University of Nairobi. MAK/A.
[87] This handbill, and the ones mentioned later, are available in the Makhan Singh Archives, Institute of African Studies, University of Nairobi. MAK/A.

"Taxes should be reduced. No taxes should be imposed on the poor."[87] The handbill dated October 31, 1936 was a news item for workers informing them that the workers of the company, Lalji Visram, were on strike until the workers' demands for an eight hour day was accepted. The handbill calling workers to a meeting on November 29, 1936 combined encouragement to workers, and asked them to be steadfast in fulfilling their historic mission with news about a strike in progress:

> ### STRUGGLE BETWEEN CAPITALISTS AND WORKERS HAS STARTED IN EARNEST
>
> Our worker comrades! Come forward! March ahead! If you do not march ahead today, then remember that you will be crushed under the heels of capitalists tomorrow. Workers should have a united stand and should stand up strongly against the capitalists so that they should not ever have the courage to attempt to exploit workers again, nor to take away workers' rights from them.
> Note: The workers of M/s Karsan Ladha have gone on strike for higher wages. It has been reported that the strike situation is becoming serious. This has now become a question of life or death for workers.
> - LABOUR TRADE UNION OF KENYA, November 29, 1936[88]

Another handbill dated March 4, 1937 gave details of a strike by Dar es Salaam workers. Printed by the Khalsa Press, the handbill gave the aims of the workers as the achievement of an 8 hour day and a one shilling increase in wages. It informed readers that the workers were picketing the works. It then made a request from LTUEA (Labour Trade Union of East Africa) to all Kenyan workers not to go to Dar es Salaam as workers, as the employers were thus hoping to break the strike. It ended by asking Kenyan workers to donate money to be sent to Dar es Salaam workers.

Yet another handbill, printed in 1935 and written in Punjabi, English, Urdu, and Gujarati was printed by Khalsa Press, Nairobi for the Labour Trade

[88] Makhan Singh Archives (translated from Gujarati by the author).

Union of Kenya (LTUK) and informed workers about a Union meeting.

The employers were not slow in following the lead of the Union in its mass communication tactics, so successful were the handbills in publicising Union activities. But the employers did not achieve much success, though they produced a few handbills. For example when the Union led the workers out on strike in April 1937 for an 8-hour day and 25% wage increase, the Indian Contractors and Builders' Association brought out a handbill printed by the Colonial Printing Works, trying to deny some of the facts mentioned in Union handbills. The workers just ignored such propaganda.

The strike for an 8-hour day and wage increases finally came to a successful end after 62 days and ended on June 3, 1937. The Union brought out another handbill informing workers about the success of the strike. All Nairobi employers agreed to an 8 hour day, and gave between 15-22% increases in wages and recognised the workers' right to be represented by their Unions. All workers dismissed during the strike were reinstated. The Union announced a demonstration to celebrate the Nairobi workers victory.

The Union was successful in the strike because of good organisation and solidarity which could only be achieved with a good communication system. The "mainstream" newspapers could not have given the Union total control over its communications during the course of the strike. Using a relatively cheap and simple technology and controlling the distribution network, the Union ensured that its communication lines were not disrupted by employers or the colonial authorities.

Besides producing handbills, the Union also started a monthly newspaper called the *Kenya Worker* with Makhan Singh as the Editor. Makhan Singh was the main person behind the consolidation of the trade unions at that time and he brought with him working class experience from India which he creatively applied to the Kenyan situation. Not only was he a good organiser and trade unionist, he was also an excellent communicator and understood well the needs of ensuring effective communications between trade unions and workers. It was largely his influence that shaped the successful strikes and publishing policies of the trade union movement in Kenya.

But the colonial government did not allow the trade union newspaper to survive. It was too dangerous a threat from the working class struggling for its economic and political rights. It used minor legal technicalities to ban it. Makhan Singh provides details:

> From 1st November 1936, the Union began publishing a monthly paper called *Kenya Worker*. Three issues were published in Punjabi and one in Urdu. The Union's plans were to publish the paper also in English, Gujarati and Swahili. Makhan Singh was its editor. A few months later the paper was named *East African Kirti*. Its Editor was Mota Singh, the President of the Union at that time. The paper stopped after three issues had been published. This was due to the Government having prosecuted the editor for not having obtained registration for the paper. He was fined for the "offence". Both the papers contained articles about the Union's policies and news about workers' struggles and national and international news of general interest.[89]

The Annual Return made under the Newspaper Registration Ordinance indicated that *East African Kirti* was published weekly and that the average circulation was 1,000 copies per week.

By 1948, there were 16 trade unions affiliated to the Labour Trade Union of East Africa, with a total membership of 10,000 workers. The economic conditions of Kenyan workers and peasants had worsened after the Second World War. More land was being taken over for settlement of British (ex) soldiers, and peasants were left landless and forced to work as cheap labour for the settlers. Workers' conditions were also deteriorating. While the workers were continuing to organise and to go on strikes, political organisations were also being formed. In February 1946, the African nationalist organisation, the Kenya African Study Union changed its name

---

[89] Singh, Makhan (1969), p. 56.

to Kenya African Union (KAU). There was a close co-operation between the trade unions and the KAU with many trade union officials being active in the political organisations.

The year 1947 saw the struggle of the squatters from Kijabe, Kiambu and other areas culminating in the squatters' demonstration on the lawn of the Government House in Nairobi. Similarly the struggle of workers was gathering strength. This was shown clearly by the General Strike in Mombasa from 13-25 January, 1947. The strike led by Chege Kibachia was an important achievement for the working class in Kenya. It set the scene for the intensifying struggles of the people of Kenya in the following period. Sicherman, in her "chronology of Kenyan history and politics", captures the mood of the period:

> **1947 (13-25 January)** - General Strike of 15,000 of the 20,000 workers in Mombasa, during which city is paralysed and 400 people arrested. Strike is notable for its discipline and for involving "even the most atomised of employees - domestic servants and Africans who performed odd jobs". Led by Chege Kibachia, African Workers Federation (soon renamed Transport and Allied Workers Union) is formed during strike; it calls strikes and organises union branches all over country, stressing solidarity of workers across lines of craft and industry...government arrests Kibachia on 22 Aug. and on 5 Sept, police kill three strikers and wound six others at Uplands Bacon Factory near Lari. Mombasa strike and widespread rural protests make 1947 "key year" in which government loses control in Nairobi and Gikuyuland.[90]

Throughout the colonial history of Kenya, there has been a very close link between trade unionists and those involved in national politics. Many trade union activists saw that the only way to achieve their aims was to be active in direct political activities. In addition, trade union and political activists were involved in the publishing field as well. Earlier, we saw Makhan Singh's involvement in trade union work, which inevitably involved him in

[90] Sichermann (1990), pp. 72-73

publishing. Similarly, Chege Kibachia carried out his trade union and political work through the publishing field as well. In 1947 he was an assistant editor of *Sauti ya Mwafrika*.

The next period, 1948-63 to which we now turn, was in many ways the most dynamic and revolutionary period in the history of Kenya. Many forces that had been preparing the people for active resistance to colonialism were in place by the end of 1947. A long history of struggle at different levels had been leading to one conclusion: that there could not be any meaningful change for the majority of people without an armed struggle. Various peaceful methods had been tried, but with limited success. The lesson of past struggle was that a strong organisational structure, leadership, and a correct ideological stand were necessary if Kenya was not to become a "settlers' colony" as happened in Zimbabwe.

The experiences of a creative alliance between trade union, working class, and progressive nationalist movements showed what can be achieved with patient planning and with mass popular support. But for all these to succeed, it was essential that there should be a free flow of information among the people, and between the people and their trade union and political organisations. The trade union experience had also shown that it was possible to build a new publishing sector with worker control over content, production and distribution of material. In addition the importance of oral communication was shown when news of strike and worker struggles was carried by word of mouth over large parts of the country – often by railway workers, taxi, bus and lorry drivers.

All these lessons and experiences were to prove invaluable in the next period even in the face of one of the most brutal suppressions seen anywhere in the colonial world.

Before we turn to the final period before independence (1948-63), we shall examine the well-established publishing industry at the Kenya coast. Many lessons have been learnt from this experience which has been a pioneer not

CHAPTER FOUR

Kiswahili Resistance Publishing at the Coast

One of the oldest and well established languages in Eastern Africa, indeed in Africa, developed at the East African coast. Kiswahili has a long history of literature and culture associated with it. Some background on its early development is given by Ali and Juma:

> The earliest known document recounting the past situation on the East African coast written in the 2nd century AD (in Greek language by anonymous author at Alexandria in Egypt and it is called the Periplus of Erythrean Sea) says that merchants visiting the East African coast at that time from Southern Arabia, used to speak with the natives in their local language and they intermarried with them. Those that suggest that Swahili is an old language point to this early source for the possible antiquity of the Swahili language.[91]

EARLY KISWAHILI EPICS

Ali records the early history of written Kiswahili:

> The oldest surviving documents written in Swahili date from the early 1700s. They are written in an Arabic script, reflecting the

[91] Ali and Juma (n.d.).

influence of Islamic culture on Swahili society. Most of these documents are transcriptions of Swahili epic poetry, recording on paper an oral tradition of works intended for chanting or singing. The most common of these poems are called Utenzi (Utendi), drawing upon conventions of both Arab verse and Bantu song. Its earliest composers most likely worked in Kenya, in the Lamu Archipelago, using one of the northern Swahili dialects. The tradition later spread south to Mombasa and Pemba, where the focus of the verse shifted from religious legends to social commentary, which continues to be a theme used by contemporary Swahili poets. The classical poetry still plays a major role in Swahili culture; it is recited on special occasions and regularly quoted; newspapers often devote space to poetry that has been submitted by their readership.[92]

Some other sources date early Kiswahili written material to at least AD 1600. Almost half of these were religious works. Of the rest, approximately 20 percent were written in East Africa while the remainder consisted of material written outside, but copied in, East Africa.

Early Kiswahili texts were written in Arabic script and consisted of manuals of religion, law, medicine, astrology and linguistic works. As is true of other publications world-wide, Kiswahili literature reflects social contradictions. A study of Kiswahili literature shows the contradictions at different times in the society. It reveals, for example, the battles that the Waswahili undertook against the Portuguese invasion of East Africa and against the Germans and the British in later years; it reveals the continual struggle for political and economic freedom, right up to, and beyond, independence. Each social and political struggle and its representation in literature influenced subsequent struggles. Thus the Maji Maji rebellion in Tanzania against German colonialism, influenced all Kiswahili-speaking people in Eastern Africa.

A popular Kiswahili literary form is the mshahiri, both written and oral. Some of these are based on Islamic religious traditions while others reflect

---

[92] Ali (n.d.).

people's social, cultural and economic struggles. These include some written in the 18th and 19th centuries, such as:
- Utenzi wa Fumo Liyongo
- Utenzi wa Tambuka
- Utenzi wa Shufaka
- Utenzi wa Mwana Kupona

Kiswahili literature provides not only vivid details of daily lives but records of historical events as well. In broad terms, it reflects struggles within societies. This literature is a vast reservoir of pre-colonial history in Africa. There are over 70 Kiswahili epics providing rich source material of life stretching over many centuries. These reflect internal as well as external struggles in the society. The internal ones, for example, show conflict between urban and rural people, between the well off in society considered "civilised" - "Utamaduni" or "Uungwana" - who lived in stone houses and those not so well off who lived in mud and thatch houses: in essence a basic class struggle.

Utenzi wa Fumo Liyongo, for example, tells the history of Fumo Liyongo who was a leader of the coastal people and who fought to safeguard the interests of his people. His leadership stood in contradiction to the tyrannical rule of some of the later coastal rulers. The title 'fumo' means 'spearlord', indicating the importance of the weapon used against enemies:

> The story of Fumo Liongo (sic), in many ways the national epic of the Swahili and evidently dating originally from an earlier era, is in large part the tale of a typical African warrior, roaming the countryside with spear, bow and arrow, constantly at odds with his town-dwelling relatives of the Pate Court; fighting, dancing and versifying until he meets with a hero's death... His title, fumo means 'spearlord'... [The spear] is generally identified as a broad spearblade and is also an emblem which appears constantly in the decoration of houses and mosques, even in the centre of the stone towns like Gedi and Pate itself. The Fumo Liongo tradition, as

symbolised by this spear, lived on side by side with the urbanising traditions within Swahili culture.[93]

King'ei quotes Dundes on the role of poetry as a tool of resistance: "One of the most important functions of folklore is its service as a vehicle for social protest. Whenever there is injustice and social oppression, one can be sure that the victims will find some solace in folklore"[94] Makokha goes on to examine Fumo Liyongo:

> It is clear that Fumo Liyongo was largely treated as a hero by his kinsfolk because his struggle to the throne of the Pate sultanate symbolised their collective urge to rid themselves of an evil and dictatorial leadership. This is the light in which the poem must be read and interpreted. Today, the epic of Liyongo can be described as a "dramatic account of heroism, wit and strength."[95]

Another major Kiswahili work, Al-Inkishafi, written by Sayyid Abdalla Bin Ali Nasir (1720-1820)[96], depicts the decline of the rule of Pate during the second half of the eighteenth century. The rulers of Pate had at one time controlled the wealth of the coast as far as Dar es Salaam. The poem documents a period when their wealth and, with it, their social and cultural dominance, was declining.

KISWAHILI BOOK PRODUCTION

Kiswahili publications have used antiquarian book production techniques. Many scholarly works were copied in East Africa, many others were written in East Africa. Some of these were written on loose sheets of paper, others were compiled in well bound volumes, which survive even today at the Kenya National Archives, University of Nairobi Library, in private collections and at the National Museum in Kenya. Allen says that there are

---
[93] "The earliest known Swahili poet of note is Fumo Liyongo, who is dated by various writers anywhere from the 14th to the 17th century" (Allen, (1971), p. 22.
[94] King'ei (2001) who quotes from Dundes, A. (1965).
[95] Makokha (2000).
[96] Nasir (1977).

possibly thousands of these earlier works privately owned today and discusses their binding:

> Many of the volumes have considerable aesthetic appeal. Digby noted that the illuminations on the London half quatrain were distinctive examples of Swahili art. Many others surviving in East Africa have far more elaborate and beautiful illuminations. The craftsmanship in some of the bindings is also well worth conserving and studying. Most of these books were written and put together, bound and decorated in Siyu, a town on Pate Island which still retains some unique and fascinating art forms. It is also possible to trace links with other examples of traditional Swahili art: door carvings, plasterwork, coral carving, etc. And these can in turn be linked up with the art of some non-Swahili peoples.[97]

These early literary achievements are not given their due place in African literature nor is their contribution as literature of resistance been fully recognised.

KISWAHILI AS A LANGUAGE OF RESISTANCE

Ali and Juma show how British colonialism came to see and use Kiswahili as a way of reaching the people through their language:

> Christian missionaries learnt Swahili as the language of communication to spread the Gospel in Eastern Africa. So, the missionaries also helped to spread the language. As a matter of fact the first Swahili-English dictionary was prepared by a missionary. During the colonial time, Swahili was used for communication with the local inhabitants. Hence the colonial administrators pioneered the effort of standardizing the Swahili language. Zanzibar was the

[97] Allen (1981), p.20..

epicentre of culture and commerce, therefore colonial administrators selected the dialect of the Zanzibar (Unguja) town as the standard Swahili. The Unguja dialect (Kiunguja) was then used for all formal communication such as in schools, in mass media (newspapers and radio), in books and other publications.[98]

Kiswahili orature developed further during the colonial period. The oral forms of the language began to be used by progressive people to struggle against foreign and local enemies in order to rid the land of exploitation. In this respect, Kiswahili was called upon to serve the concrete needs of its speakers, in common with other languages of the people of Kenya. This reflects the universal aspect of language: helping the communication process of its users so as to solve the particular contradictions of a particular historical period. During the same period, written Kiswahili continued to develop and the Roman script began to replace the earlier Arabic script.

The language, and its publications, developed in an environment of sharp contradictions between those who supported colonialism and those who sought to destroy colonialism and exploitation. Each side developed the Kiswahili language in this struggle.

Those who supported colonialism got their ideological support from their colonial masters and their language use reflected the culture and forms of the British capitalist system. The values of the British ruling class had given birth to a new culture reflecting its own world outlook which was in sharp contradiction to the world outlook of those struggling against colonialism and imperialism. Ruo shows how the publications of those who supported colonialism reflected their class interests:

> During the colonial rule, [there was] a reign of terror in this part of the world. The writers of this period [included] educated people...who accompanied their explorer masters to the interior. What they wrote shows clearly that they were only one of the many of that time already mentally castrated by the European

[98] Ali and Juma (n.d.).

standards...This group also consisted of puppet Liwalis and Jumbes who were either Africans or Arabs appointed to rule instead of local leaders. Since they could read and write reasonably well, they were expected [by their colonial masters] to write poetries with themes which played the role of drugs, religion or booze, i.e. providing momentary relief from the consciousness of the oppressive environment. Poems with love and beauty themes were, therefore, abundant during this time.[99]

The colonialists thus sought to encourage publications of material which would take people away from all thoughts of resistance to colonialism. Colonialism sought to enforce a culture of silence and acceptance of foreign domination. But the difficulties of people's daily existence ensured that they broke this silence. Within this contradiction, Kiswahili publications advanced to new heights.

Just as with the Mau Mau freedom songs, so too with Kiswahili literature there developed a form of language with double meanings: one for the oppressors, who could understand only the surface meaning; the other, deeper, meaning was for the oppressed who forged a new culture of resistance. Thus Ruo (1984) talks of "Kiswahili cha ndani" which is understood only by the people but not by the oppressors. He quotes the following example of an anti-colonial saying: Mgeni Siku ya Kumi.

The full text is: Mgeni Siku ya Kumi, mpe jembe akalime akirudi muagane (On the tenth day, give the guest a hoe to go to the garden and when he comes back he will say good-bye!) This is a reference to getting rid of the colonialists. Not only was the meaning not clear to the colonial administration but the form used to pass on this message was also new. Such messages were written on women's khangas and so reached a wide audience right in their homes.

The colonialists, of course, sought to suppress all resistance publications. Ruo (1979) explains how people overcame the censorship:

[99] Ruo (1979), pp. 8-9..

The writers of this period were politically aware that they were being oppressed. Some writers wrote using symbols . . . Many other people wrote poems in the Kiswahili papers of their time (Mambo Leo, for instance) while others used women's names for fear of repercussions (women did not have "pass-books" or Kipandes, and so could easily evade colonial justice). We have Saadani Kandor writing under the pseudo name of Mary Binti Rajabu in 1949.[100]

The Kiswahili speaking people of the coast have used their language in its different forms (oral and written) to express their anti-colonial feelings. Kiswahili poetry has served this social function. It has expressed the aspirations of the people for a life free from domination and oppression. For example, Muyaka bin Haji (1776-1840), often considered the father of Kiswahili poetry, used poetry to support the people's struggle against foreign invasion at the beginning of the 19th century. Kiswahili poets have strong links with people's struggles and did not generally write "abstract" poetry in the Western tradition of "art for art's sake". Theirs was people's art at the service of the people.

The best known poem of the "great Mombasa poet", Muyaka is "Mugogoto wa Zamani" in which the poet becomes a politician and urges the freedom fighters of Mombasa to struggle against domination:

> *Jifungetoni masombo mshike msu na ngao,*
> *Zile ndizo sambo zijile zatoka kwao,*
> *Na tuwakalie kombo, tuwapigie, Hario!*
> *Wakija tuteze nao wayawiapo ngomani!*
>
> *Na waje kwa fungi we pupate kuwapunguza*
> *Waloata miji yao ili kuja kujisoza!*
> *Na hawano waiyeo wana wa Mwana Aziza,*
> *Sijui watayaweza au ni k'ongeza duni!* [101]

---

[100] Ruo (1979), p.10.

NEVER BE SILENT

ENGLISH TRANSLATION
Gird up thine loins; take up thine swords and shields
Behold, those are their ships arrived from their homeland
Let us await them in readiness, let us hail them on
So that when they come to battle we may shoot at them.

Let them come in their great hoards so we may reduce them
They have forsaken their own towns to seek self-destruction here,
They and their Zanzibar companions;
Can they succeed or are they merely after more humiliation.

This same spirit of struggle against oppression is also found in the works of Ahmadi Nassir, "the Mombasa writer and indisputably the greatest Swahili poet alive"[102]. The message of resistance comes out clearly.

UWATAPO HAKI YAKO

Simama uitetee, usivikhofu vituko
Aliye nayo mwendee, akupe kilicho chako
Akipinga mlemee, mwandame kulla endako
Uwatapo haki yako, utaingiya motoni
Teteya kwa kulla hali, usiche misukosuko
Siche winge wala mali, sabilisha roho yako
Unyonge usikubali, ukaonewa kwa chako
Uwatapo haki yako, utaingiya motoni

ENGLISH TRANSLATION
Stand up and fight for your right, fear not the

---
[101] Hichens, W (1970), p.10
[102] Mulokozi (1972), p.16

perils!
Tell whoever has it to give it back;
Should he refuse, rise upon him! Pursue him everywhere!
If you forfeit your right you will end in the fire.

Fight for it in every way, care not about the hazards!
Fear not their numbers, their wealth; be ready to sacrifice your life;
Submit not to oppression; defend that which is your own;
If you forfeit your right you will end in the fire.

Although many such Kiswahili poems were printed and published much later, they became popular through the oral medium. This was a form developed over centuries and served well the propagation of progressive message during colonialism when there was strict censorship of progressive ideas. Through this form, the political message circulated among the people undetected by those it sought to uproot. This tradition survives even today. Mukimbo gives the example of the Amu women's political songs which she recorded in 1974/75. These songs were created by women to defeat the forces of exploitation by exposing the oppression of the people by the rich.

One of the songs compares those politicians who have corrupted and destroyed the town with wild dogs and hyenas; an unwanted, destructive element which had to be removed from the society:

Aloufisidi mui
Mola memrufaisha
Mbwafanya
Mbwai mbwai
Magofu kutobakisha
Akifumiwa na mai
Asipate pa kuegesha[103]

---
[103] All the Amu songs are taken from Mukimbo (1978).

Other songs show how the people have awakened to the tricks of the rich and how their time of exploitation had come to an end:

> *Mwalitukuwa khatuwa* You took steps
> *Ya Kututiya tandini* to trap us
> *Tukawavika shingoni.* We entangled the trap
> We put it round your necks.
>
> *Komeshani udarai* Stop hypocrisy
> *Ubepari umekwisha* Exploitation is finished.
> *Na mapesa hayafai* And money will not help.

Yet another song shows the social awareness of the working people about the forces of exploitation in the society, and the steps necessary to end this exploitation:

> *Tulipokata shauri* When we the oppressed
> *sisi wanyonge* decide with one mind
> *Hela hawa mabepari* to defeat the capitalists
> *Natuwapige* the exploiters are left with nothing
> *Waateni waipare* scratching their dirty bodies.
> *Wana Uwambe.*

This brief look at Kiswahili oral and written material shows the highly developed communications sector at the coast. These achievements, suppressed during the colonial presence, need to be examined afresh in their proper context of the total communication system of the people of Kenya and as part of the resistance activities of the people.

CHAPTER FIVE

1948-1963: Mau Mau Revolutionary Struggle

> ### THE BURNING OF THE BOOKS
>
> When the Regime commanded that books with harmful knowledge
> Should be publicly burned and on all sides
> Oxen were forced to drag cartloads of books
> To the bonfires, a banished
> Writer, one of the best, scanning the list of the
> Burned, was shocked to find that his
> Books had been passed over. He rushed to his desk
> on wings of wrath, and wrote a letter to those in power
> Burn me! he wrote with flying pen, burn me!
> Haven't my books
> Always reported the truth? And here you are
> Treating me like a liar! I command you:
> Burn me!
>
> Bertolt Brecht (1898-1956)
> "The Bookburning" (Die Bücherverbrennung)
> http://www.ifla.org/faife/litter/subject/bookfire.htm
> (Accessed: 17 April, 2004)

It was during the period 1948-63 that Kenyan publishing developed to its highest level ever. This was in keeping with other levels of production, for example the development of industries such as gun making, clothing industry, Mau Mau medical system, liberation cultural activities, the science of guerrilla warfare, all of which rose to new heights in the areas controlled by Mau Mau. In keeping with this accelerated development in every field, publishing also saw rapid development during this period. Kinyatti provides the background to the publishing scene:

> Along with the deepening of contradictions between the progressive forces and the forces of reaction, the period witnessed the development of a militant, anti-imperialist press. Some of the newspapers and pamphlets it produced were in English, but the majority were printed in various nationality languages. Although the political contents of these national papers and pamphlets differed, essentially all of them were patriotic, anti-imperialist in nature and content. They expressed the Kenyan people's indignation at and hatred for British imperialism.[104]

The publishing activities of this period are examined against the background of people's contradictions with the colonial regime, as well as internal contradiction among Kenyan people.

A HIDDEN HISTORY

BRUTAL AND SHOCKING

- "To the British, the uprising was such an outrageous attack on colonialism that it justified any response, and that response, when it came, would be brutal and shocking".
- By the end of the Second World War, 3,000 European settlers owned 43,000 square kilometres of the most fertile land, only 6 percent of which they cultivated. The African population of 5.25 million occupied, without ownership rights, less than 135,000 square kilometres of the poorest land. On the "native reserves" much of the land was unsuitable for agriculture.[105]

After the Second World War, Kenya became the scene of a major war

[104] Kinyatti (forthcoming).
[105] Slaughter (1999).

between Kenyan workers and peasants on one side and British colonialism, on the other.

Paul Maina provides background to the emergence of a new revolutionary situation which led to the formation of Mau Mau:

> In 1947 a very militant group headed by very young men emerged. It was an extension of the more elderly statesmen of the "underground" KCA (Kikuyu Central Association). This was called the Forty Group (Riika ria 40) or "anake a forty". They were ... ex-servicemen who had fought either in the Burma forest, India or Madagascar during the Second World War. These men returned home with a lot of experience of the outside world. Soon after their return they found themselves without employment and without land. Their European war counterparts had been rewarded for their services with big farms in Kenya as retirement benefits.
>
> Men of the "Forty Group" became more politically militant and committed men. They no longer could accept the government's oppressive measures... The Group threatened to take up arms against the government if KAU's demands were not met.
>
> At the beginning of 1950 a Mau Mau Central Committee was formed in Nairobi. This was to co-ordinate Mau Mau activities in the city as well as in the reserves... After the start of the Emergency the Central Committee changed its name to "War Council". This became the "war office" of the whole movement. Contacts were established with Mau Mau fighters in the forests and in the reserves and supplies in the form of guns, clothing, medical supplies and new recruits were passed on to them.[106]

"Independent Kenya" continues the history of resistance thus:

> By the late 1930s and early 1940s there were organisational links

[106] Maina, Paul (1977), pp. 13, 17-18.

between the unions in the towns and the majority of our people in the countryside. Resistance to various aspects of colonial policy was often nation-wide. For instance, the trade unions, and such organisations as the Kenya African Union, the Kavirondo Taxpayers Welfare Association, the Ukamba Members Association, the Taita Hills Association, and the North Kavirondo Central Association, all took up the issue of land alienation and demanded a better deal for the African people. Protests became more militant after World War II. Nationalist feelings nurtured by such bodies as the Forty Group, the Action Group within KAU, and the unions under Chege Kibachia and Makhan Singh, must be seen as a part of a general world-wide Afro-American movement against colonial domination."[107]

The Channel Four film, Mau Mau gives relative military strength of the two sides at the start of the war:

> Although conceived in the early 1940s, it was not until 1952 that the Mau Mau launched attacks on white farmers - the first wave was, in fact, targeted against African chiefs and headmen who were loyal to the British. In October 1952 - when there were some 12,000 African guerrillas in the field - a state of emergency was declared by the governor, Sir Evelyn Baring.

> Simultaneously, British troops began arriving by air from Egypt and the United Kingdom to reinforce the British-officered King's Africa Rifles. Eventually despatched to Kenya were naval, artillery engineer and RAF elements, the last equipped with light bombers. The Kenya Regiment, whose ranks were filled with the sons of white settlers, was also mobilised, and the Kenya police reinforced until they were as heavily armed as the army regulars. At its height, the campaign involved five British infantry battalions, six battalions of the King's Africa Rifles, two RAF bomber squadrons and a greatly expanded police force.[108]

[107] Independent Kenya (1982). p. 10, 12.
[108] Slaughter (1999).

The real strength of the Mau Mau movement and its contribution in dislodging colonialism from Kenya can be seen better today through the release of new documents of the history of the period, hitherto kept secret to hide the brutality of the colonial regime. We take a brief look at some documents which reveal the need for more research in the real history of Mau Mau.

McGhie reports on the release of new evidence:

> Dramatic evidence has been unearthed of such systematic British brutality in the former colony of Kenya that it may require the rewriting of imperial history. Hitherto secret files show that the then colonial secretary, Alan Lennox Boyd, sanctioned a policy of violence towards interned guerrilla suspects.
>
> A former colonial official, Terence Gavaghan, now living in London, was, according to a memo written by the governor, Sir Evelyn Baring, authorised to use force. Some detainees allegedly had their mouths stuffed with mud and were beaten unconscious by his men.[109]

A special report in the International Press Institute summarises the situation of the press in Kenya in early 1950s:

> The size and variety of the Kenya press are considerable in relation to the literate population. Apart from a European press, whose standard is as high as any in a British colony, there are 12 Asian-owned and 26 African-owned vernacular papers circulating in daily or weekly editions.[110]

The report goes on to analyses some aspects of South Asian and African press:

---

[109] McGhie (2002).
[110] International Press Institute (1953).

The Asian press caters for Gujarati and Urdu readers whose newspapers are published half in English and half in one of these languages. ...in the past its editors have encouraged racial bitterness against the European community.

The African press has developed swiftly since the end of the World War II. Its growth has been stimulated by the social revolution proceeding in one of the Kenya (nationalities), the Kikuyu. The Kikuyu have passed out of the traditional control of their elders into the hands of the young men... Among the urbanised Kikuyu, there is a more advanced class with a developed and violent political consciousness. Numbers of them have set their own small printing establishment where they edit newspapers in their own [nationality languages].

> ### MONUMENTS FOR THE MAU MAU
>
> The struggle of the Mau Mau against the British colonists in Kenya brought independence in 1963. But it is only now that some of the Mau Mau's significant sites are being recognised and signs put up to explain to people what exactly happened.
>
> The sites include a fig tree which the fighters used as a post office. They hid letters and requests for supplies in a hollow in the trunk. There is also a cave where the fighters lived, a mass grave and also a trench where the renowned Mau Mau leader, Dedan Kimathi, was shot, wounded and finally captured.[111]

---

[111] Jenkins (2004).

LEGAL ASPECTS OF PUBLISHING
THE BARBARISATION OF WARFARE

WHAT HAS HAPPENED TO ME?

- In the 'free fire zones' any African could be shot on sight…Rewards were offered to the units that produced the largest number of Mau Mau corpses, the hands of which were chopped off to make fingerprinting easier. Settlements suspected of harbouring Mau Mau were burned, and Mau Mau suspects were tortured for information.

- Reports of brutality by the British forces began to appear in the press. The Daily Worker carried a report under the headlines: "Officer who quit says, 'Its Hitlerism'. The officer concerned was 19-year-old Second Lieutenant David Larder, who after killing an African, chopped off his hand. Afterwards he wrote home in anguish asking, "What has happened to me?"

- Other reports told of officers who paid their men five shillings a head "for every Mau Mau they killed". One soldier testified in court that his officer had said he could shoot anybody he liked as long as they were black, because he wanted to increase his company's score of kills to 50.[112]

The resistance of Kenyan people to colonialism gave rise to brutal attacks

[112] Slaughter (1999).

from colonial armies. This was not the first time that an occupying force resorted to brutal force to suppress a people taking up arms against an occupying force. Overy (2004) sets the Mau Mau struggle in its historical perspective:

Since the 1940s, all instances of asymmetrical warfare – where local populations have sustained irregular campaigns against an occupying army – have occasioned a brutal, sometimes atrocious, response. This was true of British forces fighting the Mau Mau in Kenya, US troops in Vietnam, Russian armies in Chechnya, and it now turns out, coalition forces in occupied Iraq. The term used…the "barbarisation of warfare", can be used in many other contexts.[113]

With the increasing militancy of Kenyan people after World War II, the colonial administration attempted to control Kenyan forces of liberation and turned to its legal system to control free flow of ideas and information as well as freedom of association and assembly. Control of free press was part of this attack on the Kenyan people. Thus Kenya Legislative Council passed a number of emergency bills on 25 September, 1952, the chief provisions of which included attack on the press:

- Control of the African press and organizations
- Restriction of the movement of Africans suspected of belonging to the Mau Mau Society
- Licensing of printing presses, unless specifically exempted, and powers to seize and destroy newspapers printed on unlicensed presses
- Registration of organisations with ten or more members, except co-operatives, trade unions and Freemasons. Societies with international affiliations could be prosecuted
- Confessions made to police officers may be used as evidence against Africans and evidence can be taken on affidavit
- A British provincial commissioner who is satisfied that any African is a member of Mau Mau may order his arrest and deportation to a restricted area

[113] Overy (2004).

A number of other similar acts were soon enacted. One such act held the Africans jointly responsible if any African village failed to surrender persons accused of being associated with Mau Mau. Another act empowered the Exco member for security affairs, if he deemed it necessary in the interest of law and order, to evict the African population of any district, and even to destroy the livestock and other personal property of the evicted people.[114]

The legal foundation of British colonial activities in Kenya was based on "wholesale violation of human rights." While every attempt was made to give a formal "legitimacy" to atrocities committed against the people of Kenya, the basic illegal nature of colonial activity were exposed by the International League for the Rights of Men:

> The International League for the Rights of Men has sent a letter to the Secretary General of the United Nations protesting against the "wholesale violation of human rights by the Kenya Government". The league, which has a consultative status with the United Nations Economic and Social Council, alleged that the Kenya administration had violated six articles of the declaration of human rights…(including) the extraction of forced labour, the use of torture to obtain confessions, discrimination before the law, the arbitrary arrest and detention of thousands of Africans…without any form of trial, the institution of the pass system, the institution of enforced villagisation, and the deprivation of property of political detainees and suspects.
>
> The evidence available demonstrates that the violation of human rights in Kenya has passed far beyond what might conceivably be termed 'unavoidable' limits.[115]

The legality issue was raised by the Moderator of the Church of Scotland in East Africa, the Rev. David Steel, in a sermon to a large Nairobi congregation:

---

[114] Sik (1974).
[115] Daily Worker (London) 21 August, 1956.

A judicial commission of experts in constitutional law is called for to pronounce on the legality of much of our emergency legislation. Kikuyu employees in the residential areas of Nairobi had been repatriated to the reserves – although their papers were in order...we don't kill babies, we can only put father out of employment and reduce them to starvation, and then we will have a save-the-children fund. The indiscriminate removal of Kikuyu from the Rift Valley early this year had disastrous results...60,000 Africans were detained as part of Operation "Anvil"...these were not ways to end the emergency, and even the European community was becoming accustomed to injustice by the Government's practices...The Government could not do what it liked because that was the road to tyranny.[116]

One aspect of the oppression of Kenyan people was the exceedingly high number of hangings on minor "offences". Even the Times was alarmed by some aspects of this use of "laws". The following report reveals the extent of such hangings:

The toll of hangings in Kenya continues to mount at an alarming rate. About 50 men are hanged a month and the total number since the Emergency began 2 _ years ago is now over 800...Examination shows that 250 were charged with murder...by far the largest number, amounting to about 320, were hanged for being in possession of arms and ammunition. Another 200 were hanged for consorting with terrorists, and about 50 for miscellaneous offences, mainly administering the Mau Mau oaths......nobody indeed who is not blinded by prejudice or hatred can seriously regard the consequences of these regulations, as they now stand, with anything but revulsion.[117]

The following section on publishing therefore needs to be seen against the above background.

---

[116] Times (London) 10 January 1955
[117] Times (London) 19 February, 1955

"HIGHLY SEDITIOUS" AND "BITTERLY RADICAL"

A key factor in promoting political activity in Kenya was the African press, which grew rapidly from 2 newspapers in 1945 to 12 in 1946. According to F. D. Corfield, the African press, by 1952, had mushroomed to about 50. All were considered "highly seditious" and "bitterly radical". All were suppressed by the Colonial Government in 1952.
- By 1956, there existed 29 independently owned news sheets: 21 in Kiswahili, 2 in Gikuyu, 1 in Kimeru, 3 in Dholuo, 2 in Kikamba.[118]

TWO LAWS

MOBILE GALLOWS

Taking the Mau Mau oath was made a capital offence. Between 1953 and 1956 more than 1,000 Africans were hanged for alleged Mau Mau crimes. Public hangings, which were outlawed in Britain for over a century, were carried out in Kenya during the emergency.

Professor Lonsdale explains, "A mobile gallows was transported around the country dispensing 'justice' to Mau Mau suspects...Dead Mau Mau, especially commanders, were displayed at cross-roads, at market places and at administrative centres.[119]

The selected lists of banned material in the Appendix A show that a large quantity of material was published by Mau Mau in early 1950s. The technical aspects of publishing had largely been solved with a large capacity to print, publish and distribute publications to meet the needs of the movement. Thus two printing facilities were established in Nairobi, one at Mathare Valley and another one at Parklands, opposite the Parklands Police Station, organised by Ambu Patel. The content of this material also reflected

[118] Huff (1968), pp.62, 99..
[119] Slaughter (1999).

the needs of the people. The publications helped to unite the workers and peasants of Kenya in their anti-imperialist struggles, gave encouragement to them, passed on important military and other information and countered colonial propaganda about the struggle. In general, they helped to create an anti-colonial world outlook among the people.

It was this progressive content of Kenyan publishing that the colonial government objected to and tried to suppress. They used the colonial laws to suppress all means of social communication open to Kenyans. They thus banned newspapers, books, records, and fined or jailed their writers, publishers and printers. They strictly controlled radio broadcasts to reflect only their own colonial point of view. They even banned or prevented importation of progressive films from overseas. An example is that of the anti-imperialist Indian film, Jhansi ki Rani, which was prevented from showing in cinemas. This was the story of Laxmibai the great anti-imperialist South Asian nationalist and revolutionary who devoted her life to defeating British imperialism in India. The film was made in India and proved a major success with South Asian communities in Kenya. The Kenyan colonial government decided that the message of the film was too revolutionary for the Kenyan audiences who had started their own armed struggle against British imperialism. But the progressive Kenyan South Asians defeated this imperialist embargo by going in large convoys across the boarder to Moshi and Arusha in Tanzania to see the film.

The emergency laws enacted by the colonial government were aimed against the African press. Enacted on October 19, 1952, the new laws allowed the colonial government to prevent the printing, publishing and distribution of any material which might be "prejudicial to public order". They empowered the police and administrative officers to search, seize and ban the publication of information which they decide can create alarm or despondency. Once the emergency laws were passed, they were used to suppress nine African newspapers.

This 'legal' embargo on progressive publications was rejected by the Kenyan people. Although the colonial administration banned some newspapers and publications two or three times, the liberation forces either ignored them and continued publishing their material, or changed the format from newspapers to other forms, e.g. to cyclostyled papers and handbills which were not covered by the laws. Thus the process of anti-colonial communication continued.

It is thus obvious that there were two laws in operation at the time: one 'passed' by the colonial administration; the other enacted by and serving the class interests of Kenyan workers and peasants. These laws reflected not only the needs of the people but also served the war time needs of a people up in arms against a heavily armed foreign power, working at local level in conjunction with its "homeguard" allies.

It is in this context of colonial and Kenyan laws in contradiction that we should see the development of publishing in Kenya. So long as Kenyan people ignored colonial laws, there was no way that colonial authorities could enforce them. Concentration camps, imprisonment, detention, physical punishment, confiscation of property - all these methods were tried by the colonial authority, but activists found ways of overcoming these obstacles.

COLONIAL LAWS CREATE A POLICE STATE

"NOT GUILTY" AT HOLA MASSACRE

- On 3 March 1959, 85 prisoners were marched out to site and ordered to work. One of the detainees, John Maina Kahihu, speaking with quiet dignity described what happened: "We refused to do this work. We were fighting for our freedom. We were not slaves".
- "There were two hundred guards. One hundred seventy stood around us with machine guns. Thirty guards were inside the trench with us. The white man in charge blew his whistle and the guards started beating us. They beat us

> was covered by other bodies – just my arms and legs were exposed. I was very lucky to survive. But others were still being beaten. There was no escape for them".
>
> ♦ Afterwards 11 men lay dead and 60 were seriously injured. The prison officials attempted to cover-up by claiming that the men had died from drinking contaminated water. But the story found its way back to London and the truth could not be suppressed.
>
> ♦ Cowan's remarks, looking back on those terrible events, are chilling. "I didn't feel guilty, I don't think. I don't think that quite the word...I felt extremely sorry that it had gone wrong, but not actually guilty." (John Cowan was the Senior Superintendent of Prisons in Kenya from 1957 to 1963).[120]

The Kenyan colonial laws were made and used by the colonial administration to create a false legitimacy in order to support their rule. They were essentially used in an attempt to suppress the movement for national liberation of the Kenyan workers and peasants. It was their class weapon against Kenyan worker-peasant alliance and its organisations. The colonialists used both the weapons mentioned by Lenin:

> In all capitalist countries throughout the world, the bourgeoisie resorts to two methods in its struggle against the working-class movement and the workers' parties. One method is that of violence, persecution, bans, and suppression. In its fundamentals, this is a feudal, medieval method [used] in highly critical moments in the workers struggle, [and] the entire bourgeoisie is agreed on the employment of such methods.
>
> The other method the bourgeoisie employs against the movement is that of dividing the workers, disrupting their ranks, bribing individual representatives or certain groups of the proletariat with the object of winning them over to its side.[121]

One example of the use of violence and persecution was when it was

---

[120] Slaughter (1999).
[121] Lenin (1972), p.455.

reported that "shoot to kill" orders have been issued in certain areas to prevent sabotage on the railways; again, anyone suspected to be Mau Mau could also be killed and the killer soldier would earn money for each "terrorist" killed.[122]

The colonial-controlled mass media was used for the second method to spread colonial propaganda. The method of "persecutions, bans, and suppression" is what we will look at in this section.

The liberation forces had always rejected colonial "law and order". The Kimaathi Charter and other publications made this clear. So fierce and successful had the resistance to colonialism been in Kenya, that the colonialists had to resort to violence, bans, suppression, and persecution on a vast scale. In the process, the façade of the rule of law faded away. This fact was documented by certain progressive British newspapers. We take a brief look at two – The Tribune and The Socialist Leader:

LABOUR TO FIGHT KENYA THUGS: LABOUR DECLARES WAR ON KENYA 'POLICE STATE'

In the heart of the British Empire there is a police state where the rule of law has broken down, where the murder and torture of Africans by Europeans goes unpunished and where the authorities pledged to enforce justice regularly connive at its violation. And at last the Labour Party has declared war on this.[123]

HANGMAN BUSY IN KENYA

Ten days before Christmas, nine Africans were hanged in one night in the prison at Nairobi. Described as Mau Mau terrorists, the crimes for which the

---
[122] Manchester Guardian 23 February, 1954.
[123] The Tribune (UK), September 30, 1955.

men were executed were listed as follows:
- Five were executed for murder.
- One for being in illegal possession of ammunition.
- One for carrying a pistol illegally.
- One for carrying a home-made gun.
- One for 'consorting' with the man carrying a home made gun.

With this bloody act, Kenya enters its fourth year of blood, repression, brutalities, mass imprisonment of the lawless enforcement of unjust laws by agents of its government and of the British Government.

For three years and two months, this has gone on, so that the Whites in Kenya shall have privileges, living standards, and rights denied to Africans forming the overwhelming majority of the population.[124]

PUBLISHING AND COLONIAL LAWS

From the earliest times, the colonial administration had controlled every publishing activity in Kenya with a view to banning any publication it thought might endanger its colonial rule. Thus the Newspapers and Books Act (1906) made the registration of newspapers a legal requirement.

By 1950, there were many Kenyan publications which attacked British colonialism in Kenya. The colonial administration was alarmed as these publications were raising the political consciousness of the people. The 1950 penal code was intended to allow confiscation of printing presses which published materials considered seditious. This move was aimed to intimidate the progressive printers (many of whom were South Asians) from printing liberation material. This move, however, failed. Many printers preferred to face colonial 'justice' rather than stop printing such material. Others continued printing 'illegally' so as to avoid detection by colonial authorities. Other publishers started cyclostyling their material to avoid and defeat the colonial laws.

[124] The Socialist Leader (UK): December 31, 1955.

Undeterred by colonial threats, progressive Kenyan publishers continued publishing even more and by 1952, over 50 newspapers and a large number of monographs were published regularly. The next legislation from the administration sought to overcome the "unfavourable" conditions created by this growth of liberation publishing.

On 6th October 1952 (just before the formal declaration of Emergency), the colonial administration issued the Printing Presses Rules, 1952. This "gave the [colonial] government broad powers to refuse, or cancel, a licence to a printer in order to prevent publication of material believed even possibly prejudicial to public order." The Rules also required "any person . . . to furnish the Registrar with information on any matter connected with the use of any printing press."

The need to pass the Printing Presses Rules points to the fact that the colonial officers not only could not attack the actual publishers; they did not even know who they were. There were many publishers issuing various materials, many being organised skilfully by the Mau Mau High Command. The colonial officers sought to control these publications through a tighter control over printing presses. But even this did not work. The Kenya Committee records "nine African newspapers, mostly in Kikuyu language, [were] proscribed by the Nairobi District Commissioner, October 24, 1952 (just days after the declaration of emergency).[125]

Publishing was not the only activity of the Kenyan worker and peasants which began to worry the colonialists. Their other activities which directly or indirectly challenged the colonial rule were also attacked: education (e.g. the Kenya Independent Schools movement); political associations had been proscribed (e.g. the Kikuyu Central Association, the Taita Hills Association, the Akamba Members Association were all proscribed in 1940); religious movements which were basically anti-imperialist mass peasant movements (e.g. Dini ya Msambwa banned on 13-2-1948 and again on 11-11-1954; Dini ya Mariam and Dini ya Mumbo, both banned on 9-9-1954; and Dini ya Kaggia).

---

[125] The Kenya Committee, Vol. 1 p. 8: "The Kenya Committee for Democratic rights for Kenya Africans" was formed in London to support the Kenyan liberation movement. It is referred to in this book as the "Kenya Committee".

Thus the first reaction of the colonial administration to resistance from Kenyan workers and peasants was to suppress each activity individually. The Kenyan people soon became experts at dodging these bans. This forced the colonial administration to take a more drastic step - a declaration of total war called a State of Emergency - against Kenyan workers and peasants, using their own groomed homeguard as local support. This declaration then abandoned all pretences to a legal facade of 'rule of law' and allowed the colonial armed forces a free hand in killing, looting and raping Kenyan workers and peasants and confiscating their property.

The Emergency Regulations, 1952 (Colonial Government Notice No.1103) and the Proclamation (No.38) were dated 20th October, 1952 and were issued under the Emergency Powers Order in Council, 1939. This last Order was issued by the British King under powers granted him by the British Parliament under the British Settlements Act, 1887 and the Foreign Jurisdiction Act, 1990.

The proclamation of emergency by the colonial governor of Kenya explains the reason for the need for an emergency: "A public emergency has arisen which makes it necessary to confer special powers on the government and its officers for the purpose of maintaining law and order."[126]

Kinyatti explains that the declaration of emergency was more than an emergency; it was "a war against the people of Kenya":

> In their effort to halt the KFLA offensive, the British imperialists deployed thousands of troops, police, armoured cars, warplanes, police dogs and brought white reinforcements from South Africa, North and South Rhodesia, Australia, New Zealand and Canada. White mercenaries from the United States and Europe were also employed. This was not a state of emergency, it was a war against the people of Kenya.[127]

---

[126] Kenya. Colony. Emergency Regulations, 1952 (Colonial Government Notice No.1103).
[127] Kinyatti (forthcoming).

The power taken over by the colonial authorities under the Emergency Regulations affected publishing in many important ways. The following powers are relevant:

- Detention Orders: "for the purpose of maintaining public order.. Person shall be arrested and detained."
- Power to detain suspected persons.
- Acts likely to cause sedition, impeding essential services etc.:
- If any person without lawful authority or excuse has in his possession or on premises in his occupation or under his control, any document containing any report or statement the publication of which would be a contravention of the foregoing provisions, he shall be guilty.
- Public Meetings and Processions.
- Publication of Alarming Reports: "No person shall publish any report or information calculated to create alarm or despondency ... broadcasts by the British Broadcasting Corporation shall be deemed to have been published with the authority of the governor."
- Subversive Publications (Section 7A) :
- Where an Administrative Officer is satisfied that any publication is subversive or prejudicial to the maintenance of public order he may by order apply the provisions of the Regulations to that publication.
- An order made under sub-regulation (1) of this Regulation shall be deemed to extend to all copies in whatever language, of such publication.
- Any person who prints, publishes or distributes; or is in any way concerned with the printing, publication, or distribution of; or has in his possession or under his control, any publication to which this Regulation applies shall be guilty of an offence under this regulation.
- Any police officer or any administrative officer may seize any publication to which this Regulation applies and any publication so seized shall be disposed of as the governor may direct.

These then were some of the oppressive legal power assumed by the colonial administration. Most banning orders for publications were made under Section 7A mentioned above. The penalties under this was a fine not exceeding Shs. 10,000 &/or imprisonment not exceeding two years.

Even this all-embracing law did not stop Kenyan publications. The colonial administration had to issue another Emergency (Publications) Regulation, 1953 (C.G.N. No.222), this time to overcome the increasing use of duplicating machines (this was also issued under the Emergency Powers Order in Council, 1939).

Again in February, 1953, the same emergency powers were used to issue the Emergency (Amendment) (No.10) Regulations, 1953 (C.O.N. No. 304). The purpose of this legislation was to control not only the publication but the also the possession of already published material. At the same time it targeted the entire population, reflecting the popularity of liberation literature among the people. The Explanatory Note to the Regulation explains:

> Under regulation 7A of the Emergency Regulations, 1952, which deals with subversive publications, it is an offence for any person to be in possession of a publication to which the provisions of that regulation have been applied.
>
> In a recent case the view was judicially expressed that it is not an offence to be in possession of a copy of a publication dated or issued before the date of the order . . . It is considered desirable so to amend the regulation as to make it expressly an offence to be in possession of any copy of whatever date and whenever issued, of a publication to which the provisions of the regulation have been applied.[128]

When finally it became obvious that colonialism was fast coming to an end, the authorities sought a new, neo-colonial presence in Kenya. In the publishing field, they still sought to suppress local publishing in order to clear the way for multinational publishing companies to establish themselves and to stifle the local publishing industry and to control free flow of information. Thus new legislation introduced in 1960 brought prohibitive restrictions on

---

[128] Kenya. Colony. Emergency (Amendment) (No.10) Regulations, 1953 (C.O.N. No. 304).

local publishers. This required a surety bond of £500 for registration of a new newspaper. This amount was prohibitive for local publishers who were thus prevented from establishing the basis of a free, national press - particularly in nationality languages - after independence. Yet about 15 local newspapers managed to get registered. It is probable that a large level of creativity among publishers and writers was thus suppressed.

This section on colonial laws has examined some of the colonial laws used to suppress Kenyan publishing. Publishers, printers, and other publishing industry workers suffered banning, fines, imprisonment and other harassment from colonial laws. But these hardships did not deter those to whom expressing their views was a basic human right.[129]

IMPORTATION BANS

In an attempt to curtail free flow of information between Kenyan working people and friendly people of other countries, the colonial administration sought to ban communication between the two. It used its 'legal' powers to ban importation of books, newspapers, records and other published material from overseas. These banning orders were made under the Penal Code (Cap.24) and the Emergency Legislation, 1952, Section 7A.

The banning orders were of two types, either for all publications from a particular issuing body like the British Communist Party and the World Federation of Trade Unions or individually-named publications.

By 1948, the increasing worker struggles for economic and political rights had begun to worry the colonial administration. They thus banned the importation of publications which supported worker struggles. These bans included the *Labour Monthly* (London), *New Africa* (New York), *The Guardian* (Cape Town), and *People's Age* and *Blitz*[130] (both published in Mumbai).

In 1951, the colonial administration banned the importation of all

---

[129] A publication from the British Library, entitled "Publications proscribed by the [Colonial] Government of India" gives the same picture of suppression of progressive South Asian publications as in Kenya. It explains: "The rising tide of nationalism in India in the early twentieth century found expression in a variety of propagandist literature. Published in both South Asian and Western languages, it emanated from movements in India, in Europe and the USA. The [Colonial] Government of India applied measures for the suppression of material thought likely to provoke disturbances and, from 1910 until shortly before the independence and partition of India in 1947, proscribed a variety of printed matter. Much of this banned material was deposited in the India Office library and the British Museum Library" (British Library. Publications Catalogue. 1984, p.13). One hopes a similar list of proscribed material from Kenya and other African countries would also be published.

[130] Singh, Makhan (1969), p.199 where People's Age is referred to as Peoples Age.

publications of the World Federation of Trade Unions (WFTU). This was an attempt to keep Kenyan workers isolated from progressive workers in other countries so as to keep them ignorant about their rights as workers and about struggles waged by workers around the world. The colonial regime was especially upset by a WFTU publication called *For a Pan African Trade Union Conference*.

The following were the main points of the documents, which the Government of Kenya tried to suppress by banning all the WFTU publications:

- All the peoples of Africa suffer colonial exploitation.
- The imperialist powers have seized the colonial territories by force and are maintaining their hold on them by force.
- The first task of the African trade union movement is the fight to liberate the African people from colonial exploitation. The colonial system is the cause of poverty and repression and there can be no future for the workers of Africa as long as it exists.
- Along with this struggle, African workers must fight for peace, for war is desired by their main enemy, imperialism, and they have nothing to gain either from the pre-paration for war or from war itself.
- Colour bar and racial discrimination must be strongly opposed by trade unions. The barbarous and slanderous theory of racial superiority is nothing other than an attempt to justify the most shameful and cruel form of the exploitation of man by man, to justify the right of the trusts and monopolies to establish their domination and make fabulous profits while paying labour practically nothing.

Publications of the following bodies were also banned:

- Anti-Colonial Bureau set up by the Asian Socialist Conference in Rangoon[131]
- British Communist Party
- The Kenya Committee, London "which the authorities say is sponsored by the British Communist Party".[132]

---

[131] Times (London) 15 March, 1955.
[132] Times (London) 15 March, 1955.

On October 16, 1954, the following newspapers which represented worker point of view were also banned:
- *Daily Worker*, London.
- *Challenge*, London.
- *World News*, London.

It was not only books and newspapers which were banned by the colonial government. The banning orders also included music items, both imported and locally produced. Some of these are listed in Appendix A.

The reason for bans of these papers was because they published news, articles and letters about the atrocities committed by the colonial government in Kenya. For example, the following is an extract from a letter to the *Daily Worker* about people detained in camps like Githunguri, Kiamuangi, and Uplands:

Every night two or four of them are taken out by the Kenya Police Reserve, to be shot. Three young men from Mbari ya Kihara were shot on July 18. These bad things are still going on. What should we do about this? Of course we are still being beaten and killed. Can you see some people and tell them the story?[133]

THE ESTABLISHMENT OF LIBERATED TERRITORIES

The years that followed the declaration of Emergency by the colonial government saw dramatic changes in the political and military situation in the country. Barnett and Njama sum up the position by the first half of 1954:

---

[133] Daily Worker (September 7, 1953).

It was certainly true that after almost a year and a half of fighting, and with vastly superior weapons, the (Colonial) Government seemed no closer to defeating the insurgent forces. In fact, guerrilla strength seemed to be growing, with Kenya Levellation Army units more active than ever in the reserve, a Nairobi Land and Freedom Army formed and very active, supplies flowing from the city into the forests, and Government apparently unable to launch a winning offensive against the guerrilla armies of Nyandarwa and Mt. Kenya.[134]

A report in the *Manchester Guardian* revealed the extent of Mau Mau control:

> In June 1953 things were going badly in Kenya. Parts of Kikuyuland were virtually Mau Mau republics, and the great majority of the Kikuyu [(people] were passive supporters of Mau Mau. The gangs in the forests of the Aberdares and Mount Kenya were living fairly comfortably. They were well supplied with food and clothing, with stolen arms and ammunitions, with women to tend for them, and with information of the movements of the security forces. They had effective communications by couriers with Nairobi. They were able to raid, murder and to pillage over most of Kikuyuland and into the surrounding settled areas. Nairobi was a hot-bed of Mau Mau. The greater part of the population of the city was intimidated, living in terror of the gangsters. Mau Mau were able to enforce a boycott of the buses, and on the smoking of cigarettes, and the drinking of beer.

So successful had the Mau Mau movement been that large areas of land and people had been liberated from colonial rule. These included not only the liberated forest bases in Nyandarwa and Mount Kenya - "The forests were virtually impregnable to the [British] army for about eighteen months", says Odinga.[135] In addition, there were semi-liberated rural areas in the settler farms and in the so called "reserves". There were liberated and semi-liberated areas in Nairobi itself, which was the centre of colonial rule in

[134] Barnett and Njama (1966) p. 330.
[135] Odinga (1968), p.117.

Kenya. Large parts of the city of Nairobi were under the rule of the guerrilla forces; others were controlled by the colonial army by day but were taken over by the Mau Mau by night.

The full extent of Mau Mau control in Nairobi became known to the colonial authorities towards the end of 1954:

> A severe blow was struck at the Mau Mau movement by the destruction of their base in Nairobi during "Operation Anvil". Since then, Mau Mau leaders and organisers had been unable to send the recruits, the money, the food, the weapons and ammunition, and the messages to the forest gangs and to those who belonged to the elaborate organisation in African Reserves and farming areas...At times a large roving gang could still strike a severe blow.[136]

*

> Reports so far received (as part of Operation Hammer) (reveal) the significant feature of the first phase has been the large number of hideouts found (in the Aberdare forests), some considerable size and many were skilfully constructed. One consisted of four huts capable of holding 80 men and with a piped water supply from a waterfall 30 yards away.[137]

The guerrilla forces established their own government in these liberated areas, controlled law and order in the interest of the struggling Kenyan people, ran an effective administration with its own legal system and a policy for financial control with its own taxes to finance the war effort. It was this tax levied in liberated and semi-liberated areas in the enemy territory that bought guns, ammunition, food and other supplies for the guerrilla army. It established hospitals as well as factories for the manufacture of armaments and other necessities such as clothing. The Kenya Committee Press Extracts summarises reports from contemporary papers about the destruction of

[136] *East African Standard*, 15 October, 1954.
[137] Times(London), 14 January, 1955.

Mau Mau hospitals by the British forces:

> An army patrol following in the tracks of freedom fighters discovered a 40 bed Mau Mau hospital with complete medical kits. A Government communiqué said the hospital was 5 miles east of Mount Kinangop.[138]

> On the outskirts of Nairobi, Kikuyu guards and men of the Kenya Regiment, killed four freedom fighters, destroyed a Mau Mau hospital furnished with a supply of medicine and food, and arrested six women food carriers.[139]

> Security Forces searching the Aberdare Forests found a deserted hospital which had apparently been evacuated a few days before, also a Council Chamber with accommodation for about 150.[140]

There are various accounts of Mau Mau gun factories and guns made in Mau Mau factories are still available. Kinyatti says "The Shauri Moyo and Pumwani bases played a special role as KLFA gun factories. Karura Forest was the main KFLA gun factory in Nairobi. It was also a KLFA major hospital."[141] There were many South Asian skilled craftsmen who helped the establishment of such factories and training Mau Mau cadres in gun making. One such person was Jaswant Singh who was sentenced to death for illegally possessing two rounds of ammunition. As the *Times* noted "this was the first time that the supreme penalty has been imposed on a non-African under the emergency regulations"[142]. Kinyatti provides some details:

> Jaswant Singh was storing firearms for the Movement. His house was a safe haven for the Movement. In 1954, he was betrayed, arrested and sentenced to death for possession of firearm. Despite the savage torture he underwent he refused to betray the Movement.[143]

A number of reports on Mau Mau gun factories, conference facilities, as well

---

[138] Kenya Committee. Press Extracts, Vol.1 (13 July, 1954), p.67..
[139] Kenya Committee. Press Extracts, Vol.1 (25 September, 1954), pp. 82-83..
[140] Kenya Committee. Press Extracts, Vol. 1 (6 June, 1955), p.140..
[141] Kinyatti (forthcoming).
[142] Times (London). 31 July, 1954.
[143] Kinyatti (forthcoming).

as housing and water supply systems in liberated areas were carried in contemporary newspaper reports:

- East African Command headquarters announced today that a patrol of guards and police from the Meru (nationality) led by Officer Harry Hinde discovered and destroyed a Mau Mau "arms factory" in the Meru forest.[144]
- Police today discovered a Mau Mau gun shop and store in a part of Nairobi where the city's two hundred street sweepers live.[145]
- In early days the terrorist camps were well built. The sites were laid out with solidly constructed huts of split bamboo, with kitchens and stores, quarters for women and children and signboards indicating the commander of the camp...from these camps, arms and ammunition, food, clothing and valuable documents have been recovered.[146]

Mau Mau forces had liberated large areas even before the declaration of Emergency; in fact this was one of the reasons why the colonial administration was forced to declare a state of emergency. The success of the liberation forces was documented by Corfield (1960). It admitted that by August, 1952 in large parts of Central Province, which was the primary battleground in that period leading up to independence, colonial law and law courts "had virtually ceased to exist". Their function had been taken over by the emerging Mau Mau administration, which established a revolutionary administration and legal system and carried out sentences against colonial officers, saboteurs and other anti-people elements. Thus between May and October 1952 (before the declaration of Emergency) fifty nine home guards[147], including the colonial chief Waruhiu had been sentenced by the liberation courts and the sentences were carried out by the armed forces of the people.

With the advancement of the armed struggle after 1952, there was also an increase in the areas that were liberated by the Mau Mau movement forces.

[144] Manchester Guardian. 29 Jan.1954.
[145] Manchester Guardian. 23 Feb. 1954.
[146] *East African Standard*. 20 August, 1954.
[147] "Home guards" – those who sided with the British colonial authorities.

They set up large administrative machinery which had jurisdiction over vast areas with hundreds of thousands of people for whose economy, welfare, education, health and security they were responsible. The Colonial Office Parliamentary Delegation to Kenya admitted the fact of Mau Mau control:

> It is our view based upon all the evidence available to us, both from official and responsible unofficial sources, that the influence of Mau Mau in the Kikuyu area (i.e. the whole of Central Province and parts of Rift Valley and the Highlands), except in certain localities, has not declined; it has, on the contrary, increased; in this respect the situation has deteriorated and the danger of infection outside the Kikuyu area is now greater, not less, than it was at the beginning of the State of Emergency . . . In Nairobi, the situation is both grave and acute. Mau Mau orders are carried out in the heart of the city, Mau Mau courts sit in judgement and their sentences are carried out. There is evidence that the revenues collected by (Mau Mau), which may be considerable are used for the purposes of bribery as well as for purchasing Mau Mau supplies.
>
> ...There is also a passive resistance movement among Africans, an example of which is a bus boycott under which Africans have for several months boycotted European-owned buses.[148]

The Mau Mau organisation, support structures and influence had reached outside the borders of Kenya. Thus the Tanganyika government declared a state of emergency in North Tanzania, and Kenyans from North Tanganyika and Zanzibar were returned in increasing numbers for fear of spreading liberation ideas in these areas and to cut off the supply structures to Kenyan liberation forces. The Tanzania government set up a detention centre at Urembo in Tanzania for Kenyan detainees[149]. Some other details follow:

- The Tanganyika Government arrested and expelled Kenyans living in the Kilimanjaro area on the Kenya border.[150]

---
[148] Report of the Colonial Office Parliamentary Delegation to Kenya. 1954. Quoted in Barnett and Njama (1966) pp.330-331.
[149] Kenya Committee. Press Extracts, Vol.1 (2 January, 1954), p. 49.
[150] Kenya Committee. Press Extracts, Vol.1 (10 November, 1952), p. 14.

NEVER BE SILENT

- "Over 1500 Kikuyus arrested in northern Tanganyika – a Kenyan officer taking part in the arrests had already been sentenced for the torture of captured Kikuyu."[151]
- Tanganyika Government announces that all Kikuyu women and children in the Northern Province – about 5000 in all – would be sent to new restricted areas in the colony.[152]
- The Tanganyika Government declares a state of emergency in the Northern Province.[153]
- 44 Wakamba were arrested in Tanganyika and returned to Kenya during a police round up in the Northern Province.[154]
- There were Mau Mau cells in Mombasa, Pemba, Zanzibar, and other coastal regions. In Tanzania, the movement [Mau Mau] succeeded in winning over hundreds of Kenyan migrant workers. Mau Mau cells were established mainly in northern and Tanga regions where the bulk of these Kenyan migrant labourers worked and resided... In their attempt to contain the spread of the anti-imperialist resistance in Uganda and Tanzania, the colonial authorities in both countries banned the Mau Mau Organisation and severe punishments were meted out to those who were suspected of being members. In Tanzania, a state of emergency was declared in the northern and Tanga regions and police and army were ordered to round up Gikuyu, Embu, Meru and Kamba (GEMK) workers and put them in concentration camps. Thousands were arrested, tortured and then deported to Kenya where they were further brutalised and then sent to Manyani concentration camp. In Uganda, all the GEMK students attending Makerere University were arrested, interrogated and then deported to Kenya. The GEMK traders who had established business in Uganda were also subjected to the same brutality. Both colonies worked with the colonial regime in Kenya to fight the KLFA forces. They supplied the colonial Kenya with intelligence, men and war material.[155]
- The Ethiopian intelligence is aware of what is going on in

[151] Kenya Committee. Press Extracts, Vol.1 (11 January, 1954), p. 49.
[152] Kenya Committee. Press Extracts, Vol.1 (14 January, 1954), p.50.
[153] Kenya Committee. Press Extracts, Vol.1 (19 May, 1954), p. 58.
[154] Kenya Committee. Press Extracts, Vol.1 (17 June, 1955), p. 142.
[155] Kinyatti (forthcoming).

Kenya. Mau Mau and its causes is a subject about which they frequently ask questions. On the face of it there seems a parallel with their own mountain rebels, the Shiftas.[156]

- Mau Mau influence reached South Africa as well, as shown by a letter from A. J. Simpson who wrote: "I am on holiday in S. Africa where it is considered there is an underground movement by the natives to overthrow established Government throughout Africa and this is certainly the idea of Mau Mau".[157]

We next turn to the publishing activities in the country in the context of this ever sharpening struggle at the political level.

COLONIAL GOVERNMENT PUBLICATIONS

The history of colonial publishing of this period shows that the colonial government adopted various means to have a communications monopoly. Its main objective was to disseminate news from the colonial point of view through the publication of a large number of newspapers in various nationality languages. However, it failed in areas where independent African and South Asian newspapers circulated. This failure should be seen in the context of the authority spending an ever increasing budget on its publishing programme. Thus while in 1947 the colonial administration had planned to spend £7,000 on publishing its newspapers, by 1952 funds approved for "African Information Services" had jumped to £33,150.

In just one year, 1955, the colonial Department of Information distributed about seventeen million copies of over four hundred publications. This shows the extent of the propaganda war launched by the colonial administration. It also shows the success of the publishing activities of the revolutionary forces.

[156] Manchester Guardian. 12 January, 1955.
[157] Kenya Weekly News. 19 November, 1954.

It is interesting to note that the internal contradictions between the settler community and the colonial government were reflected in their publications as well. The rich settlers wanted "Home Rule for Kenya under settler leadership" along the lines of the UDI (Unilateral Declaration of Independence) in Zimbabwe during the colonial period of Rhodesia. The colonial government did not see its interests served by such settler sentiments.

The colonial administration used a variety of publishing activities to fulfil its aims. As early as 1947, they sought to establish and distribute widely a government newspaper in Kiswahili or in Kenyan nationality languages. But they faced the opposition of the settlers on political as well as on commercial grounds. The objections were articulated by *The East African Standard*. The government had to give in to the powerful settler business interests and *The East African Standard* was given a financial guarantee to produce four newspapers, in Gikuyu, Kiswahili, Kikamba and Kiluhya. In the event only the Gikuyu one was published. It was called *Mucimania* and lasted for five months in 1948. Gadsden (1980) records the failure of *Mucimania*, which led to the launching of district newspapers:

> In spite of Government encouragement, *Mucimania* was a failure and was closed down. The failure of the *The East African Standard* to provide satisfactory counter-propaganda to the African press led Government to encourage the formation of district news-sheets controlled by the District Commissioners. Twenty one of these were founded between 1946 and 1952.[158]

The colonial government established the Kenya Vernacular Press (KVP) whose publications included:

Ngao (Kiswahili)
Thome (Kikamba)
Kihoto (Gikuyu)
Omwoya Khomuluhya (Kiluhya)

[158] Gadsden (1980), p. 530.

Ramogi (Dholuo, founded by Achieng Oneko, acquired by K.V.P.)
Mulina (Kiluhya)

It is interesting to note that the colonial authorities published its newspapers in all Kenyan nationality languages, as well as in the Kenyan national language, Kiswahili. Besides the ones listed above, in the period when it was opposed by the forces of Mau Mau, it launched a campaign to persuade the people of all Kenyan nationalities not to support or join the movement. This was done mainly through the publications issued by the Colonial Government Information Services:

Agikuyu (Gikuyu) 1955-59
Akamba (Kikamba) 1956-59
Ilomon le Maasai (Maasai)
Jaluo (Dholuo) 1956-59

But this was not enough to stop the growth of Mau Mau. Although colonial propaganda attempted to show that the Mau Mau was restricted to only one nationality, its anti-Mau Mau publishing activities showed that it was aware that the movement had spread throughout the country. Thus in addition to the above publications, the colonial administration started many District newspapers to cover the whole country. Altogether 16 such District papers were published in different languages. These included:

Siku Hizi (Nairobi, Kiswahili)
Shahidi (Nakuru, Kiswahili)
Sauti ya Pwani (Mombasa, Kiswahili)
Nyanza Times (Kisumu, Kiswahili)
Mutai (Embu)
Mshauri (Embu)
Muranga Umuthi (Murang'a)
Muei wa Mukamba (Machakos)
Mirembe (Maragoli)
Amasonga (Kisii)

Chamge (Kalenjin)
Misawa (Dholuo)

It was with the use of all these publications that the colonial government hoped to suppress Kenyan publications and to discredit Mau Mau. They sought to portray Mau Mau not as a movement for national liberation which used armed struggle to liberate the country from imperialist control, but as a "primitive" movement which was against the interest of the people. It was partly to counter this deliberate colonial misrepresentation that the Mau Mau High Command decided to increase its own publishing activity.

An aspect of cultural imperialism in this period was the use of Mau Mau activists and suspects under death sentence in the Rank film *Simba*[159]. Three days after the filming, they were all executed. The film opened at Leicester Square Theatre in London on 19 January, 1955. The Kenya Committee Press Extracts record these grim facts for 23 June, 1954 and 19 January, 1955. The Halifax Labour Party protested against the filming:

The Halifax Labour Party has protested against the filming, according to a newspaper report, of eleven Mau Mau members who three days later were hanged for possessing firearms. In a resolution carried unanimously it states that it is "shocked" by the report, and adds: "The taking of this film for the purpose of a picture called "Simba" now being made at Pinewood calls for the strongest possible protest against the callous and brutal use of condemned men in a way which seems calculated to formant race hatred".[160]

SETTLER PUBLICATIONS

"GOOD TO SHOOT…"
A former assistant inspector of police in Kenya, Peter Bostock, said he believed that it would be good to shoot every Kikuyu.[161]

---

[159] The Channel 4 Television documentary "Mau Mau" (Hidden History series shown in August 1999) describes the film "Simba" (1955) thus: "Forceful liberal-minded film, starring Dirk Bogarde, that grapples with the problems brought about by the Mau Mau rebellion and the end of the British Empire".
[160] Manchester Guardian, 28 June, 1954.
[161] The People, 7 February, 1954.

This section looks at publications from some settler groups to examine their policies and publications. They include the Electors' Union and the Kenya Empire Party. Both issued various publications of their own and also used the established settler papers like the *Kenya Weekly News* to disseminate their points of view.

The interests of the colonial government and the settlers coincided generally, but tension between the two began to increase as the liberation movement progressed and the achievement of independence under majority rule became inevitable. Yet they shared overall vision and came together when they felt their joint interests were being threatened. One incident that touches on communications was when the colonial government and settler joint action forced the BBC to cancel one of its programmes:

> The BBC was forced to cancel a re-broadcast to East Africa of a programme "Journey into Kenya" recorded early in the year by Edward Ward and his wife and which raised a storm of protest when first broadcast in Nairobi in April. The settlers and the Kenya Government protested that it would be unfair and inaccurate.[162]

The Electors' Union made its views on important issues known by circular letters and newsletters, as well as letters to newspapers sympathetic to its stand. One of its stands was that it was justified to murder African leaders. This point was made in a letter dated August 7, 1952 written by its Executive Officer, Kendall Ward to the Chairman of the Elected Members' Organisation. It dealt with the "neutralisation of political leaders." The letter reads:

> The Executive Committee (of the Electors' Union) had in the past urged on the then Member for Law and Order, Mr. Foster Sutton, the need to neutralise certain African leaders. It is not necessary to mention names . . . In light of recent events the Executive Committee consider that their opinion of three or four years ago has now been vindicated and that in the case of subversive leaders

---

[162] Kenya Committee. Press Extracts, Vol. 1, (15 July, 1955), p.153.

it is quite clear that steps must be taken in some way for their neutralisation or liquidation.[163]

When considering the political and publishing activities of Mau Mau, it is important to keep such sentiments as those of the Electors' Union in mind.

The Electors' Union also issued its own *Electors' Union Newsletter* which was published from 1950 to 1952. The annual subscription rate was Shs. 10/-. The November 1952 issue, (probably) the last issue of the Newsletter is headed "Not for Sale". It urges readers to "Please circulate to a friend". This issue explained the Union's slogan, "we are here to stay", a reaction to Mau Mau's armed struggle. The *Newsletter* sets out the Union's political platform:

> The Electors' Union has represented European interests in this Colony for 8 years. Our policy, outlined in "Kenya Plan", has been vindicated time and time again and never more clearly than in our request, made in 1949, for the appointment of that very Royal Commission which has now been set up.
>
> Our old slogan - "We are here to stay" - criticised at the time, has been reiterated in the House of Commons by the Secretary of State... Our suggestions for dealing with the present Emergency have been extensively implemented by Government - and we hope more will be. This Newsletter indicates some of our work - will you pass it on to a friend?[164]

Another 4-page (undated) leaflet of this period reveals the internal contradictions between the settlers and the colonial office. The former wanted independence from colonial government so as to run the Colony in its own interest. The colonial office, on the other hand, had its own economic and political interests to protect and so wanted direct or indirect control over the country.

The leaflet sets out its demands: "The time has come to demand from HM

---

[163] A copy of the letter is reproduced in Koinange (1955). Koinange's book itself was banned by the colonial government in the same year it was published. It was reprinted in 1969.
[164] *Electors' Union Newsletter.* November, 1952.

Government an equivocal statement that European settlement is a permanency in Kenya and that the maintenance of British European leadership is paramount[165]." The last page of the leaflet carries the aims of the Electors' Union:

Permanency of British settlement

- British leadership and inter-racial co-operation.
- Control over our own affairs.
- Increased European settlement.
- Liberty of the subject.
- A British East African Dominion.

The leaflet was printed for the Union by Kingsway Press, Ltd. Nairobi.

As the progressive African-South Asian forces made progress in pushing their agenda forcefully on the political scene in Kenya, cracks began to appear in the colonial government-white settler front. An example of this was the time when the colonial government, under military pressure from Mau Mau, made a "surrender offer" to the Mau Mau – which it promptly rejected. But the settler community was greatly upset by this offer. They staged a "silent march" on Parliament Building in Nairobi protesting at the Government surrender offer in February, 1955. In addition, some of them started a leaflet campaign against the offer:

> A leaflet campaign against the Government's surrender offer to resistance forces, started by white settlers in the Aberdare Forest area. Leaflets printed in Kikuyu threatening death by hanging to all resistance forces and signed "European Settlers" were picked up in the past week in the forest where the Government last month dropped millions of leaflets giving details of the surrender offer.[166]

The colonial government had realised by now that it could no longer resist the demands for change and began to take a stand against settler pressure, as shown by its response to the settler leaflets:

[165] Electors' Union (Nairobi) Leaflet (n.d.) "Permanency of British settlement".
[166] Kenya Committee. Press Extracts, Vol. 1 (17 February, 1955). p.122.

NEVER BE SILENT

Government announces that its surrender offer will be kept open for at least three months from January 18th, in spite of the protests by sections of the white settlers.[167]

It followed up this announcement with a ban on the settler leaflet and announced that the penalty for violating the ban would be up to 2 years imprisonment or a fine of £500 or both.[168] Thus the contradictions within the colonial set-up were becoming more hostile and coming out in the open, thanks to the continuing militancy from the liberation forces.

The Electors' Union also used the daily press controlled by settlers and colonial administration to propagate its views. One example of this was in the form of a letter to the editor[169]. The letter was signed by Michael Blundell[170], and was on the subject of collective punishment - the practice of the colonial government to impose collective punishment on workers and peasants as a way of making them give up their support for Mau Mau. The collective punishment took the form of confiscation of land and other property (cattle, sheep, goats, bicycles, motor cars as well as food crops) from the people. This form of punishment was used extensively in the initial period of British colonialism when peasant property (land, livestock and other belongings) was confiscated by the occupying forces in an attempt to stop their resistance. The letter from Michael Blundell gives full backing of the Union and of the European Elected Members to this practice:

> European Elected members have always had the view that collective punishment is a right and proper weapon in certain circumstances and that view is obviously also shared by

---

[167] Kenya Committee. Press Extracts, Vol. 1 (18 February, 1955), p. 122.
[168] Kenya Committee. Press Extracts, Vol. 1 (22 February, 1955), p. 123.
[169] Kenya Weekly News 24 October, 1952
[170] "Sir Michael Blundell (b 1907) was educated at Wellington College, Berkshire. On leaving school in 1925 he went out to farm in Kenya, eventually buying his own property in the Nakuru district. His interest in agriculture led to his first public appointment when, in 1938, he was elected to the Coffee Board of Kenya. During World War Two he served in the Royal Engineers in Abyssinia, Asia and East Africa and, in 1945 was appointed Colonel, East Africa Command. From 1946 to 1947, as Chairman of the European Settlement Board, he initiated the post-war European Settlement Schemes.
His political career began in 1948 when he became elected member for Rift Valley, a position he retained until 1957, and again from 1959 to 1963. He was elected to the Pyrethrum Board of Kenya in 1949 and became Chairman the following year. In 1951 he was Acting Leader, then Leader, until 1954, of the European Elected Members. In 1954 he was appointed Minister Without Portfolio to the Emergency War Council during the Mau Mau crisis, later leaving it to serve as Minister of Agriculture, a post he held until 1955 and from 1961 to 1962. During the period 1954-1957 he belonged to the United Country Party of European Liberals.
A couple of years after the party's demise, he was requested to organise a moderate group of elected members of the Legislative Council, the nucleus of the New Kenya Group. In 1959 he resigned from office in order to lead it. In his role as leader of moderate opinion in Kenya he played a large part in bringing about the negotiations for constitutional developments leading to independence. These negotiations resulted in the two Lancaster House Conferences of 1960 and 1962." - Source: Bodleian Library of Commonwealth and African Studies at Rhodes House. Ref. GB 0162 MSS. Afr. s. 746. Archives Hub. http://www.archiveshub.ac.uk/news/02121203.html. Accessed: 29 June, 2004.

Government as, for instance, when collective punishment was imposed in recent months for disturbances in Fort Hall area and arson in South Nyeri. Our view was quite clearly put to (the Electors' Union) Conference by Mr. (Humphrey) Slade. There is, therefore, no difference of opinion between Elected Members and the Conference itself in regard to the advisability, in certain circumstances, of the use of collective punishment.

Michael Blundell, while talking about "multiculturalism", was to show his real feelings once again in July 1954 when he endorsed the principle of pre-emptive action:

> We do not detain people for what they have done – we detain them for what they may intend to do", said Mr. Michael Blundell, Minister without Portfolio and leader of the Kenya European land owners yesterday.[171]

This was no mere talk. The previous day (2 July 1954) the District Commissioner H.C. Wilkes described the new camp for detainees at Kapenguria as being built to absorb people against whom "no charge could be brought after screening and yet who were suspect Mau Mau".[172]

Another settler party of this period was the Kenya Empire Party whose slogan was "Coming out Fighting". The Party issued a handout setting out its programme:

> The Kenya Empire Party has come into being because it is felt on all sides that good work though the Electors' Union has done in the past, it will be impossible in the future for there to be only one political organisation to represent the different views of the whole European community.
>
> Every European must surely realise that in a world of constant change it is essential to give allegiance to some political body and

---

[171] Kenya Committee. Press Extracts, Vol. 1 (3 July, 1954). P.64
[172] Kenya Committee. Press Extracts, Vol.1 (2 July, 1954), p. 64

that only by doing so can he or she be kept informed of and take part in what is going on. Moreover in all political history individual action has very rarely proved successful whereas collective action has almost INVARIABLY achieved its objects.

Moreover, being certain that the Emergency will be brought to a successful conclusion in the near future, we are thinking ahead and are determined that all the efforts of the Empire Party must be directed...to ensuring that such a state of affairs can never return to Kenya.

. . . if we wish to make Kenya fit for our children to live in we must be prepared not only to devote thought to political issues but to work together for their solution.[173]

The Application Form for joining the Party made it clear that not only was it against the freedom struggle of Kenyan people, it also sought to maintain cultural control over Kenya by insisting on the supremacy of the English language over Kenyan national and nationality languages. The Application Form with the following Declaration had to be signed by all wishing to join the Party:

> I realise that the (Party) is political, and its purpose is to unite all unofficial Europeans in Kenya into one Party pledged to the Six Articles hereunder:
> - Complete loyalty to the Crown.
> - To maintain Kenya (and East Africa) as an English-speaking integral part of the British Empire.
> - To maintain European leadership in Kenya (and East Africa).
> - To obtain Home Rule for Kenya under European settler leadership at the earliest possible moment.
> - To maintain effective and permanent representation in England in order that the lies, calumny and ignorance so prevalent there can be combated at once.

[173] Kenya Empire Party (1953). "Coming out fighting". 23 January, 1953. The handout was printed by the English Press and was signed by C. V. Delamere, (?) Thornton and I. E. Vigar.

- To link up when the time comes with the Capricorn Society to fight for Federation of the Six Territories of East and Central Africa.

Yet another settler party was the Federation Independence Party which published the *Comment* (1949-56).

All the settler attempts to turn the tide of history were in vain. The forces for independence organised by the Mau Mau movement were too far advanced to be stopped by the last minute attempts of the settlers to stop them. In time, many settlers came to recognise the inevitability of change and joined the bandwagon of "multipartyism" as the only way for them to have a political presence in the new Kenya which was being created. Yet the regret for not having taken drastic action in early period of resistance remained. Hugh Latimer, representing the views of well established settlers, wrote:

> If only, in the early days, we had just taken the first hundred caught and strung them all up to the nearest tree, it would have been all over now. This is the proper Kenya spirit.[174]

One important aspect of colonial rule in this period was an attempt to neutralise the militant trade union movement. They used the colonial laws to prevent the trade union organisations to function. Besides jailing and deporting progressive trade union leaders, they began to promote conservative trade union organisations such as the Kenya Federation of Labour (KFL) and pro-Western leaders such as Tom Mboya. They supported such "leaders" in a number of ways, by providing them with scholarships for their supporters for overseas training, by giving them almost limitless funds to groom a pro-Western trade union movement. They also gave huge amounts of money to set up a moderate trade union press to oppose the militant ones which were gradually being strangled by jailing editors, journalists and printers as well as by forcing them to make higher deposits before they were allowed to publish papers. Needless to say, few could afford such high costs. Kinyatti, quoting various sources, records some

[174] Observer 23 June, 1954.

activities that supported the conservative trade unions and press:

> The C.I.A., through the fund for International Social and Economic Education, contributed more than $25,000 to Mboya's political operations. Another CIA-sponsored organisation, Peace with Freedom under the direction of Murray Barton contributed $40,000 to the KFL for publication of its weekly [anti-Mau Mau] newspaper, *Mfanyi Kazi*. Similarly, the Kennedy Foundation contributed $50,000 to the KFL anti-Mau Mau, anti communist campaigns.[175]

EDWARD RODWELL AND THE MOMBASA TIMES

Edward Rodwell was born in 1907. His father worked in a furniture store and they moved from Sittingbourne, to Folkestone, Deal and Dover, before settling in Herne Bay, where Rodwell went to school. Edward's father apprenticed him to a local printer in Herne Bay where, after a five years apprenticeship, he was appointed manager of the press in 1926. He learnt "how to print, to publish a book, do the bindings and make the cover, and even got to do a bit of writing". He then went to the London School of Journalism and applied for a job with the *East African Standard* Newspaper Group. In 1933 he was appointed the managing director of the daily newspaper "The Mombasa Times". Aldrick takes up his story while providing an interesting insight into newspaper publishing during this period:

> On arrival in Mombasa he was appalled by the age and condition of the printing machinery with which he had to work, most of which dated back to 1902 when the newspaper had first started. The main production of the *East African Standard* had moved to Nairobi in 1910 leaving the old plant behind for the paper in Mombasa, which in 1933 had a circulation of just 380 . . . Reuters sent them a daily cable of some 300 words and the rest was

[175] Kinyatti (forthcoming).

concocted by Rodwell and his editorial staff and then printed on his antiquated press with the help of three aged Swahili printers who had been trained at the Heidelberg school of printing before the First World War.

The war catapulted Rodwell into the centre of events as Mombasa became an important Allied naval base after the fall of Singapore in 1942 and later a troop collection point prior to the Burma Campaigns. He found himself meeting and interviewing important dignitaries and military commanders and his newspaper carried reports of increasing weight and international interest. It was he who was now cabling Reuters with important news communiques. The circulation of the *Mombasa Times* soared dramatically as the population of the town was swelled with service personnel busy in the preparation of war.

After the war Rodwell continued to run the *Mombasa Times* until 1956, when he resigned and joined the *Kenya Weekly News* as Coastal and special correspondent under the charismatic Mervyn Hill. But he continued to write his Causeries and was Coast correspondent for the *Times* and *Manchester Guardian* as well. He also became a radio broadcaster and did a weekly slot for the KBS, (Kenya Broadcasting Service), which lasted for 20 years, earning him the title of the Alistair Cooke of East Africa. Two publications also belong to this immediate post war period 'Gedi the lost City' (1948) and 'Ivory, Apes and Peacocks' (1949).

The Mau Mau years were difficult ones for all who lived through that period in Kenya. Newspapers were strictly censored and journalists had to be very careful what they wrote. The Kenya Weekly News was a newspaper with pro-settler views which did not always see eye to eye with Colonial Government. Edward Rodwell"s column 'Along the Waterfront' reported on the unfolding political scene and how it affected the Coast.

The *Mombasa Times* folded in 1966 and the *Kenya Weekly News* in 1969. Edward Rodwell became a Kenyan citizen in 1963 and continued to write his Coast Causeries for the *East African Standard* Newspaper. He started a Public Relations Compnay, founded the Rodwell Press and edited and published house magazines for businesses at the Coast. Passionately interested in his library, he still collected books and archival material, which he meticulously documented and indexed. In 1970 the Kenya National Archives recognising the importance of his collection acquired some the rarest items for the nation. His present library, though missing the choicest material, remains a unique archival resource and first point of call for memorabilia of Mombasa and the Coast.[176]

SOUTH ASIAN PUBLISHING

Following from the high achievement of South Asian press in the previous period, the South Asian press continued to develop and expand further during this period. In general, all South Asian papers were anti-colonial, as Kitchen says:

Kenya alone among East African territories has developed a strong Asian press…The editorial policies of the various Indian-edited papers derive from a mixture of social, political, and business considerations. News and comment from India are featured prominently and most Indian papers follow a strong pro-Nehru line. Many tend to veer towards the left and, in the case of the *Daily Chronicle*, towards the extreme left. Attempts are made, probably both for political reasons and to increase circulation, to appeal to African readership.[177]

---
[176] Aldrick (1999).
[177] Kitchen (1956), p.28.

Yet there were internal contradictions within the South Asian community and these were reflected in the press ownership and editorial policies. The South Asian press reflected the community's external contradiction with colonialism, and also its internal contradictions among themselves, between the petty-bourgeoisie and the working class interests. Seidenberg discusses the "three categories" among the South Asian community in Kenya:

The Asians, in their response to Mau Mau, tended to fit into three categories. There were no Asians who fought in the forest, but one group which might be called the radicals was strongly sympathetic and gave covert aid to the movement . . . many of the new activists had been educated abroad [and] were influenced by the libertarian ideas of John Stuart Mill and the socialist precepts of Karl Marx.

On the other side of the political spectrum, there were the conservatives, a group which was vehemently anti-Mau Mau and generally pro-British in outlook.

In the middle, there were the moderates [who] admittedly rendered a great service to African nationalism but were not committed to Mau Mau. This last group was probably in the majority.[178]

The South Asian worker, lower petty-bourgeoisie and some professional people saw their conditions as being aligned to those of African working people. Their world outlook and their publications were thus anti-imperialist and reflected their working class conditions.

A point to be noted about South Asian press is that it reflected the changing class positions that the community as a whole experienced. Many South Asian newspapers changed their outlook and editorial policies from the beginning to the end of the period. As national politics and capital relations changed, class alliances began to be more clearly defined. Racial differences came to be less important, although remaining significant, and class divisions began to assume primary aspect.

[178] Seidenberg (1983) pp. 111.112.

This change of alliances and class outlook were reflected in the publishing field. Thus papers like *The Colonial Times* and *Kenya Daily Mail*,which had been progressive and had taken an anti-colonial stand at the beginning of this period, later began to reflect the views of their new owners who saw their financial and thus political interests linked with those of the newly emerging African petty bourgeoisie. While the working people at the time were demanding immediate political and economic independence, the African petty-bourgeoisie led by the "moderates" was asking the colonial authorities to "grant" them constitutional self-government. Thus a section of the South Asian press joined forces with the moderate elements among the African people.

This clear change of stand on the part of once progressive South Asian newspapers forced many committed journalists and other press workers to give up their jobs rather than compromise their principles. Initially, many such progressive, committed workers moved from a conservative newspaper to a progressive one. This did not last long as economic pressure forced more and more papers to compromise and give up their principled stand.

The committed press workers then realised that the only possible way of action was to establish their own newspapers which would reflect their views without restriction. The paper some of them established in 1947 was *The Daily Chronicle* "founded by radical members of the *Colonial Times* staff who had become disillusioned with that paper's policy and direction."[179] Seidenberg gives the political thrust of the paper:

> Taking its philosophical thrust from Marx and Lenin and the political activities of Gandhi, the *Chronicle* was dedicated to a common franchise for all people in East Africa, to socialism, and to independence in the colony. That it was outspoken in its views was borne out by the number of sedition charges that the newspaper incurred during its first three years of existence. By 1950, according to its editor Haroon Ahmed, the paper had accumulated

[179] Haroon Ahmed, quoted by Seidenberg (1983), p. 97.
[180] Seidenberg (1983), p. 97.

over 50 charges of sedition.[180]

Among the prominent progressive South Asian newspapers of this period were The *Colonial Times, Daily Chronicle,* and the *Kenya Daily Mail.* These and other South Asian publications took a strong anti-imperialist stand. They also provided printing facilities for Kenyan African publications and for this the editors and printers were often fined and jailed by the colonial courts of law. Odinga records their contribution:

The Daily Chronicle was the first and the only English language newspaper in Kenya to advocate a militant nationalist policy, and to issue a call for total independence of the colony under majority African rule. There were continuous police raids on the offices of the newspaper and a succession of persecutions for sedition against the paper, its editors and publishers. It was *The Daily Chronicle* group that had sold us the flatbed printing machine on which the Luo Thrift and Trading Corporation ran off the first African language newspapers in Nairobi and later in Kisumu. Pio Gama Pinto (the editor of *The Daily Chronicle*) helped, too, with the preparation of KAU (Kenya African Union) memoranda, leading up to KAU's representations to the East African Royal Commission in 1951, but by then the period of petitioning to commissions was being overtaken by a far more inflammable method of struggle [the armed resistance led by Mau Mau] in which Pinto was to play an invaluable role.[181]

SOUTH ASIAN PRESS PROFILES

A good way of understanding the work and social context of South Asian publications is to take a "snap shot" look at some of the important publications. The following section sums up the history of some South Asian newspapers of this period by looking at what has been written about them as well as looking at contents of some numbers in order to show the progressive stand they took on various issues. Material for this section has been collected from various sources listed in the Bibliography.

[181] Odinga (1968), p. 110.

(1) The Colonial Times (1933-1962)

An English-Gujarati weekly, started by G.L. Vidyarthi in 1933. From its first year, *The Colonial Times* was recommending direct African representation in the Legislative Council and on committees and commissions dealing with African affairs. It supported African trade unionism and was indignant at the Government's policy of forced destocking in the Akamba reserve. Wide and sympathetic coverage was given to the Akamba march on Nairobi and the allied protests of the Kikuyu Central Association.

By the end of the Second World War the *Colonial Times* had begun to recognise the community of interest between the two communities (African and South Asian) in opposition to white privilege. It supported the attempts to co-ordinate the activities of the Indian Congress and K.A.U. Much publicity was given to K.A.U. and its pages were opened to African writers.

The Colonial Times advocated an inter-racial tax, jobs and pay according to merit, more and better education for Africans, and the allocation of land in the "White Highlands" to landless Africans. It continued to stress the need for a well organised trade union movement. By 1957, *The Colonial Times* was devoting much space to African politics. Many Africans were among its readers, and its correspondence columns suggest that it was taken seriously by African politicians. It offered them a platform for their opinions, both in the articles they were invited to write and in the wide coverage given to their speeches and meetings.

The Colonial Times Printing Works printed many African newspapers, for example *Luo Magazine*, and Ramogi. It also financed and published a Kiswahili paper, *Habari*, whose first editor was W. W. W. Awori, then a leading member of K.A.U. After the declaration of Emergency, they financed another Kiswahili paper, *Jicho*, which helped fill the gap created by the suppression of African papers in 1952.

Budohi sums up the activities of the newspaper, its editor and their general publishing activities:

> Mr. Girdhari Lal Vidyarth plunged into publishing business in the early 1930s without any experience of the trade. His retirement from the colonial Civil Service due to the great Depression of 1930, made him manage his father's printing business.
>
> The Colonial Printing Works became the printer of several journals, magazines and weeklies. The first publication launched by the Press was *The Colonial Times*, an English-Gujarati bilingual weekly, which started on July 1, 1933. In a short time, the paper became very popular with readers in East Africa, but the colonial regime was suspicious of its intentions.
>
> Its motto was "Free, Frank and Fearless Press". It lived up to its motto, earning a four-month jail sentence for its Chief Editor, Mr. G. L. Vidyarthi.
>
> In 1935 Mr. Vidyarthi owned and co-edited the first ever Kiswahili newspaper in East Africa, *Habari*. It was a mere four-page octavo leaflet, 1,000 copies of which were printed and distributed free every week.
>
> By 1946, *Habari* had become a political paper and its content invoked the colonial government's displeasure and as a result *Habari* was charged with sedition. Mr. Vidyarthi and his co-editor Mr. Francis Ruhinda were respectively sentenced to 18 months and six months imprisonment.
>
> Undeterred by this, in 1952, Mr. Vidyarthi again started a Kiswahili newspaper by the name *Jicho* (the Eye) which became extremely popular. It closed down in 1962. This publication used to be edited by the present Editor-in-Chief of *The Standard*, Mr. Henry Gathigira."[182]

[182] Budohi, Dome (1979).

(2) The Daily Chronicle (1947)

The *Daily Chronicle* was founded in 1947 by former members of *The Colonial Times* who needed a progressive forum for their radical views. Among them were Pio Gama Pinto, Makhan Singh, Chanan Singh, Haroon Ahmed and D.K. Sharda. The group represented the progressive, worker-allied section of South Asian Kenyans. Benegal Pereira recalls the part played by Salim Yakub in setting up of the *Daily Chronicle* as well as other activities of the progressive young people:

In 1947 Salim Yakub also took keen interest in journalism. He formed a company of seven young men and established a daily newspaper the *Daily Chronicle*. The seven directors were Harun Ahmed, D.K. Sharda, Pranlal Sheth, Raval, Ambalani and Nathu and himself as the Chairman. In 1948 Harun Ahmed, Nathu, and Ambalani were charged for writing sedition, and jailed...In 1956 Salim got a flair for politics, activated in the Kenya Freedom Party with Joe Murumbi, Pio Pinto, Harun Ahmed, Tom Mboya, and P.C. Shethi - all hot heads. P.C. Sheth got deported in 1967 . . . [183]

The group used *The Daily Chronicle* to support their activities at the East African Trade Union Congressand also their nationalist, non-racial anti-British, worker-orientated activities. Their demands were "independence now" and for a socialist and anti-imperialist political line. Indeed, Makhan Singh was the first Kenyan to make a public demand in 1950 for "immediate independence for Kenya at a joint meeting of the Kenya African Union and the East African Indian National Congress in April 1950".[184]

This group of activists were opposed not only by the colonial government, but by a section of South Asians who had aligned themselves to the colonial administration. This included A.B. Patel who then was a Member of the Legislative Council. Patel lost no opportunity to attack Makhan Singh and *The Daily Chronicle*. Thus when Makhan Singh was attacked by the colonial authorities for organising the trade union movement, A. B. Patel joined in

---
[183] Pereira, Benegal (1999).
[184] Sicherman (1990), p.179

the attack. He said:

> I myself am aware that in this Colony there are one or two Indian communists, supported by the Indian communists' daily paper[185] here who are misleading the labour movement in the country. I am also fully aware that, instead of encouraging the labour movement in the right manner, those gentlemen try to take their orders from Stalin in Russia and try to misguide these poor people. I may say further that there is need for supervision of trade unions and their accounts, because I have strong reasons to believe that this Indian daily communist paper, and one or two Indian communists, receive financial assistance from communists abroad.[186]

It is thus clear that internal contradictions among the South Asian communities were along class lines, with Makhan Singh, Pio Gama Pinto and others leading the working class cause and petty-bourgeois elements like A. B. Patel ready to compromise with colonialism against the interest of working people.

The *Daily Chronicle* supported African politicians, just as in early 1920s *The East African Chronicle* had done. The Colonial Governor in 1950 clearly saw the trade union activities of Makhan Singh and the publishing and writing team at *The Daily Chronicle* as anti-imperialist, for which he would have preferred all of them to be sentenced to death:

> I am giving anxious attention to the position of law here in the Colony, for it appears to me that the obstacles in the way of obtaining convictions for sedition are at present excessive when the persons involved are . . . deliberately engaged in what is in fact waging war...up to about 150 years ago agitators such as Makhan Singh and the Editor and writers of *The Daily Chronicle* would have found themselves quickly on Tower Hill.[187]

By the end of 1954 *The Daily Chronicle* was arguing that the interests of the

---

[185] Presumably *The Daily Chronicle*.
[186] Quoted in Sidenberg (1983), p.99.
[187] Dispatch from the Colonial Governor to the British Secretary of State in April 1950. Quoted in Corfield (1960).

South Asian communities should not be seen in isolation from the rest of Kenya, and that the community should be subordinated to the general interests. Some examples of how the paper's stand landed its writers and publishers in court are given below:

- Haroon Ahmed, the Editor of *The Daily Chronicle* was sentenced to six month's imprisonment for writing a 'subversive' news item about the General Strike in Mombasa of 1947.[188]

- Towards the end of 1947, repression intensified. The editors of two prominent nationalist papers *Mumenyereri* (Henry Mworia) and *Daily Chronicle* (Govind Dayal Rawal) were fined for "seditious articles". Rawal was clearly aware of the danger posed by the "divide and rule" policy pursued by the colonial authorities and wrote: "The Government is infinitely more interested in the division of Indians among themselves than their uniting with other citizens of the country"[189]

- When the Uganda Government banned importation into Uganda of *The Daily Chronicle* in May 1950, the East African Trade Union Congress protested and explained: "The ban is victimisation of the paper for its support of working class and trade union movement and its solidarity with the demand for freedom and democratic liberties."[190]

The colonial government's views of some Kenyan South Asian papers were summed up in an official report:

> The policy adopted by these vernacular periodicals was supplemented by the efforts of the Indian-owned and edited *Daily Chronicle*, with its blatant bias against both Government and the European, never missing an opportunity of supporting African claims, however fantastic or subversive. A similar contemporary, *The Colonial Times*, not only subscribed to the same policy but

[188] Singh, Makhan (1969), p. 144..
[189] Quoted in *East African Standard* 3 September, 1948, p. 5 (Seidenberg ,1963 p. 68)..
[190] Makhan Singh (1969), p. 266.

sponsored both *Habari* and *Mwalimu* throughout their comparatively brief existence.[191]

Kinyatti sums up the achievements of the *Daily Chronicle* and other South Asian anti-imperialist press:

Besides helping in the production of this anti-imperialist literature (*Mumenyereri, Sauti ya Mwafrika* etc), Pio Gama Pinto, Makhan Singh, and a militant, anti-imperialist group of South Asian youth were involved in publishing an anti-colonial newspaper, *The Daily Chronicle*, which vigorously supported the struggle for national independence. In a sense, *The Daily Chronicle* and other South Asian anti- imperialist literature enriched and deepened Kenya's anti-imperialist struggle by their radical defiance and exposure of the British tyrant rule.[192]

(3) Forward (1946)

Forward was founded by Chanan Singh. The paper's primary concern was with South Asians in Kenya and elsewhere, but it also devoted a lot of space to international affairs, particularly the 'third world'. Its outlook was anti-colonial. It supported African opposition to the *kipande*, and supported demands for elected representatives and equality in employment.

(4) Tribune (1951-52)

- Founded by D.K. Sharda, *Tribune* held that "it was the responsibility of Indians in Kenya to fight for equality, and urged its readers to accept a democratic solution to Kenya's racial problems. It wanted a common electoral roll and inter-racial political parties. It considered that K.A.U. occupied a position similar to that of Congress in India, but recommended that it should be better organised and more consistent in its policies.

- *Tribune* was among the 50 Kenyan publications banned by the colonial government when it declared emergency in October, 1952. *Tribune*'s

[191] Corfield (1960), p. 195.
[192] Kinyatti (forthcoming).

licence was withdrawn by the colonial government. The colonial government was empowered to refuse printing licences by one of the emergency measures introduced in September 1952. The colonial government had justified these measures by pointing to the need to combat growing 'lawlessness' which, *Tribune* had argued for six months, was the product of an unjust society.

* *Tribune* frequently attacked those South Asian councillors and members of Legislative Council who failed to support African political demands. It called for a boycott of the Legislative Council which was dubbed as a 'minority view'.

* The Tribune Press printed the following three Kenyan publications, although this has been 'outlawed' by the Colonial Government Ordnance of 1950:

    * *Afrika Mpya* (1952-1953) Edited by Bildad Kaggia, and later by S. R. Kimani.
    * *Wihuge* (1952-1953) Edited by Isaac Gathangu.
    * *Njokia-Gwitu* (19?-1953) Published by Mbugua Book Writers.

* The above three newspapers were also suppressed by the colonial government under the emergency regulations in 1953.

(5) Kenya Daily Mail (1926-1963)

Kenya Daily Mail was established in Mombasa by Jaganath Bhavanishankar Pandya. In 1951 the paper declared that none of the immigrant races had any right to flout the unanimous wishes of the sons of the soil. "This land belongs to the African and in all affairs, political and economic, it is their word that must count", it said[193].

---

[193] Kenya Daily Mail 20 April, 1951.

(6) Africa Samachar (1954-1974)

Started by Haroon Ahmed and Hirabhai Patel, *Africa Samachar* was published weekly in Gujarati. It continued to "advocated the struggle of equality, democracy, and common franchise, and urge its readers to forget race, religion and provincialism."[194]

*

The above brief survey gives a brief view of the positive role played by the South Asian press. But the role of South Asian publishing during this period was not confined only to publishing newspapers which supported the democratic rights of Kenyan people. It also printed a large number of other publications for progressive working class organisations and other political organisations. In fact almost all Kenyan publications of this period were printed at least once during their life span by presses run by South Asian Kenyans.

In common with other democratic activities of Kenyans, South Asian publishing was attacked by the colonial government when it declared a State of Emergency in 1952. But "the radical tradition of the South Asian press was continued during the Emergency."[195] The committed Kenyan South Asian journalists, writers, press workers and printers had to change their tactics in order to continue printing, publishing and writing. As the economic and political forces changed the outlook of the owners of South Asian press, these progressive press workers moved from paper to paper, finding temporary homes at the most progressive ones. Thus Haroon Ahmed left the *Daily Chronicle* for the *Colonial Times*. In 1959, when a change in the ownership of the *Daily Chronicle* resulted in a shift of policy, Rodrigues and Inde Desai left to continue the radical tradition in a new paper, the *National Guardian*.

Some further achievements of South Asian publishingare given below:

---

[194] Haroon Ahmed, quoted in Seidenberg (1983), p.117.
[195] Carter (1970).

The editorial policies of *Colonial Times* and *Daily Chronicle* consistently favoured African constitutional advance and the improvement of the economic and social conditions of African people. Both gave much publicity to Kenya African Union (K.A.U.) before its suppression in 1953, and afterwards D, K. Sharda campaigned for its continued existence as a national party. Their pages were available to African writers. Both papers argued that the violence used by the Mau Mau was as a result of social, economic and political grievances. Their achievement included:

- Pointing to the inevitability of African majority rule.
- Contributing to the growth of the nationalist movement, for these papers were important in arousing and extending political consciousness and opposition to the colonial government. The terms offered to African publishers by the South Asian printers were better than those of the European printers and they were more sympathetic towards African editors than the Europeans, many of whom were not even prepared to print African nationalist literature, particularly in the decade after 1945.

- Tom Mboya[196] commented in 1959: "It was fortunate for the Indian community (in Kenya) in this period of confusion that they had a clear-minded press. *The Daily Chronicle* and *Colonial Times* have not wavered in their stand and attitudes."[197]

It is not possible in this short study to cover all South Asians who were active in the political and press activities of this period. However, a mention needs to be made of one such activist - Eddie Pereira. The following section is taken from his short biography written by his son, Benegal Pereira (Pereira, n.d.):

- Eddie Pereira was opposed to the authoritative British rule in India as well as the Portuguese dominance in Goa. Add to that his

---

[196] Tom Mboya (1930-69) The son of a Luo farmer, he was born in the "white highlands" of Kenya and educated at Roman Catholic mission schools. Early involved in trade union activities, he joined Kenya African Union and soon became one of its leaders. In 1953 he was elected general secretary of the Kenya Federation of Labor. After studying in India and England, Mboya returned (1956) to Kenya and, under the first elections held (1957) for African members of the Kenya Legislative Council, was one of eight elected.
After Kenya gained (1963) its independence, Mboya served as minister of labour (1962-63), minister of justice and constitutional affairs (1963-64), and minister of economic planning and development (1964-69). He was assassinated in 1969. Source:http://www.encyclopedia.com/html/M/Mboya-T1h.asp. Odinga says: "The British Government nurtured (him) as the rising star of Kenya's trade union movement...Mboya became general secretary of the Kenya Federation of Labour (KFL)....which lost the support of many nationalists...KFL was affiliated to the American dominated ICFTU (International Confederation of Free Trade Unions)...KLF was never a rank and file movement...KFL alone was never suppressed by the colonial government. (Odinga, 1967, p. 109).
"Mboya was seen as an important link-man in the extension of American influence over East Africa." (Independent Kenya, 1982).
[197] *Colonial Times* 5 March, 1959

fierce opposition to the imperial British regime in Kenya. His convictions about the ill effects of colonialism ran so deep that one gets the impression that he wanted to take on imperialism with his bare hands.

- The nationalist and freedom-loving Eddie Pereira was a natural supporter of Kenya's Mau Mau rebellion. Their quest for Kenyan independence justified their methodologies for Eddie. Indeed, in the years that followed, he became a constant thorn in the sides of the British and Portuguese rulers of Kenya and India. He was imprisoned for his overt anti-British views and actions. His staunch anti-colonial stance would eventually result in his deportation from several provinces of British Kenya. His characteristic full tilt manner frequently clashed with pro-Portuguese Goan loyalists and there were strong indications that the Portuguese would bar him from ever returning to Goa The "loyalists" in Goa who preferred to emulate the Portuguese elicited sharp criticism from Eddie who saw in them fellow Indians who had turned their backs on their own traditions.

- His continued opposition to British imperialism in Kenya, the inflammatory anti-British articles he wrote for Kenyan newspapers etc resulted in Eddie's imprisonment by the Kenyan authorities in 1957.

- Eddie wrote: "I had written over 100 articles in the press against British and colonial rule in Kenya, and had coughed out fines several times for writing sedition. My political agitation against the British started from 1940 and openly I donned Khadi.

- At the time of death, Eddie left behind the manuscripts of three books. One was to be his autobiography, while the other two were entitled, "A trail blazer century: the history of Indians in Kenya" and "Goans in Kenya: a New Breed". Unfinished, they are awaiting publication.

- Kenya and India lost a true son in Eddie Pereira. His unsolved murder in Nairobi on January 25, 1995 left an immeasurable void.

Further developments and contribution by activists from the South Asian communities are recorded below as part of liberation publishing during the Mau Mau period. This is a reflection of the coming together of progressive sections of South Asian communities and progressive sections of working people and progressive nationalists.

THE MAU MAU COMMUNICATION STRATEGY

The Kenyan people's struggles at the end of the 19th and beginning of the 20th centuries had gone through various stages. The early struggles for national liberation had been waged through armed resistance by various nationalities directly affected by colonial plunder. Later, some sought a solution through peaceful means along constitutional lines: petitioning and asking colonial authorities to grant people their rights. This line of struggle was abandoned by many people after the mass murder of Kenyan workers and peasants following the peaceful General Strike of 1922. The struggles of workers from the 1920s to around 1948 led to the emergence of the proletarian line, which was influenced by experiences around the world. This maintained that the only way to resolve the contradiction with colonialism was through an organised, armed struggle based on a strong organisation and a clear ideology. The lessons of these earlier struggles were clear to the workers and peasants: the only way to remove colonialism imperialism from Kenyan soil was through an armed struggle. This realisation began to be put into practice by around 1948, by which time both the subjective and objective forces were ready for an armed confrontation with imperialism.

The Second World War helped to sharpen the contradictions in Kenya between the colonised and the coloniser. It also consolidated the working class which began to organise anew to struggle for their economic rights. But the activists also realised that their aims could not be achieved without a political struggle. There thus emerged a qualitatively different contradiction amongthe people opposed to colonialism. On the one hand was the "traditional" political way represented by those active before the War. The new way was represented by the working class which gained a new momentum after 1945. The former sought change through seeking colonial administration's agreement to change; the latter maintained that only armed struggle could dislodge imperialism from the soil of Kenya.

The change in national outlook was reflected in a new revolutionary atmosphere in the country, manifested at the political level by the formation of many small organisations which sprung up all over the country. The trade unions soon emerged as the leading revolutionary force giving shape and direction to the new mood in the country. They could back their demands by using their main weapon, strikes, which had already proved successful in achieving their economic demands. The colonial government had to come to terms with this new militant power base in the country. The danger for the colonial government arose from the fact that the trade unions were not only waging a struggle for the working class; they soon became the leading force in the national liberation struggle with a forceful economic, as well as political, platform.

The workers began to organise around 1948 along two battlefronts: the secret, underground movement and the open trade union front. They were, in reality, two aspects of the same militant political movement which soon took the front stage in the anti-imperialist struggle in Kenya. This united movement attacked imperialism from two fronts simultaneously: first, was the preparation for an armed struggle under Mau Mau. Its activities were planned and organised in Nairobi from the secret, underground, Mathare Valley HQ. It had its own publishing programme and included printing and distribution facilities.

The second front was the trade union movement which used all "legal" methods to organise and politicise the working class so as to attain its political and economic goals. It made skilful use of the strike weapon to achieve its goals. This was the democratic, open face of the militant struggle. Although led by advanced working class cadres, the movement soon began to influence other progressive classes and racial groups which were opposing colonialism in different ways and who were their "natural" allies: peasants, progressive professionals and intellectuals, students, as well as the lower petty-bourgeoisie who had been kept in the margins of the society. This alliance also included progressive South Asian intellectuals, trade unionists, publishers, printers as well as sections of the business community. There arose powerful vanguard from this broad mass of people who were to play a crucial role in many Mau Mau activities: bus and taxi drivers, prostitutes, market women, hawkers, children and young people from the "dispossessed" classes. Perhaps one of the greatest achievements of Mau Mau was the forging of this national unity of various progressive classes and different Kenyan nationalities.

The activities of this disciplined and united group broke the artificial barrier created by colonialism – the "divisions" between workers and peasants, between progressive people on the basis of race, between the African and South Asian people. The colonial "divide-and-rule" policy sought to hide the real factors which divided people – class divisions – and instead focused on artificial divisions so as to encourage unnecessary fights among people, thereby destroying the unity of those struggling against imperialism for a just society.

Trade union activities were organised from Kiburi House in Nairobi. Kiburi House was the centre of progressive political and trade union activity in the country.

Plans of anti-colonial activities such as meetings and strikes made at the Kiburi House were spread throughout the country in short time. It was also from Kiburi House that Mau Mau cadres were organised and recruitment campaigns launched. If there is one Kenyan institution that symbolised the strength of Mau Mau it is Kiburi House. It represents the strength of working class organising in total secrecy its anti-imperialist strategies right in the heart of the colonial capital, under one of the most sophisticated and well-organised intelligence and military forces in the colonial world. It symbolised the unity of the trade union movement and political movement for liberation waged under the Mau Mau movement.

It was also from the Kiburi House that ideas about liberation and how to struggle for it were spread throughout the country. As Ngugi says:

> The building is well known to the older generation of politicians who were actively involved in the freedom struggles for it was here that they lay down their plan on how to deal with the whites...The Kenya African Union (KAU) had its offices in Kiburi House soon after its formation in 1946. The building was a haven for the African politicians in the 1940s and 1950s . . . All trade unions that existed before emergency had their offices in Kiburi House. These unions did not have "offices" as such at this place, but since there were many, each of them used to operate from a desk . . . many politicians and trade unionists who operated there were detained during the emergency.
>
> Kiburi House also served as a base for the Mau Mau freedom fighters as they organised and coordinated their strategies there. This building also acted as a printing office for many nationalist newspapers such as *Wiyathi, Inoorio ria Gikuyu,* and *Afrika Mpya*.[198]

The combatants realised that any serious confrontation with a technically superior power required good organisation and planning. A key requirement for this was the need to establish an efficient communications strategy. The organisational structures of the liberation forces had to be strong. These had to be created in secret and on a national scale. The task was made more difficult as the enemy they faced had the resources of its whole colonial empire. Under the leadership of the workers and progressive nationalists, the Kenyan masses organised throughout the country, with the first armed struggle taking place in Central Kenya.

[198] Ngugi, P. (1987).

As the number of people involved in the anti-colonial struggle was very large and spread out over a vast area, the problems of communications had to be solved first. An organisation of this vast magnitude could not function unless its various components could communicate with each other: the leadership needed to get intelligence and other reports from the smallest units and pass down instructions for action. At the same time contacts with sympathetic masses of workers and peasants had to be maintained, together with links with nationalities from all parts of the country.

Different methods of communication were developed and used at different stages of the struggle and in different areas of the country, depending on the level of struggle in each area and on whether the area was liberated, semi-liberated or under British control. The Mau Mau High Command developed an information strategy which was controlled at the centre.

ASPECTS OF LIBERATION PUBLISHING

Here we shall look at the following aspects of the Mau Mau information strategy:

1. Oral communications.
2. Revolutionary publishing.
3. Use of pamphlets and handbills.
4. Establishments of a people's press.
5. Information gathering and dissemination.

ORAL COMMUNICATIONS

The use of oral communication systemswas well established before the colonial government declared a state of Emergency. Fred Kubai explains how this developed:

> In November 1951 the colonialists and white settler newspapers stopped covering KAU public meetings. [In order to overcome] this, the militants started mouth to mouth bush-radio information service. Songs were composed carrying revolutionary and 'subversive' messages and were sung by both young and old. Kinuthia Mugia of Olenguroine became champion in the composition of new Kikuyu songs. J. J. Gakara, among others, printed the songs into 'hymn books'. Kikuyu and Kiswahili newspapers and pamphlets were started. I revived the official KAU organ, *Sauti-Ya-Mwafrika*. Other militant papers included *Afrika Mpya* which was edited by Kaggia, *Hind ya Gikuyu* and *Muthamaki*, which were edited by Victor Wokabi, *Muramati, Mumenyerer, Kayu-ka-Embu, Wihuge, Gikuyu na Mumbi*.[199]

The content of these publications reflect a high awareness of what mperialism meant for Kenya. For example, *Muthamaki* explained the conditions which gave rise to Mau Mau in an article in July 1952:

> Mau Mau will never be destroyed by the imposition of fines, imprisonment or torture. Mau Mau is the product of the exploitation and racism which our people experience in their daily lives. Eliminate exploitation and racism and there will be no Mau Mau.[200]

There was a need to organise secretly against colonialism. This was achieved by using oral communication, a method developed during an earlier period when the colonialist regime had banned Kenya-wide nationalist movements, in order to keep Kenyan nationalities in isolation from each other.

The problem of how to communicate effectively, but secretly, was solved by the Mau Mau High Command, using its organisational network, centred at Mathare Valley in Nairobi. Since the largest concentration of workers was

[199] Kubai (1983), p. 98.
[200] Kinyatti (forthcoming).

in Nairobi, a new communication network was organised from here. Workers of various nationalities were recruited in Nairobi. One aspect of their work was to act as links with their nationality areas. Thus the worker-organised Mau Mau movement established deep roots among peasantry, without which the whole movement could have been crushed by imperialism within a short time.

This early organisational work, together with the task of establishment of communication links with the rest of the country, was done so secretly that it was almost five years before the colonial government became aware of the movement and were forced to declare a State of Emergency - in effect a state of war - against Kenyan workers and peasants in October, 1952.

Before the Emergency was declared, the nationalist and the worker forces had been using the "legal" press to organise and communicate, although this had to be done in coded languages which outsiders could not understand. One aspect of the political work was to organise mass political meetings which could both organise people and give direction to the political movement. It was thus necessary to communicate times and places of such anti-imperialist meetings to the people who were ever eager to be active. Barton examines this early period to assess how the communication needs were satisfied:

> The mushrooming of the African press was an important factor in fostering political action in the urban centres of Kenya after the Second World War. Publications appeared in several (national) languages and also in English. Most of these were printed in Nairobi, although Mombassa had the *Coast African Express* and on the shores of Lake Victoria, in Kisumu, there was the *Nyanza Times*.

> All were nationalist and highly militant, expressing bitterness at colonial discrimination and poverty and insecurity of the African [people] against the affluence of the settlers.

The Kikuyu papers around Nairobi were the most successful, and the most influential was *Mumenyereri* ("Defender"). This was a weekly edited by the Kenya African Union's assistant general secretary, Henry Mworia, and with a sale of 10,000 was probably read by six times that number.

As the tension grew which was to ignite finally in the Mau Mau, it became more and more uncompromising in its nationalism. The colonial government had banned political meetings but *Mumenyereri* was regularly referring to 'tea parties' in the shanty towns (Mathare, Kariobangi, Bahati and Majengo worker areas) around Nairobi, which were, in fact, occasions for the secret [anti-imperialist] oathing ceremonies.[201]

Kinyatti gives even a higher estimate of the circulation of *Mumenyereri*, based on recent research:

> As channels of political communications, and using our own languages, these anti-imperialist newspapers were vital in developing anti-imperialist consciousness amongst the Kenyan masses. Some of them were widely read and had great political influence in the country. For instance, *Mumenyereri* was the most popular paper in Central Kenya and the squatter areas of the Rift Valley, with an average circulation of 20,000 copies. It played a patriotic role in agitating against British colonial land and labour policy, vehemently opposed white racism and cultural imperialism, and supported the underground movement.[202]

After the declaration of Emergency by the Colonial authorities, it became necessary for the Mau Mau to reorganise as an underground movement. But it continued to function very efficiently as an organisation. This is shown, for example, in its communication activities. The colonial administration took over total control over all the mass media upon declaration of Emergency. Until then, the Mau Mau had been publishing directly or indirectly over fifty

---

[201] Barton (1979), p. 74.
[202] Kinyatti (forthcoming).

newspapers in Kiswahili and in various nationality languages, and had published a large number of liberation songs and other anti-colonial material. The Emergency measures were now used by the colonial power to suppress all these publications which had functioned as important means of communication for the liberation forces.

The reorganised Mau Mau soon found alternative methods of communicating not only with the active fighters, but also with the masses who supported it and whose armed fist it was. The oral medium was used extensively. At the same time, new printing presses and cyclostyling machines were installed at its Mathare Valley Headquarters to issue hand bills, posters and newspapers. It published the *High Command* which was issued regularly between 1952 and 1957. This was initially printed by South Asian cadres and supporters of Mau Mau, as they could initially escape colonial suspicion.

Later, the High Command was printed at the Mathare Valley printing works of the Mau Mau. It was anti-imperialist in content and circulated underground among the 35,000 freedom fighters. It provided a basic forum for the politicisation and advancement of the combatants. It informed them on the ideology, the organisation, the strategies, and activities of the Revolution.[203]

When the British colonial administration became aware of Mau Mau as an organisation, with its specific ideology and strategies for liberation backed by a political and military power, they began to investigate the background and organisation of the movement. It is interesting to see what they found out about the movement. Leakey had this to say about Mau Mau's intelligence gathering, and its development and use of the oral medium:

> The value of good intelligence system has always been appreciated by the Kenyan people. The Mau Mau organised a system of getting their own followers into key positions where they could find out what was happening and report to their leaders. Chosen men

[203] Mirii (1979).

obtained positions as houseboys and chauffeurs in the household where there was the greatest likelihood of being able to learn things about the plans of Security Forces. Others were encouraged to get jobs in Government Offices, in the Police, and in the Home Guards and Telephone Service. Since the Kikuyu have always supplied a very high proportion of the employees of these categories in normal times and since there are generally loyal Kikuyu in such jobs, it was and still is very difficult indeed to distinguish between the spy and the genuine loyalist.

Moreover, by no means all those employed on such intelligence work were drawn from the ranks of the Kikuyu. Enough members of other tribes had been won over to the Mau Mau cause to make it possible to use members of these other tribes in this intelligence organisation.[204]

It is interesting to note that when the colonial authorities wanted to minimise the national significance of Mau Mau, their propaganda described Mau Mau as purely a Gikuyu movement; yet, as the above clearly indicates, the national spread of the movement is freely acknowledged by colonial sources. Oral communication was considered a safe means of communication by the liberation forces because of the high security risks in written communications. It was common for a team of two or more Mau Mau activists to carry messages from the Mau Mau High Command in the heart of Nyandarua to different Mau Mau centres, and its armies, or to the progressive workers and peasants throughout the country. The art of the progressive Wakamba wood carvers (carving no. 1) depicts the scene:

> Two couriers carrying orders from the Kenya Defence Council are caught in the enemy ambush. One courier rushes at the enemy so that the other may escape and deliver the orders. The dying fighter digs deep the soil and exhorts his companion to continue. The courier crosses many ridges and valleys across Kenya.[205]

---
[204] Leakey (1954), p. 38..
[205] History of Kenya, 1952-1958 (1976).

These activists performed many tasks: soldiers, librarians (with duties ranging from collection, storage and making available the intelligence from different units), social workers and hunters (to obtain food while on missions). The soldier-information workers avoided carrying any written material on their bodies. They had developed their memories and could carry detailed instructions in their heads. They were under specific instructions that should they meet the enemy, they were not risk their lives but ensure that their messages were delivered. Many brave soldier-information workers gave their lives during the struggle while ensuring that communications lines were kept open.

The Mau Mau movement had developed a large number of such soldier-information workers who knew the land routes for safe travel. At the same time they had developed a network of small libraries and archival units in the liberated areas which contained much useful information. The colonial authorities were surprised to find details of some advanced Mau Mau practices in the course of one of their mass arrest campaigns:

> Arrests made in operation "Broom"...The search revealed that the Mau Mau had begun to use as couriers persons not likely to be suspected, among them a large number of young boys and old men. One deformed elderly man who was identified as a collector of funds had £40 hidden among beggars' rags when arrested.[206]

And again:

> Brigadier Boyce, general secretary of the Save the Children Fund, said that in the reserves there are children whose fathers have been killed, others whose families had left their homes, and many more whose fathers had gone away. In Nairobi, it was estimated that there were up to 1,000 such children. "Many of the orphans and homeless boys are acting as food carriers and couriers to the Mau Mau gangs, and eventually become recruits to Mau Mau," he added.[207]

[206] Times (London). 11 August, 1954.
[207] Times (London). 30 September, 1954.

Oral communication was used in other areas as well. It was particularly useful in working with the masses, for example, in passing messages about meetings or plans about specific military engagement. It was in this way that active and progressive workers and peasants passed on news about enemy movements to the military command. Children and women played a central part in this as, initially at least, they were not suspected to be Mau Mau activists. The use of resistance songs continued in detention camps. The Kenya Committee records:

> Most of the women showed quite openly their support for the freedom fighters while detained in screening camps. At one camp the women danced and sang Mau Mau songs. When some of them were escorted to the trains they hurled their rations of tinned meat, milk and biscuits at the railway staff.[208]

The colonial administration was so concerned about singing of Mau Mau songs that it sentenced people to solitary confinement for this "crime", as the following report shows:

> ...Cases which Miss Eileen Fletcher (a former rehabilitation officer in Kenya) described yesterday included one in which Kikuyu women were given sixteen days' solitary confinement in small dark cells made of corrugated iron, for singing Mau Mau hymns.[209]

Another aspect of Mau Mau's guerrilla and communications strategy was to feed incorrect information to the colonial forces. They also deprived the colonial forces of information altogether, so that often the colonial forces acted in total ignorance about Mau Mau movements, force strength and plans. This obviously could not have been achieved without the support of the masses in towns as well as in the countryside. This was acknowledged in the Kenya Police:

> The year opened with the initiative in the hands of Mau Mau

[208] Kenya Committee. Press Extracts, Vol. 1, (7 May, 1954) p. 57.
[209] Manchester Guardian. 30 May, 1956.

which... had virtually put a stop to the flow of information to the authorities. The vast majority of the Kikuyu (people) was either, actively or passively, assisting the Mau Mau movement.[210]

This was confirmed by the British Parliamentary delegation which visited Kenya. Its report, published on 23 February 1955, contrasts the use of information as a weapon by the two opposing forces:

> The delegation considered that insufficient use is being made of the weapon of information and propaganda. To some extent, the Mau Mau by using the traditional African channel of spreading rumours, the "bush telegraph" held the initiative in this field.[211]

The Mau Mau also used creative communications as a way of achieving their political and military aims. They forged symbols of colonialism to infiltrate enemy lines. They were supported in this by their members who had special skills. The Kenya Committee provides details and commentary which gives a glimpse into this aspect of Mau Mau strategy:

> African tailor, making white arm bands similar to home guards, arrested. Bands used by Freedom Fighters as disguise.[212]

> New emergency regulations making it an offence for anyone to wear naval, military, air force, police and other official uniforms without authorisation.[213] [214]

> A number of fishing boats operating from villages on the Kavirando Gulf have been the subject of a report to the authorities. The name "Jomo Kenyatta" is painted on one boat, another bears the name, "Mau Mau".[215]

> The Kenya Government announced today that a Kikuyu woman who had been crowned "Mau Mau Queen" on Coronation Day, June 2, had been imprisoned for ten years for taking the Mau Mau

[210] Kenya Police. Annual Report. 1954.
[211] Times (London). 24 Feb.1955.
[212] Kenya Committee. Press Extracts, Vol. 1 (7 April, 1953), p. 29.
[213] This was in response to the tactics used by Mau Mau combatants to launch attacks wearing British army uniforms. Kinyatti (2002) records an event in 1953: "the KFLA unit disguised in enemy uniform ambushed a patrol of the KAR traitors at Ihuririo in Uthaya killing three of them".
[214] Kenya Committee. Press Extracts, Vol. 1 (29 May, 1953), p. 33.
[215] Kenya Committee. Press Extracts, Vol. 1 (8 July, 1955) p. 151.

oath and for being chair of a women's terrorist movement.[216]

THE DEVELOPMENT OF LANGUAGE

The need for oral communication led to the development of a special language that only the liberation forces could understand. It thus became possible to pass on oral messages even in the presence on enemy forces and to use enemy controlled or censored newspapers for the same purpose. Even the colonial sources admitted the skilful use of such methods, as Leakey observes:

> In view of the risk of written messages being intercepted by security forces, documentary methods were only seldom used [by the Mau Mau cadres], and when they were, they were nearly always so worded as to be seemingly innocuous.
>
> To this end Mau Mau developed a most complex system of everyday words to indicate things other than what they seemed to mean and these code words were frequently changed. Examples of these code words are '*makara*', which normally means charcoal, for ammunition; '*muti*', which normally means a tree, for a gun; '*kamwaki*', which means a little fire, for a revolver or pistol; and '*kihii*', which means an overgrown boy, for a gunman.
>
> Constant communication was maintained between the army in the forests and various councils at upper level in Nairobi and elsewhere, responsible for collecting food, supplies, etc. [Additionally] an organisation was set up - mainly with women as couriers - to make and maintain contact with detained leaders in detention camps.
>
> As a part of the arms business, it became necessary to have all sorts of special code words, so that the verbal and written messages could be sent about the (procuring), hiding, or distribution of firearms,

---
[216] Kenya Committee. Press Extracts, Vol. 1 (2 January, 1954)

that would be clear to the recipient, but not appear in the least suspicious to the ordinary security investigator.[217]

Further examples of the development of language to suit the needs of waging an armed guerrilla movement are given by Barnett and Njama, most of these dealing with military terms:

Banda	Guerrilla terminology for home-made guns
Bebeta	Derived from the Swahili term *pepeta*, meaning to winnow or sift. It was the guerrilla term for Stan gun.
Gathec	Literally, 'sharp instrument'. It was the guerrilla term for Home Guard, derived from the fact that Home Guards were initially armed with spears.
Gathugo	Literally, 'throwing weapon'. Guerrilla term for Home Guard.
Gatimu	Literally, 'small spear'. Guerrilla term for Home Guard, derived from the fact that Home Guards were initially armed with spears.
Gatua uhoro	Literally, 'the decider'. Guerrilla term for big-game shooting guns ranging from .375 to .450.
Gicakuri	Singular of *icakuri*, meaning 'heavy pitchfork'. Guerrilla term for any government personnel or European.
Gikonyo	'Protruding navel'. Guerrilla term for British bombers, derived from the impression conveyed by the open bomb doors.
Ihii cia mititu	'Forest boys'. Guerrilla term for warriors.
Kamwaki	'Small fire'. Guerrilla term for pistol.
Kariiguru	'It is up'. Guerrilla term meaning that an air-plane was approaching.

[217] Leakey (1954), p. 37,39.

Kenya Ng'ombe	Guerrilla term for (British) Kenya Regiment personnel, derived from the fact that Ng'ombe (cow) was the KR symbol.
Kuri hono-i ndirara?	A guerrilla signal to camp guards signifying that one was not an enemy.
Makara	'Charcoal'. Guerrilla term for ammunition.
Mbuci	Guerrilla terminology for a camp, derived from the English 'bush'.
Muhimu	A code term for the Mau Mau, meaning 'most important' in Kiswahili.
Muingi	"Community" or "people" (as opposed to "enemy"). A term used by the Mau Mau for workers and peasants.
Muirigo	'A clear forest path'.
Nakombora	'The destroyer'. Guerrilla term for Bren gun.
Nyagikonyo	'The bearer of a protruding navel'. Guerrilla term for the Lincoln heavy bomber.
Nyamu Ndetu	'The heavy animal'. Guerrilla term for the Mau Mau.
Tie-Ties	African white collar worker; a pejorative term for Europeanised Africans who were least likely to assist in the revolutionary struggle for land and freedom. Refers to those who wore ties, a symbol of foreign culture.
The Townwatch Battalions	The guerrilla term for all those who fought in the towns, most of whom carried on their normal jobs during the day and fought at night.[218]

---

[218] Barnett and Njama (1966), pp. 493-504..

COMMUNICATION IN DETENTION CAMPS

The use of oral communications was developed further by Mau Mau activists in detention camps. The living conditions were very harsh, and lack of proper food, housing conditions and hard labour made the lives of the inmates even more difficult. They were also deprived of contacts with the outside world. No newspapers, radios or any news from outside the detention camp were allowed.

But the detainees developed their own oral news services and oral newspapers, with regular news services, and were thus able to communicate with each other and to get news about the struggle outside as well as world news. Kariuki describes some of these oral information services:

> In many ways the most important nourishment we had was from the two news services that we operated (at Manyani Detention Camp). *The Manyani Times* was the news that was known to be true which had been picked up from newspapers by those cleaning in the warder's lines or had been heard on a wireless by someone working near an officer's house. We were extremely cunning at obtaining news without being seen to do so.
> *The Waya Times* was the news that was largely speculation, rumours or light relief. In the evenings, after food, each 'club' in every compound would send a representative to the barbed wire partitions to get the news. We were extremely lucky in Compound 13 since we could converse with five other compounds. Anyone who had any news would stand up and say *giteo*, which is Kikuyu for 'respect' and brought instant silence all around him. Then he would say, "I now begin my words of *Manyani Times* (or *Waya Times*) which are that . . ." This immediately told his listeners how much credibility to place in what was coming. *Waya Times* news items might include the dismissal of the Governor, the date of Independence (never later than 1956), the revocation of unpleasant

regulations by the Commissioner of Prisons, our imminent release...

The warders disliked our news service intensely and whenever they saw us eagerly listening to it someone would throw a few stones to break us up. The evening news hour was also used for throwing tobacco to friends in other compounds.[219]

Other detention camps also had similar communications network, for example the *Kamongo Times* at Saiyusi and *The Mukoma Times* at Lodwar. Pio Gama Pinto and Ramogi Achieng Oneko's contribution to the development of oral communications in detention camp is also significant. Oneko gives an interesting insight:

[During detention on Manda Island] there came a time when the authorities had begun to engineer confusion in the camp in order to demoralise us. We realised that if we did not organise counter measures and propaganda many of us (numbering about two hundred) would be wrecked. We therefore started a counter propaganda move. Pio was one of the editors and played a big role in a well organised network. It was his job to dish out information to the Lower Camp by word of mouth to our own propagandists. To the astonishment and surprise of the Camp Administration the morale of the detainees was restored and we remained hard and impenetrable.[220]

It is noteworthy that the detention centres came to be known as "Mau Mau Universities"[221] as there was a well developed programme run by experienced cadres to educate new inmates on the ideology and world outlook of Mau Mau. They also acted as recruitment grounds for new members.

McGhie reveals yet another use of oral tradition in detention camps as a form of resistance and records the brutality with which the colonial regime treated such resistance. The incident below took place at the Mwea

[219] Kariuki (1975), pp. 73-74..
[220] Oneko (1966), pp. 22-23.
[221] Kenya Weekly News. 18 March, 1955.

detention centre:

> Mr Gavaghan explained, however, that there had, in past intakes, been more persistent resistors who had been forcibly changed into camp clothing. Some of them had started the 'Mau Mau howl', a familiar cry which was taken up by the rest of the camp, representing a concerted and symbolic defiance of the camp authorities. In such cases it was essential to prevent the infection of this 'oath' spreading throughout the camp, and the 'resistor' who started it was put on the ground, a foot placed on his throat and mud stuffed in his mouth. In the last resort, a man whose resistance could not be broken down was knocked unconscious.[222]

More information about such atrocities by the occupying British forces are coming into public domain as part of the war crimes inquiry launched by the Scotland Yard following the move by the Mau Mau veterans to start a potentially huge legal action for compensation for atrocities during the war of liberation.

REVOLUTIONARY SONGS

Revolutionary songs were another aspect of Mau Mau's use of people's oral culture. They served a number of purposes. Songs became a powerful expression of people's culture in the struggle with colonial culture. They broke the colonial monopoly over means of communication and took the anti-colonial message right into people's homes. The content reflected the political needs of the struggle. Songs were a tool of organising the people against colonialism, a rallying point for people to identify with. They encouraged people to oppose a common enemy in an organised way and as a united force. Songs became a source of information and a record of history which was passed on to the new generation.

New songs were made to record Mau Mau activities and events. For

[222] McGhie (2002).

example, General Kariba's soldiers of the Kenya Levitation Army composed and sung songs to commemorate the battle of the Tumu Tumu Hill.

Songs were used to propagate ideas about liberation which could not be openly published due to colonialist censorship. Describing the 26th July 1952 KAU meeting at the Nyeri Show grounds, attended by over 30,000 people, Njama says:

> The organisation (Mau Mau) was given considerable publicity because most of the organisers of the meeting were Mau Mau leaders and most of the (audience), Mau Mau members. They were given the opportunity to circulate Mau Mau propaganda songs when both coming and leaving the meeting ... As I was pushing my bicycle uphill towards Muthuaini School where I was teaching I enjoyed many Mau Mau songs which were sung by the crowd as they left the meeting.[223]

There were still other types of songs, the Marari, which were warrior songs encouraging the people to fight for their rights. Many such songs were published by the Mau Mau when the movement began to spread over larger areas. One of these Mau Mau songs was published by Tamaduni Players:[224]

Utavumilia Kifo?
Watoto wa Kenya huishi mwituni
Wakinyeshewa na mvua
Wakipata njaa, mateso na baridi nyingi
Kwa upendo wa udongo.
Uui, iiyai, uui iiyai
Uui, iiyai, uui iiyai
Kuuawa na taabu na kufungwa
Mara nyingi
Je utavumilia?
Ni akina nani hao wanaimba kwa sauti kubwa

---
[223] Barnett and Njama (1966), p. 78.
[224] Tamaduni Players (1978).

NEVER BE SILENT

> Ngambo ya pili ya mto
> Wakiwaimbia Kago na Mbaria
> Watafutaji wa haki.
> Uui, iiyai, uui iiyai
> Uui, iiyai, uui iiyai
> Kuuawa na taabu na kufungwa
> Mara nyingi
> Je utavumilia?

> Are you prepared to face death?
> Sons and daughters of Kenya
> live in forests
> enduring thunder, starvation, torture, cold
> for the love of their soil.
> Enduring torture and jailings
> time after time
> Are you prepared?
> And who are those
> on the other side of the river
> singing in fearless voices
> praises and exploits of Kago and Mbaria
> Seekers of our rights.
> Enduring torture and jailings
> time after time
> Are you prepared?

Kinyatti discusses the importance, purpose, and content of songs and oral medium as used by the Mau Mau. He identifies three aspects of oral communications which developed during the changing contradictions of the times:

> Within a span of five years the Mau Mau produced most formidable political songs which were used as a weapon to

politicise and educate the Kenyan worker and peasant masses. This helped heighten the people's consciousness against the forces of the foreign occupiers, and, in the process, prepared them for armed struggle. The role of these songs in educating the workers and peasants against the dictatorship of the colonialists was an undeniable catalyst in the development and success of the movement.

[The second aspect] consisted of detention and prison songs from the early war years. They highlight the suffering in the camps and prisons. They express the people's bitterness against the "Home Guard" traitors who were hunting, spying on and torturing them in the camps and who superintended their eviction from the settlers' plantations. The songs make it clear to these traitors that they will pay with their lives for their treachery. Some of them also eulogise the Mau Mau guerrillas in the forests of their heroism and express their confidence and faith in Field Marshall Dedan Kimaathi's leadership. Finally, they articulate the people's optimism that they will win the struggle against the forces of the occupation.

[The third aspect consisted of] lyrics by guerrillas. One can sense the very flames of war in them. They glorify the revolutionary aspects of the Movement: its dialectical relationship with the worker and peasant masses on the one hand and its principles contradiction with British colonialism on the other.

One of the Mau Mau guerrilla songs reproduced by Kinyatti shows the freedom fighters' awareness of the sufferings of the people under colonialism; it mentions the fact that colonialist laws were used to ban Kenyan newspapers; and the leadership's call "to unite and fight"; and the heroism of the people against the foreign enemy: the song is entitled *Declaration of War in Kenya*:

When the war was declared in 1952
Our country was turned into a huge prison.
Innocent people, men, women and children,
Were herded into concentration camps,
Under all kinds of harsh repression.

Our livestock were confiscated
And our crops in the fields were destroyed.
All public markets were closed down
And all people's newspapers were banned.

Meanwhile Kimaathi in Nyandarwa called for total mobilisation,
He told people to unite and fight
These foreign murderers with heroism
And drive them out of the country.

In spite of harsh enemy repression
The revolutionary flame was maintained and developed.
And people's hatred towards the British oppressors
Grew from day by day,
And proudly they declared:
"It would be better to die on our feet
Than to live on our knees."[225]

Many songs were written by Kinuthia wa Mugia, Muthee wa Cheche, Gakaara wa Wanjau, J. M. Kariuki, Karari wa Wanjau, and Mohamed Mathu. These songs were then circulated to people as orature. Many were also printed and published as booklets by activist organisations such as Gakaara Book Service. An example of a song book is *Witikio*, which became extremely popular. Others were printed and distributed as individual cyclostyled sheets.

The success of the oral sources of information was proved when the highest

[225] Kinyatti (1980), pp. 81-82.

level of confidential British information reached the Mau Mau before it became public knowledge. This happened, for example, when the colonial government declared a State of Emergency. The news had already reached the combatants through the organisation's well placed activists, even before an official announcement was made. The Kenya Committee records the events:

> On Monday, October 20th, the State of Emergency was declared . . . over 100 African leaders were arrested...There was one hitch however in the Government's elaborate plans. News of the impending arrests leaked out causing the Government to advance the arrests by one hour. In spite of this advancement, many Africans on the list for arrest were warned in time to make their escape – most likely to the forests! [226]

This was also the case when the colonial authorities made a surrender offer to Mau Mau in 1955. The London Times expresses colonial frustration at the ease with which information reached Mau Mau combatants before it was officially sent:

> In both cases, as now, there has been a breach of security, and the news of the impending offer has leaked out ahead of schedule. The fact that such leakages can still occur scarcely inspires confidence in the ability of the authorities to handle these surrender offers in the best circumstances.[227]

REVOLUTIONARY PUBLISHING

The revolutionary publishing of this period was aimed at satisfying the communication needs of the guerrilla army to maintain links among themselves, as well as with the masses which provided it support. Three different levels of publishing activities were used in keeping with the

[226] Kenya Committee. Press Extracts, Vol. 1 (? October, 1952), pp. 6-7.
[227] Times (London) 17 January, 1955.

particular conditions of the time. These were:

1. The use of existing 'legal' newspapers which were sympathetic to the Movement to pass on their messages to the people and to receive intelligence reports through coded messages.

2. The establishment of many new publications which functioned 'legally' for a time before the colonial government suppressed them. Others would then be started to replace the suppressed ones.

3. The third level was the establishment of Mau Mau's own publishing industry with its own printing works, editors, reporters and technical experts. They developed a network of printing presses in liberated and semi liberated areas which were completely under the control of the people's forces. This was supplemented by an independent distribution network.

THE USE OF "LEGAL" PUBLICATIONS

The 'legal' publications were newspapers, books and other printed material which were published with the full knowledge and approval of the colonial government. The colonial government was not, however, aware of the real purpose served by these publications. Although these publications were censored very strictly by the intelligence branch of the colonial police, the liberation forces managed to pass on much information to its supporters. We had seen earlier how *Mumenyereri* used to pass on messages about anti-imperialist meetings to its supporters under the guise of 'tea parties'.

These 'legal' publications developed in contradiction to the colonial controlled publications. Specifically they helped the liberation forces to counter colonial propaganda broadcast over radio stations, newspapers, books, and educational systems. It was the specific conditions of this period which shaped the publishing activities of this period.

In the meantime, the well organised workers continued their struggles and strikes with increased vigour. This included the strike of 2,000 workers called by the Transport and Allied Workers Union on 3rd October, 1949 in protest against the Nairobi Municipality's taxi-cab by-laws. The strike lasted sixteen days and was a demonstration of worker unity and solidarity.

The workers of Nairobi and surrounding areas boycotted celebrations of the 'Charter Day', when Nairobi was given a City status by the colonial authorities. Makhan Singh describes the boycott as "a national protest as well as a workers' protest. It increased the tempo of the national struggle for freedom and also strengthened the trade union movement for further struggles to achieve workers' demands."[228]

The reporting of the boycott by newspapers demonstrated an important fact about publishing in Kenya - newspapers and publishing as a whole were weapons in the class and national struggles. Newspapers run by workers, or those sympathetic to the workers' struggle, praised the boycott and gave publicity to workers' achievements; newspapers run by settlers quoted their own leaders who condemned the actions of the workers. An examination of the different ways in which newspapers represented different interests in reporting the boycott, provides useful lessons on the importance and use of publishing in the national struggle.

The trade union movement developed its own publishing sector in order to disseminate its point of view. They developed further the tradition of handbills and circulars which became a very important aspect of publishing in Kenya. It represented a declaration of independence from the colonial controlled media in a practical demonstration that the workers were taking their destiny in their own hands.

The East African Trade Union Congress (EATUC) became a publisher in its own right in order to disseminate its position on different matters, including the City Charter. It produced cyclostyled handbills and circulars calling for a boycott of the Charter celebrations. These were published in English,

[228] Singh, Makhan (1969), p. 256..

Kiswahili and were widely circulated. One such circular explained the Union's position on the boycott:

> Huge mass meetings of Nairobi workers held under the auspices of the EATUC have unanimously decided that the workers should totally boycott the forthcoming 'city' celebrations in Nairobi. The decision of the boycott is of the utmost importance.
>
> It has arisen from the indignation of the workers and the trade union movement against the anti-working class, anti-trade union anti-democratic and racial policies and practices of the Nairobi Municipal Council and the Kenya Government.
>
> How can the workers feel the pleasure of expansion and 'progress' of Nairobi, which has been built by exploiting the toil and sweat of hundreds of thousands of workers by a handful of moneylords, and in which progress the workers have no voice.
>
> The workers cannot be pleased with the Nairobi of the rich. By their boycott the workers wish to demonstrate that the so-called 'progress' is not the progress of the millions of toiling people but of a handful of capitalists.

The proceedings of the meeting of workers held on 5th March, 1950 were also reported fully by *The Daily Chronicle*:

> A total boycott of all civic week celebrations in Nairobi was unanimously decided upon by over a thousand Africans who met in the Pumwani Memorial Hall yesterday in a meeting which had originally been intended to be that of the Domestic and Hotel Workers Union but which soon developed into a full workers' meeting.
>
> The boycott was voted following a vigorous speech by Mr. Fred

Kubai who described the celebrations as "a mere propaganda trick" designed to make it appear to the outside world that democracy was on the march in this country.

'We see no change in our status', declared Mr. Kubai, adding that housing for the worker was still expensive, wages were low and even so basic a need as water was not available to him in adequate quantity. How could the workers under such conditions, honestly join in the celebrations? [229]

Similar sentiments were echoed by Mr. Makhan Singh, General Secretary of the East African Trade Union Congress, who declared that there were 'two Nairobis - that of the rich and that of the poor. The status of the latter Nairobi had not changed and there is nothing for us to celebrate. 'Celebrations will be justified on the day when this country's Government becomes truly democratic, with the workers fully sharing in the tasks of Government,' he said.[230]

The views of the workers on the boycott contrasted with those of the settlers which were given publicity by their newspapers:

Under the heading 'Wicked Mischief'", the editor of the settlers' paper, *Kenya Weekly News*, wrote:

> [the EATUC statement calling for a boycott] "strikes a discordant note and it is a wicked piece of attempted mischief. But I deem it better that people know of the evil in their midst rather than remain ignorant of that evil. I doubt if it will influence more than a few subversive agitators and malcontents . . . "[231]

Similarly, the *East African Standard* of 22 April, 1950 reported on a speech made by Mr. (later Sir) Michael Blundell, settler Member of Legislative Council for Rift Valley at a meeting held at the Gilgil Country Club, under the auspices of Kenya National Farmers Union (KNFU):

---

[229] *The Daily Chronicle* (7th March, 1950), quoted in Makhan Singh, p. 253.
[230] Ibid.
[231] *Kenya Weekly News*, 31st March, 1950.

Mr. Blundell referred to the manifesto issued by (EATUC) just before the visit of the Duke of Gloucester. The manifesto called upon the workers to boycott the Royal visit as their acknowledgement of the capitalist oppression under which they suffered. 'It was most utter claptrap,' he declared. 'Anybody who can write about capitalism, workers of the world, and so on, in that manner is living in the world of 1870. We are not prepared to accept persons in our midst who follow a road which would lead to misery.

The *Daily Chronicle* again took up publicising workers' achievements when it published the May Day message of the General Secretary of the East African Trade Union Congress on 1st May, 1950:

> The East African Trade Unions Congress is celebrating the May Day also as its first birthday. It was on 1st May, 1949, when it was formed by five registered trade unions, whose number has now risen to nine and membership from about 5,000 to about 12,000. The preceding year was an historic year for the unity and struggles of workers of East Africa.
>
> The strike of 300 Indian and African shoe-makers for 38 days, 180 sweetmeat workers' strike for 28 days, 2,000 transport workers' strike for 16 days . . . and hundreds of meetings attended by thousands of workers - all these strikes and huge meetings demonstrated the growing unity and militancy of East African workers to fight unitedly for their just rights and demands against the growing onslaught of the employers . . . This influence of the workers and trade unions in politics would go on increasing, because the problems facing the workers and the trade unions cannot be finally solved without the complete freedom of East Africa and ending of exploitation of man by man.[232]

The victories won by workers and their organisations were making the

[232] *Daily Chronicle* (1 May, 1950).

settlers and the colonial government uneasy. In order to break worker unity they arrested Fred Kubai and Makhan Singh on 15th May 1950. The following day the worker leaders met at Kiburi House and decided to declare a general strike for the following economic and political demands:

1. Release of Makhan Singh, Fred Kubai and Chege Kibachia.
2. A minimum wage of Shs 100/-.
3. Abolition of the municipal by-laws regarding taxi drivers.
4. We do not want workers arrested at night in their houses.
5. We want freedom for all workers and freedom of East African territories.[233]

Their past experience had taught the workers that communication was an important aspect of their work and could not be left to colonial-controlled newspapers or radios. They therefore wrote the strike notices in Kiswahili. These notices were cyclostyled and distributed and stuck on walls and trees throughout Nairobi at night and were sent out to other places in Kenya.

The general strike began the next day and continued up to 24th May. During this period, the strike spread to all major towns, including Nairobi, Nakuru, Mombasa, Kisumu, Kakamega, Kisii, Mombasa, Thika, Nyeri and Nanyuki. During the strike, more than a hundred thousand people participated in the strike. In addition, peasants and other working people had shown great sympathy and solidarity with the strike. They donated food (maize, potatoes, sweet potatoes and sugar cane) as well as cash donations for the striking workers and their families. As Makhan Singh says, the workers and their supporters "had shown unprecedented courage and heroism in defying the colonial authorities and employers. It was a great general strike in the history of Kenya's trade union movement as well as the national movement."[234]

Progressive newspapers meanwhile continued to report on the on-going struggles. Thus *Daily Chronicle* reported extensively on the activities of the EATUC. One such example was at the court proceedings for a restriction

[233] Singh, Makhan (1969), p. 270.
[234] Singh, Makhan (1969), p. 277.

order against Makhan Singh. In his report, the judge quoted from the *Daily Chronicle*:

- The defendant alleged in the newspaper, the *Daily Chronicle* (of 21.3.1950) that secret plans were being hatched in order to take away land belonging to Native Land Units in order to add them to the City area.

- The defendant admitted writing an article in the *Daily Chronicle* (of 2.3.1949) under the heading 'Repression is Mounting' alleging in effect that it was the intention of the British and United States Governments to develop Africa as a vast base for "keeping the African under subjugation and also for the purpose of re-conquering the people of the world who are either free or have recently won a partial freedom, such as the people of India."

- The defendant also wrote and published a statement in the *Daily Chronicle* (of 12.3.1949) referring to the proscription of certain Kenya societies including the Dini ya Msambwa and the Dini ya Jesu Kristo. He, in the same article, stated that the only "crime" of these organisations "is that they wholeheartedly support the cause of, and defend the true interests of, the colonial people and work for their emancipation and democratic rights."

- The defendant described His Majesty's Government as "a foreign power" with no right to be the governing body in the Colony.[235]

It is important to realise the close co-operation during this period between progressive South Asian press workers and their African counterparts in the liberation front. Spencer records their contribution:

> ...There were other Indians (besides Apa Pant) who did even more but whose importance has been overlooked. These were the men

[235] Quoted in Singh, Makhan (1969), p. 279.

in the newspaper business: printers, publishers, and editors, whose machines produced the African papers. It would be difficult to overstate the significance of these new publications...all these papers helped build a political awareness that had not existed before. Because European printers obviously would not touch them and since, for several years after the War, no African could afford to publish them on their own, it was left to the Indians . . . to print these new African papers.[236]

The use of the existing publications was one way in which the revolutionary forces communicated with their supporters. These were not controlled by Mau Mau but they managed to use whatever openings there were to pass on their messages through the columns of local papers. But given that they controlled large administrative machinery which had jurisdiction over vast areas with hundreds of thousands of people, other methods of communication had to be developed.

One such method used by Mau Mau was the establishment of 'legal' newspapers. This was possible in the late 1940s and early 1950s. By 1954, about fifty such newspapers were established by the liberation forces. As soon as the colonial administration became aware of the reality that they were controlled by Mau Mau, they were banned. Most of these were in one of the nationality languages or in Kiswahili and supported Mau Mau and the independence movement. They were in fact, directly or indirectly, controlled by the Mau Mau High Command through its Mathare Valley headquarters in Nairobi. Some of these are listed in the Appendix A.

The early newspapers were started for a political reason, to give publicity to their political demands and to organise the masses behind Mau Mau ideology and programme. The mass meetings organised by KAU were becoming very popular with thousands attending. One way in which the colonial administration tried to stop these meetings was to cut off any publicity for them. They ensured that the European-owned newspapers would not report these meetings. There thus developed an information gap

[236] Spencer (1983), pp. 78-79.

which needed to be addressed by Mau Mau.

It did so by launching a number of newspapers in nationality languages, all indirectly controlled by the High Command and run by individuals who were not known by the government as belonging to Mau Mau. Thus the organisation was protected from being known by the colonial administration and even when many newspapers were banned, the organisation remained intact.

Among papers started by activists were: *Inooria ria Gikuyu* (November 1951), *Afrika Mpya* (October 1952), *Gikuyu na Mumbi*, *Wihuge*, and *Wiyathi*. There were many song books, such as *Witikio*, all of which were spreading the same message. They gave a political interpretation to events and also publicised KAU activities.

Around this time, the old contradictions between the two ways of achieving independence sharpened. On the one hand were those who favoured petitioning the colonial government to 'grant' independence; on the other hand were those who maintained that the only way to remove imperialism from Kenya was through an armed struggle. The latter started preparations for an armed struggle soon after 1945 and represented the worker consciousness of the Kenyan proletariat. It was this line which merged with militant nationalists and trade unionists to become Mau Mau.

Kaggia records the conditions of the time:

> My newspapers and the others founded during 1951 and 1952, catered for politically conscious readers. It was the period of great strides in oath administration; it was a period of change, when people were beginning to lose their faith in gradual constitutional progress. Many young initiates were very impatient. They were always asking when we were going to take up arms and fight for our rights. The newspaper editors had to write for this audience, even if it meant being prosecuted. We had only one aim: to arouse people

[237] Kaggia (1975), pp. 82-83.

to the point where they would be ready to do anything for Kenya. We didn't consider our own safety or welfare.[237]

The activities of the Kenyan African press had begun to worry the colonial authorities as early as 1946 from which time they sought to find ways, 'legal' or otherwise, to suppress Kenyan publishing. A meeting of provincial commissioners held on 26th October, 1946 discussed the issue of newspapers and recommended that the following points be sent to the Secretary of State in Britain:

- That the present trend of the [African] press constituted a grave menace to the future of the Colony.

- That certain [African] newspapers were being financed and influenced by seditious minded Indians and that their object was purely anti-government and anti-European.

- That, as regards freedom of the press, liberty was being mistaken for licence, and that in addition to deliberate distortion of facts, many of the articles in such newspapers contained a most dangerous and pernicious form of anti-European propaganda.

- Asking for information as to what legislation existed in any other British Colony for the control of the Press, and suggesting consideration of the possibility of some form of supervision or censorship.[238]

In the following months, even more local publications emerged and the message they carried became even more anti-imperialist and militant, demanding even more urgent changes. The colonialists' concern was voiced by the Acting Chief Native Commissioner to the Member for Law and Order and the Deputy Chief Secretary on 20th February, 1947:

In my view the general tone of these tribal newspapers since the

[238] Quoted in Corfield (1960), p. 191.

date of the provincial commissioners' meeting in October last year has steadily deteriorated and the situation which was urgent enough then is worse today. As you are aware, 18 months ago there was practically no (national) Press, with the exception of the *Baraza*, which is run by the *East African Standard* and which is, broadly speaking, moderate in tone. Since that date a number of newspapers edited by Africans and published in English, Swahili, and the vernacular languages has sprung up ... To my mind a serious cause of this cleavage is the continuous stream of lies, misrepresentation and colour consciousness which is pouring out from vernacular presses, and which is inspired by a few Africans, abetted by the owners of the Indian presses who produce these papers. In my view, if we are unable to control this unpleasant stream, we are bound to have trouble in this Colony, and I do not think it is going too far to say that those troubles may well lead to bloodshed. If we are to avoid trouble, we have got to fight this deliberate attempt to drive a wedge between the African peoples and the Europeans in this country.[239]

Thus the liberation forces faced the enemy not only on the battlefield; the powerful enemy propaganda machinery kept up a continuous attack to misrepresent the national struggle. The cause of the freedom fighters and their supporters was deliberately distorted by the colonial propaganda publishing. This presented Mau Mau as a 'savage atavistic movement'. The 1950s was a period of revolutionary liberation war in Kenya, but the colonial administration presented the events as acts of barbarism, as happened in all anti colonial wars. Odinga takes up the aspect of colonial propaganda against Mau Mau:

> The sensational anti-Mau Mau propaganda of the period is a gross insult to the leadership of Dedan Kimathi and the brave men he led who defied death in a guerrilla army for the freedom cause in Kenya.

[239] Quoted in Corfield (1960), p.192-193..

The propaganda against the Mau Mau as a "savage atavistic movement" – from sensational press reports, to government and army handouts and the British Government Corfield Commission – was so fierce...The Emergency was a time of revolutionary war in Kenya. For almost a decade in the fifties only one side in this battle was able to present its case and its account of events.[240]

For its part, the Kenya Parliament, established by the liberation forces, continued to interpret events from the point of view of Kenyan masses and made it very clear what the fight against imperialism was all about:

> We are fighting for all land stolen from us by the [British] Crown through its Orders in Council of 1915, according to which Africans have been evicted from the Kenya Highlands. The British Government must grant Kenya full independence under African leadership, and hand over all land previously alienated for distribution to the landless. We will fight until we achieve freedom or until the last of our warriors has shed their last drop of blood.[241]

> Kimaathi explained in a letter he wrote from his headquarters in Nyandarua in 1955 to the Nairobi newspaper *Habari za Dunia* that "the poor are the Mau Mau. Poverty can be stopped, but not by bombs and weapons from the imperialists. Only the revolutionary justice of the struggles of the poor can end poverty for Kenyans."[242]

The Mau Mau High Command gave much importance to the communications aspect of the struggle. As Barnet and Njama (1966) record, in January 1955, when a secret meeting was held to make important organisational changes, various committees were formed with one of them being made responsible for information and publishing. The secret War Council, which had the overall responsibility for co-ordinating political and military activities, had its headquarters at Mathare in Nairobi in the mud and thatch houses among the trees. It was from here that Mau Mau publishing and printing activities were located and from where its national

---

[240] Odinga (1968), pp. 180-181.
[241] Quoted in Odinga (1968), pp. 119-120.
[242] Quoted in Odinga (1968), p.120.

NEVER BE SILENT

publicity was organised.

The early period of active revolutionary anti-imperialist war saw the build-up of armed forces which assumed control over a large part of the country. We saw earlier how some areas in Nairobi came under full control of the liberation forces. Many people like Corfield had to admit that by August, 1952, in large parts of Central Province which was the primary battlefield, colonial law and law courts "had virtually ceased to function."[243] Their functions were taken over by Mau Mau revolutionary courts which established justice for workers and peasants and carried out sentences against colonial officers, saboteurs and other anti-people elements. Thus between May and October, 1952 (*before* the declaration of Emergency) homeguard comprador traitors including Chief Waruhiu had been sentenced by Mau Mau courts and the sentences were carried out by the armed liberation forces.

It was in this atmosphere that Mau Mau established over fifty newspapers which were all banned by the colonial government using the 'emergency' powers after 1952.

PREPARATION FOR ARMED PHASE

The preparation of the armed struggle started soon after the end of the Second WorldWar in 1945. As early as 1948, activists in the armed struggle procured over 300 rounds of ammunition from the stores of the colonial armed forces stationed in the Rift Valley. It was the armed revolution that changed, and took to new heights Kenyan publishing, which had for generations been suppressed by colonial laws. Makhan Singh explains the background to the stage of armed struggle:

[243] Corfield (1960), p. 279.

> A major development in the period following the general strike (of 1950) was the rapid progress of a secret mass organisation. The organisation, which previously had been in existence for some time, could be joined by persons of any tribe who took an oath according to their customs and traditions and beliefs, pledging themselves to secrecy, dedication and sacrifice for the cause of freedom of Kenya. The aim of the uhuru-oath-organisation was to unite and mobilise the people of Kenya in the struggle for independence and to resort to armed struggle against the colonialists if and when it became obvious to the organisation that there was no other way of achieving independence of Kenya . . . When the organisation had to resort to armed struggle against the colonialists it began to be called Kenya Land and Freedom Army.[244]

And again:

> The uhuru-oath-organisation, which was now called the Mau Mau, was hotting up its struggle, especially violent struggles. It was becoming obvious to its leadership that armed force against the colonialists would have to be resorted to, because no other way was left to achieve the complete independence of Kenya. The majority of people in the Central Province had taken the uhuru-oath, and there were also such oath-takers in all other parts of Kenya. Some trade unionists in association with some other national leaders were playing an important part in the activities of the uhuru-oath-organisation.

The colonial authorities banned Mau Mau on 12th August, 1950, as a 'legally' constituted body. This did not, however, stop it operating underground. It was not until 1952 that the colonial government realised how powerful the movement had become. A full State of Emergency was considered the only way of controlling the growth of the militant organisation. This was done on 20th October, 1952. As Makhan Singh says, "A new chapter had begun. An imperialist colonial war was now on

[244] Singh, M. (1969), pp. 288-289..
[245] Singh, M. (1969), p.320.

against the people of Kenya."[245]

As the conditions were different from those of the earlier period, the publishing activities of both the Kenyan people and the settlers and the colonial government now reflected these changed conditions.

Kenyan publishing during this period developed in struggle against colonial-settler publishing. The colonial authorities gave themselves a monopoly of the means of mass communication. Kenyan liberation forces, who by this time had embarked on an armed struggle, had to develop their own publishing and mass communications network. The colonial administration reacted to this development and increased their own newspapers and radio broadcasts, using all its laws to suppress Kenyan publishing. Yet it failed to prevent Kenyans from communicating with other Kenyans or to give up their struggles for a free nation and free publishing.

The example of *Nyota ya Kirinyaga* (1949; 1951) is an important one. It was a cyclostyled paper published by S. M. Waithaka and was banned by the government on 11 January, 1954. Gadsden explains the class background of people involved in its publication:

> Among the editors were one carpenter, a shoemaker, driver, sign writer, one bookbinder, and several clerks, traders and farmers. They identified with and considered themselves the leaders of the urban and rural poor...it seems clear that it was from this class that the militant leadership was drawn, and it certainly provided the editors of the radical press.[246]

It was from the ranks of these radicals that the Mau Mau movement developed, influenced by the militant trade union ideology which itself learnt from the militancy of the South Asian struggle for working class solidarity as well as from the struggle for freedom from colonial rule.

---

[246] Gadsden (1980), p. 519.

THE KIMAATHI CHARTER

The revolutionary forces now faced their enemy in every aspect of life. The colonial and settler finance and business interests used the presses they controlled as a weapon in their arsenal. As Odinga says:

> Daily and weekly [colonial] papers slanted the news, distorted nationalist policy, destroyed or boosted African spokesman by the standards of reactionary politicians and business interests. At crucial times in the independence fight the press could be relied upon to build up 'moderates' and denigrate 'extremists'. They could eclipse a leader in the public eye by dropping him from the news columns. The freedom of the press was being used to undermine the freedom of decision of the people.[247]

The revolutionary forces were not defeated by such tactics of the colonialists. Important decisions about the whole struggle had been made at the Mau Mau Mwathe Meeting in August, 1953 and this affected the publishing field as well. The Mwathe Meeting established the Kenya Defence Council, comprising of all guerrilla leaders and headed by Kimaathi wa Waciuri. The Kenya Defence Council brought under its own unified military command all guerrilla units and also integrated all the revolutionary forces both within and outside the forest under a central governing council. Eight Land and Freedom armies were named, together with their commanders and areas of operation. An overall military strategy was agreed upon, as well as a uniform set of rules and regulations.

The Kenya Defence Council also decided to take action to counter false colonial propaganda and to encourage progressive forces throughout the country. In October 1953, the movement issued a Charter signed by Field Marshall Kimaathi on behalf of the Kenya National Defence Council. It was published in the weekly *Citizen*. The Charter which came to be popularly known as the Kimaathi Charter, publicly and openly showed what the Mau Mau freedom fighters were fighting for:

---
[247] Odinga (1968), p. 191.

We want an African self-government in Kenya.

We want an African Magistrate's Court in full authority who will judge lawfully and righteously.

We want to know who hands over the money for land from settlers and where the money goes.

We want to know why different Christian missions with different laws are brought to Kenya. Can one mission not suffice as God is one in Heaven?

We desire all authorities of gold, markets, roads, co-operative societies and auctions to be in the hands of Africans.

We desire to claim full authority of making fire-arms and various kinds of weapons.

We desire the Europeans, rascals, troops and police to be withdrawn from Kenyan African reserves.

We reject the imprisonment over Mau Mau.

We reject criminal or death cases to be judged by Europeans.

We reject dropping of poisons from the air as colonialists in Kenya are doing to Africans.

We reject the foreign laws in Kenya for they were not made for Kenya and are not righteous.

We reject to be called terrorists and demand our people's rights.

We reject the sleeping of foreigners with our wives and girls, also female imprisonment and the carrying of passes.

We reject foreign Attorney-General in Kenya for he deals with appearance rather than righteousness.

We reject colonisation in Kenya for in that state we are turned into slaves and beggars.[248]

The Charter summed up the demands of the freedom struggle. It helped to unite thousands of workers and peasants who took up arms against unjust exploitation of their labour and land. The publication of the Charter by the *Citizen* proved of immense importance in mobilising the progressive people to continue their anti-imperialist struggle.

The *Citizen* was again to publicise the views of the revolutionary forces in 1954, by which date important measures had been taken by both, the liberation forces as well as the colonialists, in the on-going struggle.

The colonial government, having failed to 'solve' the problem of armed struggle of the Kenyan people, agreed to bring in more constitutional changes, without, however, changing the system of government. This was through the so-called Lyttelton Plan, announced on 10th March, 1954. This type of cosmetic change was already condemned in the Kimaathi Charter as mere 'appearance' of change. The Lyttelton Plan was condemned by the unofficial African and Indian members of the Colonial Legislative Council, and the Kenya Federation of Registered Trade Unions as well as other progressive people. Its only support came from the European Elected Members who represented the settlers.

In a letter to a British newspaper, Shah described the Lyttelton Plan as follows:

So far as war against Mau Mau is concerned, the Lyttelton

---

[248] Kimathi Charter. Quoted from the *Citizen* by Singh, M (1980), pp.48-49.

proposals have not had any effect at all. Mau Mau is the result of a slow but steady change of mind in the African generally over a number of years on the question of land hunger, colour bar, and racial discrimination, cheap and forced labour. The African was discontented that his birth rights were refused him. Throwing little pieces of bread here and there in a form of the few schools and hospitals does not help reverse the position.[249]

The response of the revolutionary forces to the Lyttelton Plan was conditioned by developments in the liberation camp. In the main, the guerrilla war had been successful, with the liberation forces going from strength to strength. The situation by first half of 1954 was very satisfactory from the liberation point of view:

> It was certainly true that after almost a year and a half of fighting, and with vastly superior weapons, the colonial government seemed no closer to defeating the liberation forces. In fact, guerrilla strength seemed to be growing, with Kenya Levellation Army units more active than ever in the reserve, a Nairobi Land and Freedom army formed and very active, supplies flowing from the city into the forests, and colonial Government unable to launch a winning offensive against the guerrilla armies of Nyandarua and Mt. Kenya.[250]

Not only in the forest areas but also in the cities, the armies of the liberation forces won important victories. In fact, large parts of the city of Nairobi were under the direct control of the guerrilla forces and the (colonial) government forces could not even enter these areas. Other city areas were controlled by the colonial forces by day but by guerrilla forces by night. The guerrilla forces established their own, free government in these areas, controlled law and order for the benefit of the workers and peasants and the guerrillas ran an effective tax, legal and other systems. It was the taxes levied in these as well as in the colonial controlled areas that bought guns and other supplies for the guerrilla armies and ran the urban gun and other factories. The

[249] Shah (1954).
[250] Barnett and Njama (1966), p. 126.

colonial authorities had to admit their loss of control over many areas in Nairobi itself, in spite of deploying thousands of soldiers. This is what the Report of the British Colonial Office, Parliamentary Delegation to Kenya (1954) says (emphasis added):

> In Nairobi, the situation is both grave and acute. Mau Mau orders are carried out in the *heart of the city*, Mau Mau courts sit in judgement and their sentences are carried out... There is evidence that the revenues collected by the [Mau Mau], which may be considerable, are used for the purpose of bribery as well as for purchasing Mau Mau supplies . . . There is also a passive resistance movement amongst Africans an example of which is a Bus Boycott under which Africans have for several months boycotted European-owned buses.[251]

It was this control over the liberated areas that enabled the revolutionary forces to establish independent Kenyan publishing, printing and distribution network, with its nerve centre in Nairobi.

The success of the guerrilla war in cities and forests was due largely to proper organisation of the liberation forces in every field. At the same time the increasing successes required newer forms of organisation. Thus in early February 1954, the Kenya Defence Council was superseded by the Kenya Parliament, comprising twelve members and with Kimaathi as President. This was the first legitimate Government of Kenya. It marked a major political development for the liberation forces, as it separated *political* and *military* fronts, with the former taking the leadership role.

The Kenya Parliament was to take control over military, political, economic, social and educational lives of people in the liberated areas as well as some peoples in the areas still under colonial control.

The Kenya Parliament strongly opposed the Lyttelton Plan. Kimaathi wrote an open letter on behalf of the Kenya Parliament to the Colonial

---

[251] Report of the British Colonial Office Parliamentary Delegation to Kenya, January, 1954. Quoted in Barnett and Njama (1966), pp. 330-331. (Emphasis added).

Governor. Copies of the letter were sent to the British and Russian governments as well as to various newspapers. The weekly *Citizen* reproduced the letter on its front page in the issue of Saturday 5 April, 1954.

The letter made it clear that there would not be negotiations or cease fire as requested by the colonial government until the demands made by the Defence Council and the Kenya Parliament were met. The main demand was that the Kimaathi Charter should first be implemented and that any future negotiations had to be on the basis of equality. The letter said, among other things:

> General China is a sensible man, but we must state in no uncertain terms that we will not be moved by his pleas unless China and the Colonial Government agree to the Charter issued last year by Kimaathi . . . It is absolutely nonsense to reorganise the Government of Kenya today, without first acting upon the points raised in the Charter written by Field Marshall Kimaathi.[252]

Other points were explained by the *Citizen*:

> The release of all those African leaders who were detained in October 1952 is laid down as an essential condition to a cease-fire by Field Marshal Kimathi. It adds that only the release of leaders would convince the public and the world that the Government really wants peace.

The letter suggests that the basis of these negotiations would be a settlement of the future of the Africans on a basis of equality. It adds "it is useless to expect the African Members of the Legislative Council to conduct such negotiations. It must be borne in mind that up to now they are not our chosen representatives; they are [members nominated by the colonial] government. How would you expect us to have confidence in them? When matters come to a head, they have no public to call for a vote of confidence."

---

[252] Kimaathi's letter to the Colonial Governor was published by the *Citizen* from where it is quoted by Singh, M. (1980), pp. 84-85.

The period up to 1952 saw the movement of mass national resistance take root. The success of this movement was reflected in the need felt by the Colonial Government to declare a state of Emergency in October 1952. But even this failed to "contain" the situation as mass mobilisation and revolutionary action intensified. In fact, people began to see more clearly the oppressive nature of colonialism and more and more people came out in the open to oppose imperialist rule over Kenya. The mass movement grew in strength after the Declaration of Emergency and reached a peak with the Bus Boycott. The Kenya Committee (London) records the first stages of the boycott which was a response to the colonial government's efforts to "contain" activities of the Mau Mau movement:

> Thousands of Africans have been walking to and from work as a boycott against the buses. Reprisals for regulation not allowing more than one Kikuyu to travel in a motor passenger vehicle, and not riding a bicycle without it carrying the name and address in large letters.[253]

Initiated by Mau Mau freedom fighters, the bus boycott involved all the progressive people. The aim of the boycott was to take the anti-colonial struggle to a new height with mass popular mobilisation. It helped to mobilise progressive people to advance to the armed stage of the struggle. It was a protest against the imprisonment and detention of tens of thousands of people and the Government's refusal to release the imprisoned and detained national leaders.

At another level, the Bus Boycott was a national protest against the oppressive Emergency Regulations which were introduced by the Colonial government in the hope of suppressing the people's movement. The laws were used to imprison whole communities in "villages" which in effect were mass detention camps surrounded by barbed wire and police posts. Other laws were aimed at controlling the movement and communication network organised by Mau Mau. They sought to keep African buses out of many locations, cancelled drivers' passes in the Rift Valley areas and restricted

[253] Kenya Committee. Press Extracts, Vol. 1 (23 September, 1953), p. 44..

movement of members of Mau Mau. They forced the painting of names on bicycles and ordered that taxis carry the yellow band mark - all in order to identify and arrest Mau Mau activists who had developed many creative tactics of overcoming the harsh Emergency rules and of avoiding detection by the Colonial Security forces. Kinyatti explains the significance of the boycotts:

> The Mau Mau Central Committee called for a boycott of foreign capitalist businesses and prohibited any Kenyan, regardless of his or her social background, to ride British-owned city buses, to drink foreign-made beer, to practice prostitution or to socialize with the British occupiers and other foreigners. Politicization of the broad masses, combating cultural imperialism and the elimination of the national traitors and agent-provocateurs were the immediate tasks of the revolutionary movement.[254]

The bus boycott continued for several months and became a major way of continuing the struggle in spite of massive armed intervention by the Colonial forces. It showed strategic control over the anti-imperialist struggle exercised by the liberation forces. While Mau Mau waged an active armed struggle, it did not ignore the aspect of popular political and economic struggles without which the armed wing could become isolated from the people. The bus boycott helped to keep the people in tune with the armed struggle, and ensured the unity of the different aspects - military, political, economic - of the mass anti-imperialist movement. In addition, the boycott gave a very clear message to the colonial administration: in spite of colonial propaganda, the Mau Mau movement was a popular movement for national liberation and had the support of all working people and peasants from all nationalities.

The Mau Mau High Command decided the extent of its control in the content of many openly published newspapers. It allowed local freedom on some aspects of publishing, but enforced more strict control in other cases, reflecting the views of the High Command through some newspapers.

[254] Kinyatti (forthcoming).

Some Mau Mau leaders themselves started their own publications in active support of the struggle. These included Bildad Kaggia, Fred Kubai, Gakara wa Wanjau, Isaac Gathanju, Pio Gama Pinto, Ambu Patel, among others. The next section provides a brief record of the contribution by some activists in advancing the goal of national liberation through publishing.

SOME PRESS PROFILES

(1) Bildad Kaggia(1922-2005)

An overview on the work of Bildad Kaggia is provided by his biography:

> Bildad Kaggia is yet another unsung hero in Kenya's struggle for independence. His name is often mentioned alongside other Kenya's founding fathers, but just in passing. The truth is, he played a very important role in sensitizing the Kenyan masses about the evils of the colonial government.

Kaggia's political involvement can be traced to 1940 when he was recruited into the British Army, and sent to the Middle East. His assignment in the Middle East is said to have revolutionised him. For the first time he realised that the British, whom he had previously considered all too powerful, could also be defeated in battle. He immediately embarked on a plan to secure Kenya's independence from the British, first by diplomacy but if need be, by force. As a bank clerk, he formed the Clerks and Commercial Workers Union, which he affiliated with the Labour Trade Union of East Africa, an organisation he later led.[255]

Bildad Kaggia, who was on the Mau Mau Central Committee, started publishing Inooro ria Gikuyu in November 1951. Kaggia says:

> It was not easy for me to find a printer for *Inooro ria Gikuyu*. I started it on cyclostyled sheet, but it was later printed by the Tribune press. The cyclostyled format did not make the paper any less popular.

[255] http://kenya740.tripod.com/Bildadkaggia.html Accessed: 1 May, 2004)

After the government failed to curb the influence of our newspapers and song books, it decided to ban them. All of them were banned either in October 1952 or early in 1953. Inooro ria Gikuyu was one of the first to be banned, on 24th October, 1952. But it continued being published under a different name, Mutongoria. This paper in its turn was banned and the editor, Amon Gakanga who took over after my arrest, was also arrested."[256]

The other newspaper started by Bildad Kaggia was *Afrika Mpya* (in Kiswahili, published weekly) started in October 1952. This was published from Kiburi House, Nairobi and printed by Africa Press, and later by Tribune Press. *Africa Mpya* continued under the editorship of S. R. Kimani until early 1953, when it, too, was banned.

(2) Isaac Gathanju

Isaac Gathanju, Secretary General of Mau Mau Supreme Command with responsibility of the High Command administration, also started a newspaper *Wihuge* in July 1952, jointly with N. Kimani. This was also printed by D. K. Sharda's Tribune Press. *Wihuge* was banned by the colonial administration in January 1953 as being "prejudicial to maintenance of public order." [257]

(3) Fred Kubai(1915-

Fred Kubai who was also on the Mau Mau Central Committee was the editor of *Sauti ya Mwafrika* (1951). Kubai was a leading trade union organiser (1946-52) and co-founded with Makhan Singh the East African Trade Union Congress (EATUC). He was first arrested in 1950 in connection with the EATUC boycott of the celebration of the Nairobi City Royal Charter. During the period 1948-52, he was "perhaps the most feared man in Kenya because of his close contacts" with the Forty Group and other pre- or proto-Mau Mau groups.[258]

(4) Pio Gama Pinto (1927- 65)

[256] Kaggia (1975)pp. 84-85.
[257] Kenya Gazette. Notice No. 20. 6 January, 1953. Vol. LV, No.1.
[258] Throup, D (1987) Economic and social origin of Mau Mau 1945-53. London: James Currey, quoted in Sicherman, 1990, p.144.

Pio Gama Pinto was a prominent person in the struggle for total economic and political liberation in Kenya. He was a creative thinker as well as a practically-minded person who took up the cause of freedom with a rare zeal. He was active in all aspects of publishing as well – drafting, writing, printing and distributing not only newspapers but memoranda, publicity materials, posters, press and other statements. He was a journalist by profession but his publishing activities were guided by his politics. In the previous period that we examined, he was publishing and editing various newspapers, including *Colonial Times*, and *Daily Chronicle*. Pinto started *The Uzwod*, a Konkni paper in Nairobi to arouse feeling against Portuguese colonialism.

Emma Gama Pinto, Pio's widow, reflects on another aspect of his written work:

> My husband's views on current affairs were often published in Letters to the Editor in the *East African Standard* under pseudonyms, and never remained the same over the years. On occasion he used his own, but in most cases he favoured an African name. He was a prolific writer but remained the hand behind the curtain. He felt he could achieve more by not contesting in the race to jump on the bandwagon. His was a dedication to uncover the injustices perpetrated on innocent Africans who, although politically very mature, could not articulate in the lingua franca of the world, their grievances. They were men who were often hamstrung by the inability to retort rhetorically to the arguments that came thick and fast, and eventually had to resort to brute force."[259]

Pinto provided active support to the Mau Mau fighters, as Odinga recalls:

> In Nairobi Pinto was an invaluable supply man, working with the Nairobi War Council that siphoned food, money, arms and intelligence information through to the forests, and smuggling out of Kenya and into the world's press reports and photographs of

---
[259] Pinto, Emma Gamma: June 22, 1972. Material collected by Zed Press, London, for a biography of Pio Gama Pinto.
[260] Odinga (1967), p. 128.

atrocities by the security forces, until his activities were discovered and he, too, was detained.[260]

Some other facts and comments on Pinto's contribution to publishing are listed below:

- In the early 1950s Pio Gama Pinto wrote for the English-Gujarati bilingual newspapers, the *Colonial Times* and the *Daily Chronicle* becoming the *Chronicle*'s editor in 1953.

- When the armed struggle for freedom began with the declaration of emergency on October 20, 1952, Pinto increased his efforts to publicise the atrocities perpetrated by the British colonial administration, army and police.

Pinto was arrested in April 1954 and detained without trial for more than five years. On being released in July 1959 he once again actively joined the independence struggle, taking part in printing and distribution of anti-colonial posters and leaflets. It was necessary for the liberation forces to counter the new imperialist onslaught with a more powerful media strategy. In 1960, Pio Gama Pinto went to India to ask for 700,000 Kenya shillings for a KANU press. This was given by Jawaharlal Nehru, the first Prime Minister of India and thus was born the Pan African Press whose directors were Kenyatta, Achieng Oneko, O. Odinga, J. D. Kali. In 1961 Pinto and other nationalists founded the Pan African Press. He became the general manager. Among the publications brought out by the press were *Sauti ya Mwafrika* and *Pan Africa*.[261] The Press published the Kiswahili *Sauti ya Kanu* and the English *Pan African* which was edited by Pio Gama Pinto.

- Bildad Kaggia: "I can never forget his help to me and other African politicians when we decided to run our own newspapers to fight the colonial newspaper monopoly. He did all he could to see that each and every small newspaper went forward. His advice and practical help in this work will never be forgotten."[262]

[261] Noronha (1987).
[262] Kaggia (1966)., pp 12-14

- J. D. Kali mentions Pinto's activities in poster and handbill production and distribution: "Mr. Pinto had many friends among the present Members of Parliament, friendships which began years ago. He was appointed by them to act as their secretary during the last General Elections' Campaign. One of his main jobs was to draft campaign slogans and print them. Pinto even took it upon himself to display them all over Nairobi. Most often he stuck the posters at the dead of night. One of the most interesting of these posters was the 'CONGO' poster. He printed posters and pamphlets for KANU candidates all over the country."[263]

- Fitz De Souza: "History will record that Pio had a hand in the preparation of most of the memoranda and statements issued by KAU in those days. He often used to sit up to 5 a.m. in the Congress office drafting political papers in the nationalist cause.... A couple of years later when he was the Editor of the *Daily Chronicle*, the Royal Commission on Land asked for evidence and there was no one to put forward the African case for all the leaders who were in detention (or in the forest). Pio resigned his job and for three months read through the voluminous Carter Commission Report and other documents on the land issue and took statements from Kikuyu elders and others. He then wrote out and personally typed and cyclostyled, always working into the early hours of the morning, the 200-page Kikuyu memorandum as well as memoranda for other Mbaris in the Central Province.

"Pio went to New Delhi and discussed the situation on Goa with Pandit Nehru and officials of the Indian Government. He took advantage of the opportunity to ask Pandit Nehru for assistance to start a nationalist paper in Kenya. Panditji gave him funds with which Pio began the Pan African Press which published *Sauti ya Mwafrika*, *Pan Africa* and the *Nyanza Times*".[264]

- Muinga Chitari Chokwe: "Pio joined the staff of a small newspaper organisation and started whipping up public opinion in favour of the African [cause]. Pio enlisted the help of Mr. D. K. Sharda who had a small

[263] Kali (1966) pp. 20-22..
[264] De Souza (1966), pp. 28-32.
[265] Chokwe (1966), pp.35-36.

lino press [The Tribune Press] and got him to print various papers".[265]

- "The progressive, anti-imperialist elements in the South Asian community, men like Pio Gama Pinto, played a very important role in supplying KFLA with firearms, intelligence information, fund, medicine, and, above all, helped the movement to produce revolutionary literature. Pinto in particular established contacts with the illegal South Asian gun-traders who secretly sold firearms and ammunition to KFLA."[266]

- Pant sums up another aspect of Pinto's contribution:

> Pio Pinto was deeply involved with the African freedom movement in Kenya and knew all the important underground leaders. But what diminutive, brilliant highly affectionate Pio Pinto did for India and for the Indians community in Kenya during those critical days of Mau Mau rebellion can never be forgotten. The South Africans, the colonial powers and even Israel would have liked the anger, frustration and hatred of the Mau Mau to be diverted against India and the Indians. Serious and persistent attempts were indeed made to do so. Even the Church joined in smear campaign, with sermons in Swahili and passion plays depicting Africans as criminally exploited by Indians.
>
> Pio Pinto was largely responsible for having prevented the wrath of the Mau Mau from being vented on the Indian community. Had he not been able to enter the secret conclaves of the freedom fighters unnoticed, and had he not won the trust of leaders such as Stanley Mathenge, Jomo Kenyatta, Senior Chief Koinange and Tom Mboya for his sound and clear advise, thousands of Indians may well have been murdered and their property looted.
>
> After independence of Kenya, destiny's strange way led to Pio being murdered in broad daylight. It is appropriate to offer homage to Pio Pinto -- a great freedom fighter, a staunch friend,

[266] Kinyatti (forthcoming).
[267] Pant (1987).
[268] Kinyatti (forthcoming).

and a humanist.[267]

- "Pio Gama Pinto was assassinated by a government paid agent. The murderous plan was organised by the KANU circles in conjunction with the CIA".[268]

- "Pinto was assassinated by the regime on 24 February 1965 and Kenya has yet to replace him"[269]

Pio Gama Pinto was very concerned that those who sacrificed their property, educational and other opportunities, limbs or even lives in the cause of independence should be suitably honoured:

> The sacrifices of the hundreds of thousands of Kenya's freedom fighters must be honoured by the effective implementation of the policy - a democratic, African, socialist state in which the people have the right to be free from economic exploitation and the right to social equality. Kenya's uhuru must not be transformed into freedom to exploit, or freedom to be hungry and live in ignorance. Uhuru must be uhuru for the masses - uhuru from exploitation, from ignorance, disease and poverty.[270]

BE VIGILANT

Every time wetalked, Pio spoke of the need to be vigilant against the imperialists. Yes, he would say, we are marching forward, more and more countries are becoming independent, but be vigilant, for the imperialists have not been liquidated - they are here, striving to come back, to divide us.

- Romesh Chandra, a journalist for the Delhi paper *New Age*[271].

---

(5) Ambu Patel

Another prominent publisher of this period was Ambu H. Patel. His publishing activity ranged from drafting, printing and distributing various Mau Mau underground handbills and leaflets, translating a number of well known Kenyan books into Gujarati and establishing the publishing house,

[269] Barnett (1972).
[270] Pinto (1963).
[271] Pio gama Pinto (1966).

New Kenya Publishers.

With his qualification as a book binder (trained in India and in Britain) and his fierce anti-imperialist feelings, Ambubhai (as he came to be called affectionately) plunged into the publishing and political work. Patel wrote many articles for underground papers and also helped actively in printing and personally distributing these. As a South Asian Kenyan he often evaded colonial police and moved freely in areas where others could not go.

When the colonial justice sentenced some leaders of KAU to long periods of detention, the court did not release the judgement, nor did the judge think it necessary to read the whole judgement in the court. It was Patel, with help from Pio Gama Pinto, who managed to 'borrow' a copy of the 100 page judgement of the Kapenguria trial in 1953 and arranged with a progressive typist, Shirin Meghji Ahmed, to type the judgement on stencil. He had previously purchased a second-hand Gestetner duplicating machine for shs. 1500/- from a European, pretending to be a hardware merchant. He used this to reproduce 300 copies of the Kapenguria judgement. He posted 250 copies of this document to leaders all over the world as the colonial government was not willing to let the world read it.

Ambu Patel founded the New Kenya Publishers and published more books. He edited or wrote ten books which included:

- *Struggle for "Release Jomo and his Colleagues"*. Nairobi. New Kenya Publishers.(1963). New Kenya Publishers.

- 'Jaramogi' Oginga Odinga: *Two Months in India.* (1965). Nairobi. New Kenya Publishers. Compiled by Ambu Patel from the original Dholuo book *"Dweche Ariyo e India"*.

- *Pio Gama Pinto, Independent Kenya's First Martyr:* Socialist and Freedom Fighter. Nairobi. Pan African Press Ltd. 1966. Edited by Ambu H. Patel.

Ambubhai had completed work on various other books by the time of his death in 1977. These included biographies of A. M. Jivanjee and Makhan Singh, a Gujarati translation of Jomo Kenyatta's two books (including *My People of Gikuyu*). He also used to collect, 'illegally', photographs of Mau Mau freedom fighters from the colonial Information House where he had contacts. These photographs were to be the basis of a proposed New Kenya Publishers' publication entitled Mau Mau generals; a pictorial record of daring freedom fighters of Kenya.

In all another ten or so books were ready to be published by the New Kenya Publishers, all based on the anti-imperialist struggle of the 1950s. But because of the hostility from KANU after independence, none of these could be published. This ready material included:

- *Comrade Makhan Singh: fighter for freedom*. Ambu H. Patel
- *Judgement of Kapenguria:1955 Kapenguria trial judgement*.
- *Jomo the great; pictorial story of the great patriot of Africa*.
- *Badge of Kenyatta*.
- *Life of Jomo Kenyatta: a record of events in the life of our Prime Minister*.
- *M. A. Desai:a brave fighter for human rights for all in East Africa* (Illustrated).
- *Tom Mboya:the rising star of Africa*. (Illustrated).
- *'Jaramogi' Oginga Odinga: The Iron man of Kenya*.(Illustrated).
- *Vinoba sathe balpanma* (Gujarati).
- *Biography of Harry Thuku*.

Seidenberg gives an overview of Ambu Patel's contribution to the liberation struggle:

> Other individual Asians manifested a radical response to Mau Mau by carrying on underground assistance to the patriots in the forest or to the families of Mau Mau detainees. Ambu H. Patel, a staunch follower of Gandhi, who had been imprisoned in India for his anti-colonial stand, was a man with a mission "who made many

sacrifices for Kenya" [quoting Clement Lubembe]. Throughout the Emergency, Patel collected funds for food and clothing for Mau Mau fighters, and published leaflets and books concerned with Kenya's independence struggle. Patel also looked after Kenyatta's daughter, Margaret, while Kenyatta was in detention, and at great personal risk sent him clothes, food and, and shoes when no-one else would or did.[272]

(6) Gakaara wa Wanjau

The different forms that Mau Mau publishing took included newspapers, books, progressive booklets, pamphlets and song books. A prominent leader who was active in all these forms of publishing was Gakaara wa Wanjau, who was a publisher, issuing books in Kenyan nationality languages and in Kiswahili. Gakaara Wanjau was detained by the colonial government for his publishing activities in October, 1952, as the "Chief Mau Mau propagandist".

Among the newspapers published by Gakaara Wanjau was *Waigwa-atia*. By 1952, 12,000 copies of this were being published and sold at 50 cents each[273].

Gakaara Wanjau, together with Muthee wa Cheche, worked hard to collect progressive, anti-imperialist songs. These were then published by Gakaara Wanjau. Two of such song books were *Witikio* (Faith), and *Nyimbo cia Gikuyu na Mumbi* which was published in 1952. *Witikio* was aimed at advanced cadres and carried a message of "inalienable land rights" of the people. It was printed on a four page card and sold for 25 cents[274].

Gakaara Book Service (as the publishing house is called) also published progressive booklets. The purpose of publishing these was "to make the people conscious of their rights and to educate them. Some of these were distributed free while others were sold for 1/- or 2/-. Some relevant Kiswahili and English material was also being translated into Gikuyu".

[272] Seidenberg (1983), p. 118.
[273] "Gaakara wa Wanjau": a freedom fighter". Sunday Nation (Nairobi) 10 October, 1981.
[274] ibid.

Perhaps the best known progressive booklet published by Gakaara Book Service was *Witikio wa Gikuyu na Mumbi*. This was printed by the Acme Printing Press and was widely distributed by activists. In fact just when the colonialists declared a State of Emergency October, 1952, Kimaathi was personally distributing about 15,000 copies of *Witikio* in large baskets to the people in the Rift Valley.

Other progressive pamphlets published by Gakaara Book Service were:

- *Kenya ni Yakwa* (Kenya is Mine)
- *Miikarire ya Thikwota* (The Lives of Squatters)
- *Agikuyu, Mau Mau na Wiyathi* (The Gikuyu people, Mau Mau and Freedom).
- *Magerio Noomo Mahota* (Practice makes Perfect).
- *Roho ya Kiume na Bidii kwa Mwafrika* (in Kiswahili, published in 1948).
- *Kienyu kia Ngai na Ithaka* (God and Land).
- *Wiyathi wa Andu Airu* (Freedom of the Black People) written by Mwaniki Mugweru - printed by the Regal Press.
- *Kamuingi koyaga Ndiri* (Unity is strength) written by Mwaniki Mugweru.
- *Mwathanire wa Agikuyu comba utanoka* (Agikuyu Government before the coming of foreigners).

Gakaara Book Service also printed and published many handbills and posters which were distributed by Mau Mau activists and progressive people throughout the country.

Gakara Wa Wanjau reveals some of his experiences as a freedom fighter in his book, *Mwandiki wa Mau Mau Ithaamirio-ini* (1983). He also "proudly recalls how his publications passed from hand to hand under the cover of darkness in the jungle among the Mau Mau fighters." Other facts about Gakara Wa Wanjau:

- 1946: formed, with others, African Book Writers.
- *Witikio*, with its message of "inalienable land rights" of the people was printed on a four page card and was selling at 25 cents. It was intended only for advanced cadres.
- 1948: wrote *Roho ya Kiume na Bidii kwa Mwafrika*.
- Before his detention he was active in publishing, with others, *Mumenyereri*, *Agikuyu*, and a monthly *Waigwa-atia*.
- While in detention, he wrote many political songs and a play which exposed homeguards and praised Mau Mau.
- After his release from detention, he joined Pio Gama Pinto, George Githii and Joe Kadhi in publishing *Sauti ya Kanu*.

(7) Makhan Singh (1913-76)

Makhan Singh brought together the two strands in the Kenya liberation movement – trade union and politics. "He first came to prominence as secretary of the Labour Trade Union of Kenya when he organised a two-month strike in Nairobi."[275] He was detained in India for five years (1940-45) by the British and again in Kenya from 1950 to October 1961 – the longest imprisonment in the Kenyan colonial history. While in India under restriction, he worked for two years as "a sub-editor of *Jang-i-Azadi*, a newspaper published in Lahore by the Punjab Committee of the Indian Communist Party.[276]

Makhan Singh provides us with the most comprehensive history of trade union movement with his 2 volume history of trade union movement in Kenya.[277] He was thus not only a prominent trade union organiser and a politician, but a historian who did much to preserve the working class history of Kenya. He combined politics with trade union activities, as shown, for example, in the following colonial government report on him:

> Makhan published articles in the press, disseminated pamphlets and repeatedly addressed African audiences. He told them, inter

---
[275] Sicherman (1990), p. 178.
[276] Seidenberg (1983), p.44.
[277] Singh, Makhan 1969 and 1980.
[278] The secret British file on Makhan Singh. October, 1961 in: Kinyatti (2000).

alia, that His Majesty's Government was a 'foreign power who had no right to rule in Kenya', that the Kenya Government had introduced slavery, and that secret plans were being hatched to take more African land for the City of Nairobi.[278]

A member of the Indian Communist Party, Makhan Singh "embarrassed Kenyatta and Mathu by calling for immediate independence in Kenya at a joint meeting of the Kenya African Union and the East African Indian National Congress in April 1950."[279] Singh demanded, "the British Government had declared the independence of India, Burma and Ceylon; similarly it should immediately declare the independence of the East African territories."[280] Seidenberg quotes Ambu Patel: "This was the first time in the history of the freedom struggle in Kenya that anyone had actually dared to make such a demand in public."

Seidenberg sums up Makhan Singh's contribution to the trade union movement in Kenya, as well as to the struggle for independence:

> With the return of Makhan Singh in August 1947, the trade union movement also acquired a radical wing. Having spent eight years in India actively participating in the trade union movement and the political struggle for independence, Makhan Singh was well-equipped to breathe new life into Kenya's labour and freedom campaign. The Labour Trade Union of East Africa formed in 1937 and later the larger East African Trade Union Congress (EATUC) formed in May 1949 became the nerve centres for activities of the more militant Asians. From 1947 until 1952, when all trade union activities were proscribed, Makhan Singh worked behind-the-scenes activities with prominent African trade unionists including Bildad Kaggia, Aggrey Minya and Tom Mboya.[281]

---

[279] David Throup, quoted in Sicherman (1990), p.179.
[280] Seidenberg (1983), 104.
[281] ibid, p. 97.

PAMPHLETS, HANDBILLS AND LETTERS

A large number of progressive booklets were also published during this period. Some were published by Gakaara Book Service. Other publishing houses also issued such booklets and developed a tradition of Kenyan publishing. For example, Mumenyereri Press issued the following:

- *Ngoroya Mugikuyu ni ya Gutoria* ("The Mugikuyu always win").
- *Tiiri Niguo Nyina Witu* ("The Soil is Our Mother").
- *Kenya Bururi wa Ngoe* ("Kenya, the Land of Conflict") by Jomo Kenyatta was translated into Kiswahili by Henry Mworia.
- *Ithaka Ciori Ciitu* ("The Land is Ours") written by Mbiyu Koinange concerning problems he had taken abroad. Also translated into Kiswahili.

The Kenya Writers' Circle was also an active publisher. Its publications included the following, all printed by Acme Printing Press:

- Written by Gitu Kahengeri:
    - *Jifunze Siasa* (Teach yourself politics)
    - *Afrika Huru.*
    - *Shirikisho la Afrika Mashariki.*
    - *Nyambo cia Wiyathi wa Kirinyaga* (Freedom songs).
- Wiyathi ni Igai Ritu ("Freedom is Our Right").
- Written by W. K. Kahara of Uthiru:
    - Mwaria wega athuirwo nuu? ("who hates a person who speaks well?")
    - Nyatinguru.

The colonial administration also banned many progressive booklets. For example it banned *Kirira Kia Ugikuyu, (Mazungmzo ya WaGikuyu)*[282] which was published by M. N. Tahetu, and printed by Colonial Printing Works.

[282] 16 December, 1952 (Kenya Colony Government Notice No. 1400).

We have seen earlier how the publication and distribution of handbills, pamphlets and cyclostyled sheets had been used by Kenyan workers to communicate their views on their economic and political struggles. The Labour Trade Union of East Africa had made extensive use of this method of communication to maintain links with workers. This practice was developed further during the active stage of resistance to colonialism. It was being used by Kimaathi himself as well as by Mau Mau at its various levels.

Among the earliest circulars was one issued on 23rd October, 1948. This was issued by H. W. Gathithi at Murang'a and was entitled *Sons of Gikuyu and Mumbi*. An interesting feature of this circular was that it was printed on colonial government stationery. It was the Army's form letter for pay instructions, "Regimental Paymaster; Subject: Family Allotment - African Ranks". The other side of this army form letter was blank and was used to print the circular. This solved the problem of finding printing paper!

The circular provides an interesting insight into the way underground publishing worked. It shows that there were Mau Mau members working in the British colonial army, as a resistance strategy and also for earning their subsistence. They were thus able to use colonial stationery, printing facilities and resources to communicate their anti-colonial messages.

The circular stated: "People who do not do their own thinking are like a stone; they are traitors to themselves and to their country." The circular proposes the establishment of a 'Muranga African District Education Union' which should publish a newspaper, with the proposed title of *Coro wa Murang'a* (Voice of Murang'a). The Union and the newspaper were to be established on basis of the following three principles:

- Politics - "No country could make progress without politics and a country without politics is dead."
- Welfare of people.
- Education.[283]

[283] The circular is available in the Makhan Singh Archives, Library of the Institute of African Studies, University of Nairobi.

NEVER BE SILENT

One task facing Mau Mau was that of ensuring the political and ideological advancement of the cadres. Another was to demoralise the enemy troops and their European settler supporters. Many handbills and posters were issued and posted at prominent places in enemy areas as a way of achieving both these aims. We shall examine two such pamphlets. Kinyatti provides the details of the first one:

> In June 1952, the Mau Mau Central Committee instructed general Mathenge, the Mau Mau army commander-in-chief, to order his forces for military offensive. As the guerrilla army entered Nyandarwa and Kirinyaga forests, a revolutionary leaflet expressing the rage and dynamism of the struggle was secretly distributed in Nairobi, Kiambuu, Murang'a, Nyeri and Nakuru. The pamphlet read:
>
> *We are going to the mountains, but we shall return like lightening. Those who support the British are not children of our mother; they are not our brothers, they are the enemy.*[284]

The second Mau Mau pamphlet was issued just three days after the declaration of Emergency. It was sent to many settlers and posted on trees and walls in many areas of Nairobi. This shows the excellent organisational network set up by the resistance forces: while the colonial armies were busy creating a reign of terror, cadres were printing and distributing important communications under enemy gunfire. The pamphlet is important also for its content which shows the clear understanding of the situation by Mau Mau. It was addressed to the 'Murdering Colonialists' and was entitled Fascism Has Come to Kenya: *Fascism Has Come to Kenya.*

FASCISM HAS COME TO KENYA

You must feel very happy at the outward success of your cruel operation. You arrested our leaders and a lot of other people.

[284] Kinyatti (forthcoming).

Thousands of Africans leading a normal life have been stopped, searched, beaten, humiliated and arrested. Creating the Emergency, you have brutally treated us and now you cannot claim democracy and freedom. Fascism has come to Kenya.

We have been robbed of all freedom. You have destroyed our press by arresting our editors and suppressing our newspapers. But you cannot suppress the voice of the people. The brutality and oppression, the show of force and the rule of gun, will not stop us from our goal. You cannot end our political wish by arresting our leaders. We have many more men with brains and will continue to fight you and achieve our freedom. This is the voice of new Africa. We have been forced to go underground. If we are known, you will murder us. We are not afraid. We ask how many of us you will imprison, how many of us you will kill? We are six million and power is in our numbers. We shall retaliate in the method you have employed. We shall not forget the bad treatment we are suffering. When our time comes we shall not show mercy, because you do not know what mercy is. We will kill you like you are murdering us today.

This is no threat. It is how we are feeling today. Africans unite![285]

ESTABLISHMENT OF A PEOPLE'S PRESS

THE MAU MAU HIGH COMMAND

We have examined those publishing activities of Mau Mau which were 'legally' allowed by the colonial government but were controlled to a greater or lesser extent by the Mau Mau. However, the High Command could not rely on publications which were not solely under its control.

[285] The KLFA had a forceful foreign policy, one of whose aims was to publicise its interpretation of the struggle by sending important documents to friendly organizations and individuals overseas. A copy of the pamphlet was sent to the Kenya Committee for Democratic Rights for Kenya in London. Attorney General, Mr. John Whyatt prevented any newspaper from printing it on the threat of prosecution. (Kenya Committee Archives, Vol. 1, p.10: 24-10-52).

In fact the colonial administration soon realised the power of these publications. It banned about fifty newspapers, many progressive records and books published in the country as well as those imported. Some of these are listed in the Appendix.

The Mau Mau movement was well prepared for the communications battle with the colonial power. The colonial-settler government sought to maintain a complete monopoly over all information about the struggle for liberation as well as other information on national and international affairs. This was a well conceived plan in which the publication of all books, newspapers, records, and radio broadcasts were to be controlled so as to allow only the colonial points of view to be published and distributed. Even the owners of printing presses were jailed for publishing progressive material.

The liberation forces took various steps to overcome the colonial-imposed embargo on free flow of information. These steps included the use of an oral medium to exchange information with its armed forces and progressive people; the establishment of their own presses which printed Mau Mau newspapers; and issuing of handbills and posters which were circulated widely throughout the country. The success of these steps depended on a wide distribution network, which was duly created by the High Command. Such measures overcame the communications embargo imposed by the colonial forces.

The main newspaper established by the liberation forces was appropriately called the *Mau Mau High Command*, published between 1952 and 1957. This was initially printed by South Asian Kenyans in Nairobi. Later, the Mau Mau established new printing facilities at their Mathare Headquarters in Nairobi. The *Mau Mau High Command* was anti-imperialist in content. It was an underground paper circulating among 35,000 freedom fighters. Articles were signed by responsible leaders and communicated within the liberated areas and in semi-liberated and enemy controlled areas (to selected units in the latter two).

During the active war years of 1952-57, it was important for the people to know the real activities of Mau Mau. The paper carried information about colonial atrocities and explained the Mau Mau stand, as a lot of killings and destruction of peasant property were done by home guards and blamed on the Mau Mau. The Mau Mau position was to oppose colonial authorities and collaborators who worked with colonial administration, not random destruction of lives and property. The truth of these atrocities had to be communicated. Ambu Patel recalled writing various articles encouraging people and Kenyan armed forces to continue the struggle, as well as articles explaining the nature of imperialism.[286]

INFORMATION GATHERING AND DISSEMINATION

An essential aspect of publishing was gathering and storing of intelligence and information. This then needed to be stored and disseminated in the form of newspapers, oral forms songs, and pamphlets. The Mau Mau organised a whole network for distribution, which served a number of other purposes as well. A network of young activists was created with the specific task of propagating the ideology of the organisation. This consisted of children and young men and women who used oral methods to maintain contacts with people. They distributed Mau Mau song books and newspapers. They also organised cultural activities which helped to promote anti-imperialist culture and ideas. Such activities helped to recruit many young people to the organisation.

The same youth cadre who undertook this communication and political work also took up the more dangerous tasks of placing posters on trees and walls throughout the country. Such posters carried warnings to loyalists, settlers or colonial government officials and also took information to the progressive masses. For example, one such poster which was secretly placed on trees throughout the country was reported in *East Africa and Rhodesia*.[287]

[286] Oral source: Nazmi Durrani, based on information supplied by Ambu Patel.
[287] 1 January 1953.

NEVER BE SILENT

"We who rule this country are called Mau Mau", it proclaimed.

Another aspect of Mau Mau communications policy was intelligence gathering. The youth groups mentioned above were active in this work as well. Intelligence gathering activity called for the creation of a secret network called the Kenda Kenda (nine nine) which was active in Nairobi. Paul Maina explains the functioning of the Kenda Kenda:

> For the purpose of concealing Mau Mau activities in Nairobi and elsewhere, an elaborate intelligence service called Kenda Kenda (nine nine) Organisation was formed. This consisted of (people) from all walks of life in and around Nairobi. Its agents were the taxi drivers, European house servants, men working in big government offices and even beggars who sat at street corners all day. All information of value was passed on to the Kenda Kenda Organisation and then to the Mau Mau Central Committee. As a result of the success of the Kenda Kenda, Mau Mau activities went undetected in Nairobi until late in 1952.[288]

The Kenda Kenda was organised along small cell units, each of which was a tight unit of nine people who did not have information beyond their cell level. Thus each cell was large enough to make it operational, yet not too large to become a threat to the security of the movement as a whole if it was exposed. If one member was tortured for information, they could not give information beyond their own local cell of nine. This helped to keep the movement secret from the government well into 1952.

One method used by Mau Mau to distribute their messages wasthrough songs, records, and oral messages. These reflected the strength, the victories, and the future plans of Mau Mau, the weaknesses of the enemy and the inevitability of the defeat of imperialism. One such song, *We are Everywhere*, reflected the countrywide strength of Mau Mau. It translates as:

---

[288] Maina, Paul (1977), p. 17.

If you go to Nairobi
We are there.

If you go to Mombasa
We are there.

And if you go to Kisumu
We are there.

We are so many
We are everywhere.[289]

The Colonial Governor of Kenya, Sir Evelyn Baring, sent a secret message to London, summing up the situation after Senior Chief Waruhiu, who had denounced Mau Mau at a public meeting on 24 August, 1952, was assassinated:

> I have just returned from a tour and the position is very serious... clear determination by Mau Mau leaders to destroy all sources of authority other than that of Mau Mau... it is abundantly clear that we are facing a planned and revolutionary movement. If the movement cannot be stopped there will be administrative breakdown.[290]

MAU MAU STATIONERY AND DELIVERY SYSTEM

The printing facilities controlled by Mau Mau were used not only for pamphlets and newspapers but also to print its own specialised stationery, such as letterheads, envelopes, postal stamps and rubber stamps etc. More important, having rejected colonial identities and burnt the colonial *kipande*[291], the Mau Mau High Command issued its own ID cards. For example, a South Asian printer in Grogan Road in Nairobi, regularly printed Mau Mau stationery. Hundreds of Mau Mau ID cards were issued

---

[289] Reproduced in Maina, Paul (1977), p. 17.
[290] Quoted in Maina, Paul (1977), p. 22.
[291] ID cards imposed by colonial administration on Kenya.

to activists throughout Nairobi. Such printing activities increased during the course of struggles. Even the colonial kipande were forged by Mau Mau to get easy passage through enemy lines.

But it was not enough to be able to write letters and other communications. A delivery system was also needed. Mau Mau built up independent postal facilities in urban liberated and semi-liberated areas in keeping with the needs of urban situation. A similar postal system was developed in the forest liberated areas.[292] The post office system was instrumental in maintaining contact with the fighters who were living in camps scattered all over Aberdare and Mt. Kenya forests. Their letter boxes were hollow trees and only specially assigned cadres knew their location. Jenkins mentions the post office system developed by the Mau Mau:

> Nearly 40 years after Kenya won independence from the old colonial power, Britain, some of the important sites in the battles of the Mau Mau freedom fighters are to be turned into national monuments. But it is only now that some of the Mau Mau's significant sites are being recognised. The sites include a fig tree which the fighters used as a post office. They hid letters and requests for supplies in a hollow in the trunk. There is also a cave where the fighters lived, a mass grave and also a trench where the renowned Mau Mau leader, Dedan Kimathi, was shot, wounded and finally captured.[293]

---

[292] See the section, "The Establishment of Liberated Territories" of this book for further details about liberated areas.
[293] Jenkins (2001).

CHAPTER SIX

OVERSEAS SUPPORT FOR KENYA'S LIBERATION

BRUTAL THUGS

When reports of the Hola massacre reached Britain, there was political uproar. Suddenly it was the British authorities that were exposed as brutal thugs. Within weeks, London closed the Kenyan camps and released the detainees". [294]

Just as in the cases of Vietnam, South Africa, Cuba and Iraq in recent years, there was much international support for Kenyan people's anti-colonial struggle. While it is true that there was no direct military support for Mau Mau from sympathetic forces outside Kenya, the struggle caught the imagination of progressive people around the world. Their support helped to internationalise the struggle and provided an important political support. There was concrete support from India, which had links with many Kenyan activists, while Egypt provided valuable diplomatic and communications support to Kenyan people. An editorial in the *Kenya Weekly News* reflected on the international support for Mau Mau:

> There is no doubt that Mau Mau has been greatly encouraged and strengthened by expression of support from overseas; by the firm belief of the Mau Mau leaders that Russia and Communist Asia will eventually come to their assistance; and by the equally firm belief that their savage protest against colonialisation has the sympathy of many of the people of Great Britain, India, Egypt and elsewhere (21 May, 1954).

[294] Channel Four TV's Secret History – Mau Mau (screened 24 August, 1999), quoted by Barbara Slaughter "How Britain crushed the 'Mau Mau rebellion' ". World Socialist Web Site http://www.wsws.org/articles/1999/sep1999/mau-s15.shtml

Here we look at just a few cases of such support, especially in the communications context.

UK

THE KENYA COMMITTEE FOR DEMOCRATIC RIGHTS FOR KENYA AFRICANS (UK)[295]

Kenya Committee for Democratic Rights for Kenya was formed in London in solidarity with the people of Kenya in their struggle against imperialism. It was initially based at Rochester Row, London SW1 and later at Denning Road, NW3. It campaigned in Britain for liberation in Kenya. Among its founder members were Margo Heinemann and Chris Lemeitre.[296] It took up Parliamentary and press campaigns to bring real information about the situation to the notice of British people. It was in close contact with the liberation forces and made visits to Kenya on fact finding missions. The Committee's activities were attacked by the settlers in Kenya and the colonial administration banned its publications from Kenya. The Committee published annual *Kenya Reports* as well as issued monthly *Kenya Press Extracts* which were sold for 3d. to cover the cost of production and distribution. The Committee enabled the voice of Kenyan people be heard throughout Britain. For example, it circulated widely *The Kenya Terror – a Letter written to the people of Britain on behalf of the Kikuyu people* in September 1953.[297]

The Kenya Parliament, set up by the liberation forces, was in contact with the London-based Kenya Committee feeding it information about the situation on the ground. A letter dated April 4th 1955 to the Kenya Committee was signed by Karari Njama on behalf of the Kenya Parliament, Nyandarua. It refers to two earlier letters to the Committee signed by Kimaathi dated 18th and 25th March 1955. The April letter provides the true picture of the brutalities experienced by the people of Kenya:

In Kenya, there has been an average death rate of a hundred

---
[295] Referred to in this book as "Kenya Committee".
[296] Personal communications John La Rose, London, 28 July, 2004.
[297] Reprinted from the Daily Worker, 7 September, 1953 in Kenya Committee Press Extracts, Vol. 1, pp. 39-41.

persons daily since the declaration of the emergency. The deaths have been due to weapons, starvation, and treatment which are organised by the Kenya Government.

This calculation would mean about ninety thousand persons (90,000) have died and in addition to that one million pounds per month is being used in order to carry on the genocide.

The letter also exposes the colonial tactics of divide and rule used in Kenya:

> "[they have] separated the Kenya Africans into many parts and always are creating hatred between the parties and forcing the parties to fight each other and supply the groups with weapons – firearms and ammunitions".[298]

All publications by the Kenya Committee were banned by the Kenya Government in March 1955. The Kenya Government claimed that the Committee "is sponsored by the British Communist Party."[299]

The Kenya Committee came under attacks from settler interests for its support for the cause of justice and liberation. The settler publication, the *Comment* accused the Committee of "spreading dangerous propaganda."[300] The Committee also published annual reports on the repression in Kenya and this caused it to be attacked by colonial government-settler interests. Its publication, *Kenya Report, 1953* led to the call for legal action against the Committee in the British House of Commons:

> Mr. P. Williams asked the Colonial secretary yesterday if his attention had been drawn to a document entitled "Kenya Report 1953", which was being circulated by the Kenya Committee for Democratic Rights for Kenya, which was inflaming racial animosity by its inaccurate and incorrect reporting. He also asked whether the Minister would take legal action against this body in view of the subversive nature of its activities.

---

[298] The letter was issues by the Kenya Committee as an attachment to a press statement dated 15 April, 1955. Kenya Committee. Press Extracts, Vol. 1 (15 April, 1955), pp. 33(a) – 33 (c).
[299] Times 15 March, 1955.
[300] The *Comment* (Nairobi), 16 June, 1955.

Mr. O. Lyttleton stated that he had only recently seen this document. "It contains a great deal of mischievous and misleading propaganda. I am considering the point raised in the second part of the question.[301]

The Committee merged with the Association for African Freedom in September 1956. In a notice to members, the Committee explained the reason for the merger:

> In view of the recent greatly increased interest in colonial matters, and the number of other organisations now operating with similar aims to its own, the Kenya Committee decided at its last meeting to dissolve and merge into another body, because its existence as a separate organisation is no longer justified and is leading to reduplication of work and dissipation of strength . . . The Association has already done very good work on Kenya in its monthly publication, *Africa Bulletin*. It also publishes monthly Press Extracts on the whole of Africa . . . The current September [1956] edition, therefore, is the last issue of the *Kenya Press Extracts* that will be published by the Kenya Committee.[302]

Kenyan events from September/October 1956 onwards were covered by publications from the Association for African Freedom.

Many British newspapers and campaigning groups, as well as progressive individuals, have always supported the Kenyan people's struggles. This was shown, for example, when the colonial administration and colonial laws in Kenya condemned Kimaathi to death. Many newspapers, MPs, and individuals took up the case for justice for the people of Kenya. The following records from British papers provide not only a commentary on events of the last days of Kimaathi, but also show the progressive stand of some British people and press:

- Dedan Kimathi, the leader of Mau Mau...was captured

---
[301] Manchester Guardian, 18 February, 1954
[302] Kenya Committee. Press Extracts, Vol. 4 (? September, 1956), p. 4.

today...The police fired, hitting him in the thigh. Later Kimathi was operated on in Nyeri hospital and is now handcuffed under a stengun guard, with his leg in a splint . . . general Sir Gerald Lathbury, Commander in Chief, East Africa, acknowledged today that Kimathi had always been a leader of 'great resource and considerable courage.[303]

- The trial began today before the Supreme Court in Nyeri of Dedan Kimathi . . . a crowd watched him brought to court...road barriers had been erected around the town to prevent big gatherings.[304]
- Dedan Kimathi was today sentenced to death by the Supreme Court here [Nyeri] for unlawful possession of a revolver.[305]
- The President of the East African Court of Appeal has summarily dismissed an appeal by Dedan Kimathi against the death sentence passed on him last month.[306]
- Protests made on the rejection of Dedan Kimathi's appeal against death sentence by Monica Whatley, a well known Catholic publicist, and Frida Laski, widow of Harold Laski.[307]
- Thirteen leading London trade unionists have signed a letter to the Colonial Secretary, Mr. Lennox Boyd, urging "the immediate release" of Dedan Kimathi, who has been sentenced to death in Kenya. The letter declares: "An active member of the Kenya African Union before it was banned and leader of the Land and freedom Army during the last four years, Kimathi constantly made proposals for negotiations with the Government in order to bring the fighting to an end. His execution would be a further crime against the people of Kenya, 34,000 of whom are still detained in prison camps without charge or trial. It could only lead to further bitterness and bloodshed with increased suffering for the Kenyan people and more sacrifices for the British working class.[308]
- The Movement for Colonial Freedom announced last night that they have issued instructions to Messrs. T.L. Wilson & Co. Privy Council agents and solicitors, to instruct Mr. Dingle Foot, Q.C.,

[303] Times, 22 October, 1956.
[304] Times, 20 November 1956.
[305] Times, 28 November, 1956.
[306] Times, 28 December, 1956.
[307] Daily Worker, 1 January, 1957.
[308] Daily Worker, 3 January, 1957.

Mr. Ralph Milner and Mrs Evi Underhill to present a petition to the Privy Council on behalf of Dedan Kimathi, the Mau Mau leader, for special leave to appeal against sentence of death.[309]

- Kimathi's petition rejected. No leave to appeal.[310]
- A protest movement in Britain started yesterday against the Privy Council's refusal to let Dedan Kimathi, the Kenya African people's leader, appeal against sentence of death.[311]
- Kenya's leader hanged: Dedan Kimathi, Kenya people's leader, was hanged yesterday; just over 48 hours after his leave of appeal had been rejected by the Privy Council...Dedan Kimathi went calmly to his death. He was described by a senior prison official as a model prisoner. "To the last he was composed and quiet" he said.[312]
- "Kimathi execution affront to justice": Labour protest. The Labour Party National Executive yesterday passed a resolution deploring "as an affront to British Justice" the recent execution in Kenya of Dedan Kimathi, the Mau Mau leader.[313]

We leave the last word to the London weekly, *World News and Views*:

THE BURNING SHAME OF KENYA

- The statement of the British officer reported in the press on November 26, "shoot everyone who is black", has brought the feelings of indignation about what is happening in Kenya to new heights . . . every support should be given to the Kenya Committee in its activities in connection with the forthcoming national day of protest on December 9.
- With mounting ferocity, the British-led, British-equipped "security forces" continue daily deliberately to murder and terrorise Africans in their native Kenya.
- Week by week this enormous apparatus of repression[314] produces its "casualty" lists, announces more or less "successful" operations.
- We in Britain must raise a much stronger protest at the crimes

---

[309] Times, 5 January, 1956.
[310] Manchester Guardian, 15 February, 1957.
[311] Daily Worker, 16 February, 1957.
[312] Daily Worker, 16 February, 1957.
[313] Manchester Guardian, 28 February, 1957.
[314] Quoting the "Observer" of 1 November, 1953, "World News and Views" gives the following figures of British military presence in Kenya:: "Twelve British and African battalions, an R.A.F. squadron, 12,000 police and almost 20,000 Kikuyu Home Guards".

being committed in Kenya in our name, must respond with actions to the moving appeals addressed directly to us by the Kikuyu people, must demand the withdrawal of all armed forces, an end to the terror and mass murder, and the granting of democratic rights and safeguards to the Kenya Africans. *Let December 9, National Day of Protest called by the Kenya Committee, show that the united British and Kenya peoples are strong enough to defeat the imperialist policies of the Tory Government and "white" settlers in Kenya.*[315]

CANADA

LIBERATION SUPPORT MOVEMENT (LSM) INFORMATION CENTRE

Don Barnett who had in 1966 researched and published an important study on Mau Mau - *Mau Mau From Within* – set up the LSM Information Centre in Richmond, BC, Canada in 1973. The Centre published an important series of "Life Histories from the Revolution". Of the first seven life stories, three were from Kenya, on Mau Mau activists. The others were from Angola (Movimento Popular de Libertação de Angola - MPLA), Namibia (South West African People's Organisation - SWAPO), Zimbabwe (Zimbabwe African People's Union - ZAPU) and South Africa (African National Congress - ANC). Barnett thus played a crucial role in documenting and publishing histories from African liberation struggles which otherwise may not have been written at all. Barnett explains the conditions under which African peasants and workers struggle for liberation which makes it impossible for them to record their own histories:

> The vast majority of peasants and workers in the super-exploited hinterland of the imperialist system are illiterate. It is part of their oppression. They comprise almost half of the world's population, some 75% of the population in the "free world", and the emiserated broad base from which all contemporary anti-imperialist revolutions draw their essential moral and material

[315] World News and Views, 5 December, 1953. Vol. 33, No. 48.

strength. These are the masses who, under the leadership of revolutionary vanguards, are making modern history. Yet, due largely to the chains of their enforced illiteracy, these makers of history rarely have the opportunity to document their own experiences within it. Their "backwardness" condemns them to literary silence as well as to poverty, disease and a short life.[316]

Barnett continues by giving the reason for launching LSM's series, *Life Histories from the Revolution*:

> One of the objectives in launching this series is to provide a medium through which individual members of these classes-in-motion within the revolution can *speak*. We also believe it important that *they be heard* by those of us who comprise imperialism's privileged and literate metropolitan minority. Their recounted lives...offer us frees perspectives on the processes of repression and revolution from a unique vantage point: *from below* . . . These stories constitute a body of data and testimony as revealed by a few of those history-makers normally condemned to silence while others speak on their behalf.

The three books on Kenya are Muchai (1973), Kabiro (1973) and Mathu (1974). Together with Barnett and Njama's *Mau Mau from Within*, these books provide some of the best documentation on the Kenyan liberation struggle.

USSR

The support from USSR was in various forms. The positive coverage of events from a people's point of view in Soviet press is shown in the following report:

> The Soviet trade union paper *Trud* told its readers today of Britain's "bloody terror" in Kenya. The writer, G. Kulikova, declared: "Whole villages ablaze, tens of thousands killed, tortured and

[316] Barnett (1972)

mutilated people, rivers of blood, a sea of tears – this is the price the native populations of Kenya have already paid, only because they ardently desire freedom and recognition of their human rights."[317]

EGYPT

Egypt also provided moral as well as material support for the struggle in Kenya. Broadcasts from Radio Cairo provided news and views from the liberation point of view. These were heard widely in East Africa and helped to disseminate the positive point of view much wider. Britain protested about "Cairo propaganda broadcasts" in March 1956, which Cairo promptly rejected. However, the Arabic *Al Akhbar* "today repeats the very charges the British Government had been complaining about . . . (as) it speaks of British 'atrocities' in Kenya, Nigeria and other parts of Africa and wonders if Britain can delude the inhabitants of these territories into the belief that she will grant them their freedom and independence."[318]

IRELAND

Kinyatti quotes a relevant passage from "the Irish revolutionary press":

> We only get one side of the story and that, as we in Ireland know very well, is told in a way that destroys the African's case...The [colonial] papers are constantly reporting the killing of Africans while "resisting arrest", "failing to halt", or "attempting to escape." These are terms which Irish people remember as synonymous with sheer murder by British forces and police of unarmed Irish men and women. The recurrence of such expressions in reports from Kenya has a sinister ring in Irish ears...Whatever the happenings it has become evident that the mass of people are against the present [colonial] regime.[319]

---

[317] Times (London), 22 February, 1954.
[318] Times, 31 March, 1956.
[319] Kinyatti (forthcoming).

INDIA

India gave a great deal of moral and material support to those struggling for liberation in Kenya. Material support included money for setting up the Lumumba Institute and Pan Africa Press for which Pio Gama Pinto approached Nehru. India's support was given openly by its first High Commissioner in Kenya, Apa Pant. Spencer (1983) recalls the contribution of Apa Pant:

> The support (from India) increased in 1948 when the Indian Government sent its first High Commissioner, Apa Pant, to Kenya. He was so pro-KAU that the British Government asked Nehru to recall him several times before he left in 1954.
>
> Pant immediately took up the Africans' nationalist cause. For the six years that he remained in Kenya, he raised money for African causes – he was particularly successful in getting South Asian support for the Kenya Teachers College at Githunguri – obtained scholarships to India for African students, and gave KAU political advice and support. Pant publicly backed KAU on the various issues that arose, such as more African representation in the Legislative Council. In addition, his office acted as the receiver and transmitter of important messages and papers for KAU. Pant's house became a forum, practically the only one of its kind at that time, where Africans, South Asians, and Europeans could meet and talk freely.

USA

Kinyatti (forthcoming) mentions one level of support for the Kenyan struggle in the USA:

> The African-American militant movement vigorously and uncompromisingly supported the Kenyan people's liberation

struggle. For instance, a Garveyist group, the United African Nationalist Movement (UANM) staged a valiant demonstration in front of the United Nations on May 5, 1953 in support of the just struggle of the Kenyan people. It demanded the withdrawal of the British forces from Kenya.

East African Standard (27 May, 1953) quoted a statement issued by UANM: "We have been instructed by the advisory council of the UANM to request the Afro-South Asian bloc to consider bringing the dangerous situation in Kenya before the U.N. There have been undeniable violations of human rights and there continue to be unprovoked aggression against the indigenous populations by British forces and the European settlers."

TRINIDAD

John La Rose recalled the influence that the Mau Mau movement had in Trinidad during 1950s.[320] Young activists kept themselves informed about developments in Kenya through BBC reports and also from material from the Kenya Committee in London. They began to apply the lessons of the Kenyan struggle to local politics. Thus they started referring to local politicians who sided with colonialists as "loyal Kikuyus" – a term popularised by the BBC news broadcasts about the struggle of Mau Mau activists against those who collaborated with the colonialists.

[320] Personal communications, London, 28 July, 2004.

CHAPTER SEVEN

INDEPENDENCE AND NEO-COLONIALISM

The active armed and political struggles waged by Mau Mau eventually forced a change in British colonial policy, not only in Kenya, but in other colonies as well. The very approach to colonial rule had to change in face of the increasing militancy and resistance of the colonised people. While it is true that Mau Mau forces were defeated in the military field, their achievement was nevertheless considerable. Facing an enemy with the resources of the whole Empire, the Mau Mau forces kept the colonial armed machine at bay for over five years.

It has not been recognised by many that Mau Mau won the political battle for independence. Towards the end of 1960s, it became clear that independence in Kenya was inevitable. This could not have been achieved without long years of struggle by Mau Mau combatants. Yet the battle for economic liberation was not won. The departing colonial power, now joined by the new imperialist power of USA, was not about to give up economic control in Kenya and other colonies as they achieved independence. The focus shifted from military battles to the economic and political fronts. It is to the credit of Mau Mau that they recognised this changing situation and started addressing this new threat. We take a brief look at this in this closing section.

"THE STRUGGLE FOR KENYA'S FUTURE"

Towards the end of 1960s, the newly reconstituted Mau Mau organisation carried on its struggle by producing and circulating progressive material so that neo-colonial ideas would not have the field all to themselves. Two examples can be examined here. The first is a series of wall posters, eleven of which were published starting on 15th March, 1961; the second case study is the mimeographed articles published in December 1961.

The poster campaign was launched to arouse the democratic forces locally and internationally to support the cause of real liberation in Kenyn. It was undertaken to highlight one aspect of the oppressive colonial administration: the detention of hundreds of thousands of men, women and children in complete disregard of their basic human rights.

A committee called "Release Detainees Committee" was formed to undertake this struggle. It decided to highlight initially the detention of leaders. The Committee drafted, printed and posted over a thousand circulars to prominent leaders all over the world. This resulted in great moral support for the campaigns to release political detainees. The Organising Secretary of the Committee, Ambu H. Patel, records the Committee's activities:

> It was therefore decided to publish weekly posters, *World Voice on Release Jomo Kenyatta and Other Detainees* and displayed them widely. This poster campaign continued for eleven weeks and had profound effect on educating the masses and developing public opinion on a very wide scale.[321]

The spirit of the poser campaign is captured in the book, *The struggle for the release of Jomo Kenyatta and other detainees.*[322] Interesting cases of international support for the liberation struggle are recorded, for example, it documents the solidarity in "British" Guyana when the whole population observed a complete "hartal" (strike) - cessation of work and fast - for two days (p.223) when the news of the British bombers' attack on the Nyandarwa liberated area reached them.

The second example of the liberation forces continuing their political struggle through publishing activities was the circulation of progressive

---

[321] Patel, A (1963), pp. 33-34. A photograph of the wall poster is reproduced on p.222; a photograph of the five volumes of release record containing world press cuttings is reproduced on p. 224.
[322] Patel, A. H. (1963).

pamphlet in the early 1960s. The colonial propaganda machinery put out a constant message through their mass media (radio, newspapers, magazines etc.): that independence was just round the corner and thus there was no need to struggle any longer. The goals of independence struggle were won, they said; Africanization, multi-racialism, nationalism were here, they proclaimed. So why struggle? they argued.

In order to counter this propaganda and to emphasise the need to continue the struggle, the followers of Kimaathi's line prepared and published their own analysis of historical events, using a working class perspective. This was in the form of a pamphlet which was widely distributed, including at the KANU Conference held in Nairobi in December, 1961. The context was the two line struggle which was being waged within KANU – for real liberation, land and freedom or for flag independence under neo-colonial control.

The pamphlet is of major historical importance. Barnett, who reproduces the full document, gives a background: "as part of a collective effort by several Kenyans and myself, the following article was written, mimeographed and distributed at the Kenya African National Union (KANU) Conference held in Nairobi, Kenya in December 1961". The pamphlet opens with an analysis of the on-going struggles:

THE STRUGGLE FOR KENYA'S FUTURE

The struggle for Kenya's future is being waged today on three distinct though interrelated levels: political, racial and economic. It seems to us that we Africans are being allowed to 'win' in the first two spheres as long as we don't contest the battle being waged on the third, all-important, economic level.

Since the end of the Second World War, Great Britain,

knowing it could not contain the wave of nationalist revolutions spreading throughout the colonial world, has embarked on a course of "guiding" these nationalist movements down a path most conducive to the perpetuation of British and multi-national capitalist economic domination. The old colonialism involving direct political control is fast dying and a quick transition to the new colonialism is felt necessary to avert a *genuine* social revolution, which would result in economic as well as political independence and thus stop the flow of Kenya's surplus capital into the banks of the western capitalist world. The British Master Plan is thus quite simple in outline:

"Carefully relinquish political control to a properly indoctrinated group of the 'right kind' of Africans, i.e. those whose interests are similar to, and comparable with, our own, so that we retain economic control.' In short, the British Government wants to leave in political form so that its capitalist 'sponsors' might remain in economic content." Put into slogan form, this plan would be: LEAVE IN ORDER TO STAY.

What are the techniques being employed by the British to facilitate our transition from colonial to neo-colonial status? We shall mention here two of the most important. First is a technique which might be called *Racial Harmony: A Disguise for the Recruitment of African Stooges and Frontmen* . . . [There is] clear evidence of a calculated plan on the part of the economic elite to partially dissolve racial barriers in order to consolidate its position along class lines and to use Africans as frontmen and spokesmen for its interests... 'Africanization' is the term used for the process...

Let us instead struggle against a 'stability' which is in fact stagnation; let us struggle to liberate that vast reservoir of creative ability which now lies dormant amongst our people; let us, in short, create a new society which allows to each the right to eat, the right to the products of their his labour, the right to clothe, house, and educate their children, the right, in short, to live in dignity amongst equals. It is a socialist society we should be struggling to build, a system which, unlike capitalism, concerns itself with the welfare of the masses rather than with the profits and privileges of a few.

A second technique being utilised so that our rulers might 'Leave in order to stay' can be called *Nationalism: A Colonialist Substitute for Ideology*. Nationalism is essentially a negative philosophy and is no substitute for a positive ideology. The British have attempted to utilise this negative political slogan (which they themselves have popularised) to forestall or hinder the emergence of a revolutionary ideology, which they feared might mean the end of their economic domination.

Let us then fashion an ideology which will unify the vast majority of our people by articulating their needs and by advancing a program of socialist development in agriculture and industry which promises to eradicate poverty, disease and illiteracy, a program which will draw out the creative talents and energies of our people, giving them that personal dignity and pride which comes from socially constructive and productive activity.

Let us, in short, provide our people with the ideological and organisational tools necessary for the achievement of genuine independence and development.

Let us not sell them cheaply down the glittering path of neo-colonialism and social, economic and cultural stagnation.[323]

This was the ideological standpoint of the Mau Mau on the eve of

[323] Barnett (1972).

independence. It is with this important document that this record of publishing in Kenya ends. It sums up the reasons for the struggle of the whole colonial period. It also looks to the next period of independence and gives an indication of what the new struggles will be.

CHAPTER EIGHT

Conclusion: Never Be Silent

Social communications are central to any social struggle. There is a sizable body of literature from other countries on the use of oral medium, newspapers, books and other forms of communications being used as tools for organising against a powerful enemy, as a training ground for cadres and for clarifying and developing revolutionary theory, ideology, organisation and practice. All this ensures a greater unity among those resisting oppression and exploitation.

Thus revolutionary and liberation forces of Bolsheviks in the Soviet Union, the Communist Party of China, and in Vietnam had developed theories and practices of revolutionary publishing as part of their revolutionary work. This has also been the case during anti-colonial and anti-imperialist struggles in Africa, but very little of this has been systematically documented as an aspect of revolutionary communications policy and practice. While the colonial communications systems have been reasonably well documented, the resistance communication systems remain largely undocumented and ignored.

This book is an initial attempt to document this dynamic communications process in Kenya with its external struggles against colonialism and its complex internal struggles with overlaying divisions of race and class, Kenyan and foreign peoples. The main theme emerging from this experience is that people struggling to change their society always find ways of establishing their own system of communicating with the people they lead and by whom they are led. Their mission of revolution, of change, of peace, of social and economic justice requires that they should never be silent. This was well understood and practised by the liberation forces in Kenya. They were never silent.

BIBLIOGRAPHY

NOTE: Various contemporary newspapers and journals used in this book are listed in footnotes and are not recorded in this section, for example the *Citizen, Colonial Times* and *Fairplay*.

A

Abour, C. Ojwando. (1971): "White highlands no more". Nairobi: Pan African Researchers.

Abuoga, J. B and Mutere, A. M. (1988): "The history of the press in Kenya". Nairobi: African Council on Communication Education. African Media Monograph series, No. 5.

Ainslie, Rosalynde. (1966): "The press in Africa: communications past and present". London: Gollancz.

Akumu, J. Dennis. (1966): "Trade union" in: "Pio Gama Pinto, Independent Kenya's first martyr - socialist freedom fighter".

Aldrick, Judy. (1999): "Mombasa's grand old man of letters: a profile of Edward Rodwell". Taken from a posting on Namaskar-Africana on Sept. 29, 2000.

Ali, Hassan. (n.d.): "Swahili profile". Available from:
<http://victorian.fortunecity.com/louvre/88/swahili/profs04.html> [Accessed 24 March 2004].

Ali, Hassan. (n.d.): "A brief history of the Swahili language". (Revised by Juma, A). Available from: <http://www.glcom.com/hassan/swahili_history.html> [Assessed 24 March, 2004].

Allen, J. W. T. (1971): "Tendi". Nairobi: Heinemann. (Quoted in King'ei, 2001).

Allen, James de Vere. (1977): "Al-Inkishafe, catechism of a Soul" translation of Sayyid Abdulla Bin Ali Bin Nasir. Nairobi: East African Literature Bureau.

Allen, James de Vere. (1981): "Swahili book production". *Kenya past and present* (Nairobi). No.13.

Alot, Magaga. (1982): "People and communication in Kenya". Nairobi: Kenya Literature Bureau. 1982.

Anderson, David. (2005): "Histories of the hanged: the dirty war in Kenya and the end of Empire. New York: Norton.

B

Barnett, Donald L. and Njama, Karari. (1966). "Mau Mau from within; autobiography and analysis of Kenya's peasant revolt". New York: Monthly Review Press.

Barnett, Donald L. (1972): "Kenya: two paths ahead". Introduction to Muchai, K.: "Hardcore: the story of Karigo Muchai" (1973). Richmond, B.C., Canada: LSM Information Centre.

Barton, Frank. (1979): "The press in Africa: persecution and perseverance". New York: Africana Publication Co.

Bhushan, Kul (ed.) (1980): "Kenya 80-81: Uhuru 16 yearbook". Nairobi: Newspread International.

Brittain, Victoria. (1999): "Africa". *The Guardian Weekend.* 2 January, 1999.

Budohi, Dome. (1979): "Forging standards of design [and] production". Nation (Nairobi). Printing and Publishing supplement. October 26.

The burning shame of Kenya. (1953). World News and Views (London). Vol. 33, no. 48. 5 December.

C

Carter, Felice. (1970): "The Kenya Government and the press, 1906-60". *Hadith* No.2. Nairobi: Historical Association of Kenya. (Ed. B. Ogot).

Carter, Felice. (1969): "The Asian press in Kenya". East Africa Journal (Nairobi) Vol. 6, No. 10. October.

Chandan, Amarjit. (2004): "Gopal Singh Chandan; a short biography and memoirs". (Punjabi Diaspora series no. 4). Jalandar: Punjab Centre for Migration Studies.

Chandra, Romesh. (1966): "Son of Africa". in: "Pio Gama Pinto, Independent Kenya's first martyr - socialist freedom fighter".

Chege, J. W. (1978): "Copyright law and publishing in Kenya". Nairobi: Kenya Literature Bureau.

Chokwe, Muinga Chitari. (1966): "Early days". in: "Pio Gama Pinto, Independent Kenya's first martyr - socialist freedom fighter".

Cone, L.W. and Lipscomb, J.F. (1972): "The History of Kenya Agriculture". Nairobi: University Press of Africa.

Corfield, F. D. (1960): "Historical survey of the origin and growth of Mau Mau". Cmd. 1030. London: Her Majesty's Stationery Office. (Corfield Report).

Crawfurd homepage: Available from: <http://crawfurd.dk/africa/kenya_timeline.htm> [Assessed 28 June, 2004].

D

De Souza, F. R. S. (1966): "Goa's liberation". in: "Pio Gama Pinto, Independent Kenya's first martyr - socialist freedom fighter"

Durrani, Shiraz. (1984a): Gama Pinto: a Kenyan freedom fighter. The Standard (Nairobi). September 17.

Durrani, Shiraz. (1984b): Pinto backed nationalism. The Standard (Nairobi). September 18.

Durrani, Shiraz. (1986): "Kimaathi, Mau Mau's first prime minister of Kenya". London: Vita Books.

Durrani, Shiraz. (1986): "Pambana" - The legacy of resistance in Kenya, 1963-68. Unpublished paper based on a talk given at the Review of African Political Economy Conference, Liverpool, 1986.

Durrani, Shiraz. (1991): "Voices of resistance; underground publishing in Kenya after independence, 1963- 90 London: UKenya (unpublished internal document).

Durrani, Shiraz. (1997): "The other Kenya: underground and alternative literature. Collection Building. Vol. 16(2) 80-87.

E

East African Standard. 20 August, 1954. ("Mau Mau camps and documents found").

East African Standard, 15 October, 1954. (Operation Anvil).

Electors' Union (Nairobi). (n.d.): "Permanency of British settlement". Nairobi: Electors' Union.

Electors' Union Newsletter (Nairobi). (1952): Not for sale. Nairobi: Electors' Union.

Elkins, Caroline (2000): Reckoning with the past; the contrast between the Kenyan and South African experiences. Social Dynamics 26:2 (2000): 8-28. Available from: <http://web.uct.ac.za/depts/cas/sd/Articles_Vol26no2/elkins.pdf> [Assessed 4 June, 2004).

Elkins, Caroline (2005): Imperial reckoning: the untold story of the end of Empire in Kenya. New York: Holt.

Etemesi, Horace. (1980): "National policy on book promotion". (Unpublished paper) June, 1980.

Evans, Ruth. (2000): "Kenya's Asian heritage on display". BBC News Online. 24 May, 2000.

F

Finneagan, Ruth. (1979): "Oral literature in Africa". Nairobi: Oxford University Press. (See specially chapter 10: Topical and political songs. pp. 272-298.)

Frederiksen, Bodil Folke. (2000): "The Mworias in Kenya: matriarchy and social change; an essay in family biography". Seminar Paper, African Studies Seminar. University of Natal, Durban 8 November 2000. Available from: <http://www.history.und.ac.za/Sempapers/frederiksen2000.pdf>

[Assessed 27 June, 2004].

G

Gadsden, Fay. (1980): The African press in Kenya, 1945-1952. *Journal of African History*, 21 (1980) pp.515-535.

Gatabaki, Njehu. (1983): "20 great years of independence". Nairobi: Productions and Communications.

Gregory, Robert G. (1971): "India and East Africa: a history of race relations within the British Empire, 1890-1939". Oxford: Clarendon Press.

H

Healey, J. G. (1968): "Mass media growth in Kenya". University of Missouri, USA (MA thesis).

Hichens, W. (1970): "Diwani ya Muyaka bin Haji Al-Ghassaniy". Johannesburg: University of Witwatersrand Press.

Hill, M. F. (1956): "Planters' progress; the story of coffee in Kenya". Nairobi: Coffee Board of Kenya.

History of Kenya, 1952-1958. (1976): A guide to the exhibition by Kenyan artists Mule wa Musembi, Kitonyi wa Kyongo, Kitaka wa Mutua and Mutunga wa Musembi held at Cottage Crafts, Nairobi in 1976. Publicity leaflet. Exhibition organised by Sultan Somjee.

Huff, L. R. (1968): "The Press and nationalism in Kenya". Madison: University of Wisconsin, USA. (Thesis).

I

Independent Kenya. (1982). "Sponsored by the Journal of African Marxists in solidarity with the authors". London: Zed Press. ("Independent Kenya was the underground work of the December Twelve Movement" – Kinyatti, 2002, p. 42).

International Press Institute (1953): "Lost opportunities on Kenya's vernacular press". International Press

Institute Report. V.1 (9). January [by a Special Correspondent].

J

Jacques, Martin. (2004): The return of people's war. The Guardian. April 19, 2004.

Jenkins, Cathy. (2001): "Monuments for the Mau Mau". London: BBC. 22 March. Transcript available at <http://news.bbc.co.uk/low/english/world/africa/newsid_1236000/1236807.stm> [Assessed 28 June, 2004].

Jenkins, Cathy. (2004): "President Moi; opposition says it is an election ploy". BBC World Service. 22 March, 2004. Transcript available from:
<http://news.bbc.co.uk/1/hi/world/africa/1236807.stm> [Assessed 17 April, 2004].

Josh, Sohan. (1977): "Hindustan Ghadar Party; a short history". New Delhi: People's Publishing House.

K

Kabiro, Ngugi. (1973): "Man in the middle; the story of Ngugi Kabiro". Taped and edited by Donald Barnett. Richmond, BC, Canada: LSM Information Centre. (Life Stories from the Revolution. Kenya, Mau Mau. 2).

Kaggia, Bildad. (1966): "A friend". in: "Pio Gama Pinto, Independent Kenya's first martyr - socialist freedom fighter".

Kaggia, Bildad. (1975): "Roots of Freedom, 1921-1963; the autobiography of Bildad Kaggia". Nairobi: East African Publishing House.

Kali, J. D. (1976): "In Parliament". in: "Pio Gama Pinto, independent Kenya's first martyr - socialist freedom fighter".

Kamaru, Joseph. (1988?): "Migambo ya nyimbo cia Mau Mau (miaka 25 ya wiyathi)". [Mau Mau songs]. 2 cassettes. Nairobi: City Sounds Studio.

Kaplan, Irving. (1976): "Area handbook for Kenya". 2nd ed. 1976. Prepared by Foreign Area Studies of the American Universities. USA. Government Printing. Office: Washington, DC.

Kariuki, Josiah Mwangi. (1975): "Mau Mau detainee; the account a Kenyan African of his experiences in detention camps, 1953-1960". Nairobi: Oxford University Press.

Kenya. Colony. Emergency Regulations, 1952 (Colonial Government Notice No.1103).

Kenya. Colony. Emergency (Amendment) (No.10) Regulations, 1953 (C.O.N. No. 304).

Kenya Committee for Democratic Rights for Kenya (London). (1952-60): "Kenya Press Extracts". The Committee is referred to in this book as the "Kenya Committee". Photocopies of the following have been acquired by the author:
- Vol. 1: The years of the Emergency in Kenya, 1952 to 1960
- Vol. 2: (1954)
- Vol. 3 (1955)
- Vol. 4 (1956).

Kenya Empire Party. (1953): "Coming out fighting". Nairobi: Kenya Empire Party.

Kenya Gazette. (1953): Notice No. 20. Vol. LV, No.1. Nairobi: Kenya Colony. 6 January, 1953.

Kenya Police. (1954). "Annual Report". Nairobi: Kenya Police.

Khamisi, Francis. (1977): "The birth of Baraza: established to fight a war". The Standard (Nairobi) Wednesday 6 April 1977.

Kimaathi wa Waciuri. (1954): Letter to Humphrey Slade. *Citizen* (Nairobi). 20 March.

Kimaathi wa Waciuri. (1953): "The Kimaathi Charter". Citizen (Nairobi). October.

Kimali, Charles et al. (1977?): "Design theory, form content and communication in the context of the socio-economic development of rural Kenya". Nairobi: Department of Design, University of Nairobi. Project Report (1977?) (See especially Chapter 1: History of Publishing).

King, Kenneth, and Salim, Ahmed (eds.) (1971): "Kenya historical biographies" (2). Nairobi: Department of History, University of Nairobi.

King'ei, Kitula. (2001): "Historical and folkloric elements in Fumo Liyongo's epic". Folklore Vol. 16. Available from: <http://haldjas.folklore.ee/folklore> [Assessed 30 January, 2005].

Kinyatti, Maina wa. (1980): "Thunder from the mountains: Mau Mau patriotic songs". London: Zed Press.

Kinyatti, Maina wa. (1987): "Kenya's Freedom Struggle". London: Zed Press.

Kinyatti, Maina wa. (2000): "Mau Mau; a revolution betrayed". 2d ed. New York: Mau Mau Research Centre.

Kinyatti, Maina wa. (forthcoming): "History of resistance in Kenya, 1885-2002: Kenyatta and Kanu betrayed Mau Mau". (The quotations are taken from an early draft).

Kitchen, Helen. (1956): "The press in Africa". Washington, DC, USA: Ruth Sloan Associates.

Kitinya, Ishmael. (1981): "The book and newspapers trade for Africa". Nairobi: Africa Book Services.

Koinange, Mbiyu. (1955): "The people of Kenya speak for themselves". (Reprinted 1969). Nairobi: Business Forms & Systems.

Kubai, Fred. (1983): The struggle for independence; background to the nationalist movement. Gatabaki, Njehu (1983).

Kusum, K and Gross, B. (1981): Alternative communication strategies in Third World countries. Economic and Political Weekly (New Delhi) February 21.

L

Leakey, L. S. B (1954): "Defeating Mau Mau". London: Methuen.

Lenin, V. E. (1972): "The bourgeois intelligentsia's methods of struggle against the workers". Collected Works, Vol. 20. Moscow: Progress Publishers.

M

McGhie, John. (2002): "British brutality in Mau Mau conflict". The Guardian. (London). November 9, 2002.

Maina, Paul. (1977): "Six Mau Mau generals". Nairobi: Gazelle Books Co.

Makokha, K. (2000): Revered Kiswahili heroic epic on stage. Daily Nation (Nairobi). 2 July.

Mangat, J. S. (1969): "A history of Asians in East Africa, c. 1886 to 1945". London: Oxford University Press.

Mathu, Mohamed. (1974): "The urban guerrilla". Ed. Donald Barnett. Richmond, British Columbia, Canada. LSM Information Centre.

Ministry Rapped Over [Unfair] Book Deal. (1980): Daily Nation (Nairobi) Education Nation. Tuesday August 12.

Mirii, Ngugi wa. (1979): "On literacy content". Nairobi: Institute for Development Studies, University of Nairobi. Discussion paper no. 340.

Muchai, Karigo. (1973): "Hardcore; the story of Karigo Muchai". Tr. Ngugi Solomon Kabiro. Ed. Donald Barnett. Richmond, British Columbia, Canada: LSM Information Centre.

Mukimbo, Mary. (1978): "An appreciation of Amu women's poetry which was sung in the 1974/75 political campaign for parliamentary elections". Institute of African Studies. University of Nairobi. Paper No. 105.

Mulokozi, M. M. (1972): The revolutionary tradition in Swahili poetry. Maji Maji (Dar es Salaam). No.8.

Murray-Brown, Jeremy. (1973): "Kenyatta". New York: E .P. Dutton.

Mutahi, Wahome. (1981): Gakaara wa Wanjau, a freedom fighter who's turned writer, publisher and printer. Sunday Nation (Nairobi) Oct. 11.

Mwakenya. (1987): "Draft Minimum Programme". Nairobi: Mwakenya.

Mwaura, Peter. (1980): "Communication policies in Kenya". Paris: UNESCO.

Mworia, Henry. (1994): "I, the Gikuyu and the white fury". Nairobi: East African Educational Publishers.

N

Nassir, Ahmed. (1971): "Malenya wa Mvita: Diwani ya Ustadh Bhalo". Nairobi: Oxford University Press.

Ndegwa, John. (n.d.): "Printing and publishing in Kenya" (Paper presented at a conference. (A copy is available with the author).

Ndegwa, John. (1973): "Printing and Publishing in Kenya: an outline of development". London: Standing Conference of Library materials on Africa (SCOLMA).

Ngugi, Patrick. (1987): The nerve centre of struggle for uhuru. Daily Nation (Nairobi). November 3.

Njogu, Kimani. (n.d.): "A tribute to Gakaara wa Wanjau: a literary and cultural icon passes on". Network for the defence of independent media in Africa (NDIMA). Available from: <http://www.ndima.org/link129.htm> [Accessed 27 May, 2004].

Noronha, Subhash. (1987): A true son of Kenya. The Standard (Nairobi). June 22.

Nottingham, John and Okola, Lennard. (1972): Cultural armageddon. Bulletin of the Association for Commonwealth Literature and Languages. Kampala. No. 10, June.

Nottingham, John. (1966): The Book Trade in East Africa. East Africa Journal. (Nairobi). Vol. 2, February.

O

Ochieng, Philip. (1992): "I accuse the press; an insider's view of the media and politics in Africa". Nairobi: Initiative Publishers.

Odinga, Oginga. (1968): "Not yet uhuru; an autobiography". London: Heinemann.

Okwanya, Fred Ojienda. (1980): "Book publishing in Kenya". (Unpublished) Paper presented at National Communication Policy Workshop. 1st to 11th July.

Oneko, Ramogi Achieng (1966): "Detention days". "Pio Gama Pinto, Independent Kenya's first martyr".

Overy, Richard (2004): Like the Wehrmacht, we've descended into barbarity. The Guardian 10 May, 2004.

P

Pant, Apa. (1987): "Undiplomatic incidents". Hyderabad: Sangam Books.

Parekh, Bhikhu (2003): Pranlal Sheth: first deputy chairman of the Commission for Racial Equality. *The Independent*, (London). 15 July.

Patel, Ambu H. (1963): "Struggle for 'release Jomo and his colleagues' ". Nairobi: New Kenya Publishers.

Patel, Zarina. (1997): "Challenge to colonialism; the struggle of Alibhai Mulla Jeevanjee for equal rights in Kenya". Nairobi: Zand Graphics.

The People. (1954): It would be good to shoot every Kikuyu - former assistant inspector of police. Nairobi. 7 February.

Pereira, Benegal. (n.d.) "The life and times of Eddie Pereira". Available from: <http://www.goacom.com/overseas-digest/Archives/eddiep.html>[Accessed 30 May, 2004].

Pilger, John. (2004): Iraq is a war of national liberation. New Statesman 15 Apr. Also available from: <http://pilger.carlton.com/print>. [Assessed: 22 April, 2004].

Pinto, Pio Gama. (1963): "Glimpses of Kenya's Nationalist Struggle". Nairobi: Pan Africa. December 12.

"Pio Gama Pinto, Independent Kenya's first martyr - socialist freedom fighter" (1966). Nairobi: Pan African Press Ltd.

Pugliese, Christina. (1995): "Author, publisher and Gikuyu nationalist: the life and writings of Gakaara wa Wanjau". Bayreuth, Germany: Bayreuth African Studies.

R

"Report of the British Colonial Office parliamentary delegation to Kenya, January, 1954". (Quoted in Barnett and Njama, 1966).

Rosberg, Carl Gustav and Nottingham, John. (1966): "The Myth of 'Mau Mau'; nationalism in Kenya". Nairobi: East African Publishing House. 1966.

Rose, John La. (2004): personal communications, 28 July, 2004.

Ruo, Kimani Ruo. (1979): "Kiswahili poetry; its cultural and social values". Paper presented at the UNESCO sponsored seminar on Oral Traditions: Past Growth and Future Development in East Africa. Kisumu April 18-22. Nairobi. University of Nairobi. Institute of African Studies.

Ruo, Kimani Ruo (1984): Fani za Kiswahili. Taifa Leo (Nairobi). July 14, 1984.

Sareen, Tilak Raj. (1979): "Indian revolutionary movement abroad (1905-1921)". New Delhi: Sterling Publishers.

S

Scotton, James Francis. (1971): "Growth of the vernacular press in colonial East Africa: patterns of

Government control". PhD thesis, University of Wisconsin.

"The scramble for Africa; an exploration in anthropology for a new millennium". Available from: <http://www.zanzibararchives.com/vault.htm> [Acquired 16, January, 2005].

Seidenberg, Dana April. (1983): "Uhuru and the Kenya Indians; a minority community in Kenya Politics, 1939-1963". New Delhi: Vikas.

Shah, K. P. (1954): Letter to the Editor. New Statesman and Nation (UK) 1 May. (Reproduced in Makhan Singh (1980).

Sicherman, Carol. (1990): "Ngugi wa Thiong'o: the making of a rebel: a source book in Kenyan literature and resistance". London: Hans Zell. (Documentary Research in African Literature, 1).

Sik, Endre. (1974): "The history of Black Africa". Vol. IV. Translated by Sandor Simon. Budapest: Akademiai Kiado.

Singh, Chanan. (1971): "Manilal Ambalal Desai". Kenya Historical Biographies.

Singh, Makhan (1969): "History of Kenya's trade union movement to 1952". Nairobi. East African Publishing House.

Singh, Makhan (1980): "Kenya's Trade Unions, 1952-1956" (Cover title: 1952-56 Crucial Years of Kenya Trade Unions). Nairobi: Uzima Press.

Slaughter, Barbara (1999): "How Britain crushed the 'Mau Mau rebellion' – Channel Four TV's Secret History – Mau Mau". A report on the programme is available from: <http://www.hartford-hwp.com/archives/36/026.html> [Accessed: 2 April 2005].

The Socialist Leader. (UK), 31 December, 1955. ("Hangman busy in Kenya").

Sorrenson, M.P.K. (1968): "Origins of European settlement in Kenya". Nairobi: Oxford University Press.

Spencer, John (1983): "James Beauttah: freedom fighter". Nairobi: Stellascope.

T

Tamaduni Players. (1978): "Mzalendo Kimaathi" (Publicity handbill) Nairobi: Tamaduni Players.

Theuri, Mugo (1986): Stop Mau Mau debate – Moi. The Standard (Nairobi). 22 March.

Thiong'o, Ngugi wa. (1979): The national struggle to survive. The Guardian (London). 11 June.

Times (London). 31 July, 1954.(Jaswant Singh sentenced to death).

Times (London). 11 August, 1954. (Mau Mau couriers).

Times (London). 30 September, 1954. (Young Mau Mau activists).

Times (London). 10 January 1955. ("Injustice by the Government's practices").

Times (London). 14 January, 1955. (Mau Mau housing).

Times (London) 17 January, 1955. (News of surrender offer leaks out to Mau Mau).

Times (London) 19 February, 1955. ("The toll of hanging in Kenya").

Times (London). 24 Feb.1955. (Mau Mau's "bush telegraph").

Times (London) 15 March, 1955. (Anti-colonial Bureau and Kenya Committee publications banned).

The Tribune (UK), September 30, 1955. ("Labour to fight Kenya thugs"). Wanjau, Gakaara wa (n.d.): "Nyimbo cia Mau Mau; iria ciarehithirie wiyathi". Karatina: Gakaara Press. [May Mau songs].

W

Wanjau, Gakaara wa. (1988): "Mau Mau author in detention: an author's detention diary". Nairobi: Heniemann. Translated by Ngigi wa Njoroge. First published in Gikuyu in 1983 as Mwandiki wa Mau Mau Ithaamirio-ini.

Weekly Review (1980): Baraza: The end of an era in Kenya. Nairobi. January 11, 1980.

Z

Zwannenberg, Roger van (1971): "Robertson and the Kenya Critic". Kenya Historical Biographies, Eds.: King, K. and Ahmed, S.

NOTE

Many oral sources are used either to get specific details or general picture of publishing activities of different periods. These were crucial in providing important details as well as general trends of events. Material from the following Libraries has been used:
- Kenya National Archives, Nairobi.
- Nairobi City Council Library (Macmillan Library).
- University of Nairobi, especially the East Africana Collection, Institute of African Studies Library, Gandhi Memorial Library.
- Makhan Singh Archives. Institute of African Studies, University of Nairobi.
- Various personal collections, including notes, pamphlets and other collections from the personal library of Nazmi Durrani which has now been donated to the proposed "Kenya Liberation Library".

APPENDIX A
Selected Lists

Selected lists of newspapers, publishers and activists covering the colonial period in Kenya.

> ### THE PRESS WARS – THE BRITISH SIDE
> The [colonial] Information Office published nearly 1000 press handouts in 1953 distributing news of the Emergency… in 1962, 11,150 press handouts were issues.
>
> In 1956, 11 Gikuyu news sheets were directly produced by [colonial] Government. 22 [nationalist] language news organs were receiving government technical and financial assistance: 14 in Kiswahili, 2 in Kimeru, 3 in Kikamba, 1 in Kipsigis and 1 in Kinandi.
> - Huff (1968) pp. 96-97, 99, 130

> ### THE PRESS WARS - THE SOUTH ASIAN SIDE
> Indian interest in newspapers as a means to support their position vis-à-vis the white settlers led to the start of various newspapers before World War II. After the war, several of these newspapers strongly backed African nationalist aspirations.
> - Kaplan (1976) p.177

❐ NEWSPAPERS ❐

The following list is complied from a number of sources, including articles and books listed in the References. It is not intended to be a comprehensive list.

- Blue: Colonial government & settler publications
- Black: African publications
- Red: South Asian publications

◆ A ◆

Advertiser of East Africa. 1907-10. Nairobi. Weekly. Founder and editor: D. S. Garvie.
Appointed the official advertiser for the Nairobi Municipality.

Africa Mpya (New Africa). 1952-53. Kiswahili. Published by Bildad Kaggia at Africa Press, Nairobi. Printed by the Tribune Press (banned: 3-1-1953, Kenya. Colony. Government Notice [K.C.G.N.] No.20).

Africa Samachar. 1954-74. Nairobi. Weekly. Gujarati. Nairobi Africa Press. Circulation in 1970s: 16,000.[324]

Africa Times. June 1962- . Nairobi. Weekly (monthly?) Gujarati. Continuation of *Colonial Times.*

The African. 1948-49. Weekly.

The African Leader. 1946. English, Kiswahili. Weekly. Editors: James Gichuru; Joseph Otiende.

African Life. 1957-1962. Nairobi. Monthly.

Afrika Mpya. 1952-53. Kiswahili. Nairobi (Kiburi House). Weekly. Published by Africa Press, printed by the Tribune Press. Editors: Bildad Kaggia; S. R. Kimani (1953). Banned on 6 January, 1953.

African Standard, Mombasa Times and *Uganda Argus.* 18 November, 1902-. Weekly (daily from 1910. "The only non-official journal published in the English language in British East Africa". Founded by A. M. Jeevanjee. Editor: W. H. Tiller. Continued as *East African Standard* (August 1905-).

Africa Times. 1962- ? Superseded *Colonial Times*.

Afrika. 1949. Kiswahili. Weekly.

Afrika Mpya (New African). 1952. Kiswahili. Weekly. Editor: Bildad Kaggia. Proscribed in 1952 under Emergency laws.

Agikuyu. 1949? Gikuyu. Printed by Luo Thrift and Trading Corporation.

Agikuyu. 1955-1959. Nairobi. Gikuyu. Kenya Information Services. Designed to "encourage the Kikuyu, Embu and Meru people to rebuild their lives". Described as "the outstanding success of this year" in the Annual Report of the Department of Information (1955).

Akamba. 1956-1959. Nairobi. Kikamba. Kenya Information Services.

Amasonga. Bi-monthly. Kisii. Other editions published in Kalenjin (Chamge), Luhya (Miremba) and Dholuo (Misawa).

Avaluhya Times. 1947-1948. Kiswahili. Fortnightly.

Avaluhya Times. 1950. Kiluhya. Weekly.

◆ B ◆

Baragumu. ? – 1963. Nairobi. Published by *East African Standard*.

Baraza. 1939-1969. Nairobi. Weekly, Kiswahili. Published by *East African Standard*.[325]

Barua (*Post*). 1953. Kiswahili. Superseded *Mwaraniria* [*Dunia*].

Bendara ya Kenya (*The Kenyan Flag*). 1952-53. Kiswahili. Bi-weekly.

Bondeni. 1946-1947. Nakuru. English and Kiswahili. Editor: M.F. Hill.

Bondeni. 1952-1956. Monthly/fortnightly. African and Colonial Press Agency. Circulation in 1955: 10,000.

◆ C ◆

Cararuka (Frank). 1952. Gikuyu. Bi-weekly.

Chamge. Kalinjin. Other editions published in Kisii (Amasoga), Luhya (Miremba) and Dholuo (Misawa).

Chronicle. 1906-? Editor: Goss.[326]

Citizen. 1951-1956. Nairobi, weekly. Editor: Bobby Naidoo; S. T. Patwa (1956), owned by Patwa Publications. Circulation in 1956: 5,000. "During October 1953, the national liberation movement published in *Citizen*, a Kenya weekly newspaper, a Charter issued by Field Marshall Dedan Kimathi on behalf of Kenya National Defence Council".[327]

Coast African Express. 1946-1950? Mombasa. Kiswahili. Weekly. Militant, saw a class perspective.

Coast Guardian. 1933-1937. Mombasa. Editor: J. J. Robertson. Abdullah Rahimtulla Walji Hirji "went into partnership with Sir Ali bin Salim to establish a voice of the Mombasa littoral. They called it the *Coast Guardian* and it was edited by "Rab" Robertson, who published it (until his death, three years later) in Gujarati and English".[328]

Colonial Times. 1932-1962. Nairobi, bi-weekly. English on Saturdays, Gujarati on Thursdays. Editor: G. L. Vidyarthi. Publisher: African and Colonial Press Agency. Continued as *Africa Times* from June, 1962.

Comment. 1949-1956. Nairobi. Weekly. English and Afrikaans. Organ of the Federal Independence Party. Superseded *East Africa News Review* (1946-1949). "Extreme right wing European [paper], stood for indefinite White domination of Kenya and colour bar. Supported the National Party in South Africa" - Kitchen (1956).

Coro wa Agikuyu (*The Gikuyu Trumpet*). 1952. Gikuyu. Bi-weekly.

◆ D ◆

Daily Advertiser. "The only daily paper published in an Indian language throughout the East African territories". 1923. Mombasa. 4-page Gujarati tabloid.

Daily Chronicle. 1947-62. Nairobi, daily. English, Gujarati. Editors: Pio Gama Pinto, Pranlal Sheth.

- 1947: Haroon Ahmed
- 1950: Dharam Kumar Sharda (English section), Inde Desai (Gujarati section).
- "Radical Kenyan Indian paper" (Carter, 1969).
- "Working closely with the East African Trade Union Congress (led by Makhan Singh and Fred Kubai), giving it publicity and also to KAU through their independent newspaper, the *Daily Chronicle* was a small group of young Indian militants, led by Pio Gama Pinto, then on the office of Kenya Indian Congress....with Pinto were the late D. K. Sharda, Haroun Ahmed, Pranlal Sheth ..." (Odinga, 1969, pp.109-110).
- "Supported working class and trade union movement" (Singh, Makhan 1969).
- "Changes in ownership in 1959 resulted in a shift in policy – became conservative, and Rodrigues and Desai left to form the radical National Guardian" (Carter, 1969, p.33).

Daily Leader. ? – 1914. Published by Lord Bertran.

The Democrat. 1922-1930. Nairobi and Mombasa, weekly. Started by Sitaram Acharia. "It was outstanding in its stand and firght for the rights of the Indians as petty-bourgeoisie. Articles were directed towards equal opportunities... and arrogant superiority of one race over Indians and Africans. Colonialists decided that this paper should not be allowed to communicate to the African reading population. Subsequently, Sitaram Acharia was arrested and detained".[329]

Dunia [*Mwaraniria*] (*The World*). 1946-53. Nairobi (Kiburi House). Kiswahili. Editor Mwai Koigi. Printed by Zenith Printing Works. Quarterly.

Dunia Kenya (*the Kenyan Word*). 1952. Kiswahili. Monthly.

◆ E ◆

East Africa and Uganda Mail. 1899-1904. Mombasa. Weekly. Editor: Olive Grey.

East Africa News Review. 1946-1949. Nairobi. Superseded by *Comment*.

East African Chronicle. 1919-1922, Nairobi. Gujarati and English. Editor: Manilal A. Desai. Anti-colonial and for democratic rights. Supported Harry Thuku. Ceased publication in 1922 after paying a heavy damages in a libel case.

East African Kirti. 1937-38. Nairobi. Weekly. Punjabi. Proprietor: Mota Singh s/o Malla Singh. Superseded *Kenya Worker* (1936).

East African News. 1915-1916? Mombasa. Gujarati.
- "We do not ask for concessions, we scorn concessions; we do not ask for generosity, generosity is for the weak; we ask for no rewards, rewards are for slaves. We ask only for justice". - statement carried at the top of the first page of the first issue of *East African Chronicle*.
- Anti-colonial and for democratic rights, supported Harry Thuku. Ceased publication in 1922 (the year when Harry Thuku was arrested) after paying heavy damages in a libel case.
- *East African Kirti*. 1937-1938. Nairobi, weekly. Proprietor: Mota Singh s/o Malla Singh. Publication of the Labour Trade Union of Kenya. It superseded the *Kenya Worker*. Weekly circulation: 1,000 copies. The paper stopped after 3 issues. This is due to the Government having persecuted the editor "for not having obtained registration for the paper." The paper contained articles about the

Union's policies and news about workers' struggles and national and international news of general interest. (Singh, Makhan, 1969, p.56).

East African Standard. See: *African, Standard Mombasa Times* and *Uganda Argus.*

East African Star. 1950-1956. Mombasa, later Nairobi. Daily initially, weekly from 1952. Patwa News Agency in which Wm. Dawson & Sons of London acquired a substantial financial interest. Circulation in 1956: 2,000.

East African Weekly. 1931-1932. Nairobi. Amalgamated with *Times of East Africa,* continued as *East African Weekly Times.*

East African Weekly Times. 1932-1934. Nairobi. See also: *East African Weekly.*

Electors' Union Newsletter. 1950-1952. Nairobi. [An issue is reproduced in Koinange (1955, p.82)].

Equator, a magazine of East African writing. 1945. Mombasa.

Evening Leader. 1921. Mombasa. Established by Leader of East Africa.

◆ F ◆

Fairplay. 1927-1932. Editor: Dr. A. C. L. de Souza. Reported on Asian and other workers' struggles for their rights. (Singh, Makhan, 1969, pp. 41-42).

Fort Ternan Times. 1903.

Forward. 1946. Chanan Singh.

◆ G ◆

Gikuyu (Counsellor). 1946-48. Gikuyu. Fortnightly. Editor: Victor Wokabi. Continued as *Hindi ya Gikuyu* in 1948.

Gikuyu na Mumbi. 1952. Gikuyu. Monthly. Published by Gakaara Book Services, run by Jonah Gakaara; edited by V. M. J. Wokabi; printed by the Tribune Press. Proscribed in 1952 under Emergency laws - 24-10-1952, K.C.G.N. No. 1196; banned again: 2-12-1952, K.C.G.N.No.1343.

Gikuyu na Mumbi Magazine. 1952. Mathenge Wachira.

Gikuyu Times. 1948-49. Nairobi. Gikuyu. Weekly.

The Globe. 1955-1958. Weekly. English and Konkni.

Globe Trotter. 1906-1908. Nairobi. Weekly. Superseded by *The Pioneer.*

Glos Polski; tygodnik uchodzstwa polskiego w Afryce. Nairobi. Polish. [Voice of Poland, the weekly paper for Polish immigrants in Africa].

Goan Times. Radical South Asian paper.

Goan Voice. 1946-63+? Nairobi, weekly. English. A. C. L. de Souza. Circulation in 1956: 3,000 copies. "Called for the incorporation of Portuguese territories in India within the Republic of India. A well-edited paper of considerable influence among anti-Portuguese elements in the Goan community in East Africa". (Kitchen, 1956).

◆ H ◆

Habari (News). 1922-1925; 1927-31. "A newspaper for the natives of Kenya colony". Nairobi. English and Kiswahili. Monthly. Printed by Swift Press up to December 1923, then by Government Press for a few months, finally by *East African Standard.*

Habari (News) 1935-36; 1945-47. Published by G.L. Vidyarthi and distributed free. Revived in 1945 under Francis Ruhinda. Kiswahili. Weekly. Editor: W.W.W. Awori (1945) when it served as a mouthpiece of KAU. "Ruhinda and Vidyarthi were imprisoned for a total of 24 months in 1947 when Ruhinda criticised the 'discriminatory provision' for the welfare of African soldiers returning from the 2nd world war".

Habari (News). 1958-1960. first editor: Col. D. P. Watkins, Acting Chief Native Commissioner. Circulation in 1960: 15,000. "Discontinued so as to start a series of vernacular papers" (Huff, 1968).

Habari za Dunia (News of the World). 1952-54. Kiswahili; English. Weekly. Editors: W.W.W. Awori; Stephen Ruhenda. Gave a true picture of the situation during the Emergency. Published Kimaathi's letter from the forest. Banned in 1954.

Habari za Kenya. 1959. Nyeri. Publisher and editor: Wanjohi Mungau; also edited by J. M. Kariuki. Took a strong anti-colonial and anti-imperialist stand.

Hindi Prakash. 1911-14. Mombasa. Gujarati. Founded by B. H. Bhatt ("one of the reasons he started *Hindi Prakash* was to lay the grievances and requests of the Indians before the authorities" - [330]).

Hindi ya Gikuyu (*Gikuyu Times*). 1948-50. Gikuyu. Weekly. Editors: Victor Wokabi; J. C. Kamau. Superseded *Hindi ya Mwafrika*; superseded by *Muthamaki*. Kamau, Wokabi, V.G.Patel and his 3 partners were fined and sentenced several times for printing and publishing "seditious" articles.

Hindi ya Mwafrika. ?-1948. Superseded by *Hindi ya Gikuyu* in 1948.

Hingurira (Call for Freedom). 1952-53. Gikuyu. Bi-weekly.

Hodi (Hello). 1947. Kiswahili. Weekly. Mombasa. Established and edited by Francis Khamisi.

◆ I ◆

Ilomon le Maasai. 1955–1960? Nairobi, monthly. Maasai. Ministry of Information, Broadcasting and Tourism. Circulation: 400-700 (1955), 1,500 (1960).

The Independent. 1959. Nairobi. Owned and edited by E.L. Howard-Williams. Supported White settler control over Kenya, and attacked the colonial government for not supporting settler cause (banned by the colonial government).

Independent Comment. 1957. Nairobi. Printed by Welcome Press. Superseded *New Comment*; superseded by *Kenya Comment*.

Indian Voice. 1911-14. Nairobi. Editor: M.A. Desai. Portrayed the struggle between South Asian communities and European settlers.

Indian voice of British East Africa, Uganda and Zanzibar. 1911-13. Nairobi. English, Gujarati.

Inoro ria Gikuyu (The Gikuyu Sharpner). 1951-52. Gikuyu. Weekly. Founded, published and edited by B. M. Kaggia; printed by the Tribune Press (banned: 24-10-1952, K.C.G.N. 1196 and 2-12-1952 K.C.G.N. No. 1343). Superseded by *Mutongoria*.

◆ J ◆

Jaluo. 1956–1959. Nairobi. Dholuo. Kenya Information Services.

Jambo. 1942-1945. Nairobi, monthly. East Africa Command.

Jheeri's Weekly. 1924-36. Nairobi. Weekly. Publisher, printer, editor: Zaheer-ud-Deen.
• Represented the interests of the young generation of Indians – "we have issued strict instructions to our salesmen that not a single copy is to be sold to non Indians".
• Supported Isher Dass.
• Attacked European elected members for asking for loans of £5 million for European farmers.
• Demanded self-government for Kenya.

Jicho (Eye). 1952- 1963. Nairobi. Weekly. English/Kiswahili. Editor: Henry Gathigira. Circulation in 1963: 20,000. "Helped to fill the gap created by the suppression of African press in 1952".[331]

◆ K ◆

Kaguiri. 1952. Gikuyu. Weekly.

Kalenjin. ?-1960? Nairobi, monthly. Colonial Government Printer.

Kamongo Times. Early 1950s. Oral newspaper developed by freedom fighters at Saiyusi Detention Centre.

Kamuingi Koyaga Ndiri (Unity in Strength). 1952. Gikuyu. Bi-weekly.

Kenya. 1947. Kiswahili; Gikuyu. Weekly/fortnightly. Established and edited by Francis Khamisi.

Kenya Comment. 1957-1958. Superseded *Independent Comment.*

Kenya Critic – see: *Outlaw.*

Kenya Daily Mail. 1926-63. Mombasa. Gujarati/ English. Daily/ weekly. Established by: J.B. Pandya. Radical, anti colonial in content, interviewed African leaders who were overseas. Circulation: 3,000 (1955).

Kenya Guardian. 1944? Nairobi. Electors' Union, P. O. Box 1975. Monthly.

Kenya ni yetu (Kenya is ours). 1952. Kiswahili. Weekly. Proscribed in 1952 under Emergency laws.

Kenya Observer. 1923-1925? Nairobi. Printed by Swift Press. "Succeeded the Leader as the leading settler paper" (Scotton, 1971, p.111).

Kenya Star. 1948?-1950. Gikuyu. Fortnightly. Editor: Samson Kamau.

Kenya Weekly News. 1928-1969. Nakuru. [later renamed: *Weekly News*]. Founder and editor: jack Couldrey. "An outspoken settler newspaper; it gradually lost its leadership and advertising with changes in the White Highlands after independence" (Kaplan, 1976).

Kenya Worker. 1936. Monthly. Punjabi. Urdu. Nairobi. Kenya Labour trade Union. Editor: Makhan Singh, Mota Singh. Planned to publish in English, Gujarati and Kiswahili, but superseded by *East African Kirti.*

Kihoto. 1952-1957. Weekly. Gikuyu. Kenya Vernacular Press. Circulation in 1954: 1,500. One of a range of nationality language papers started by the colonial administration after suppressing progressive Kenyan papers following the declaration of Emergency in 1952. Others included *Mulina* (Kiluhya); *Ngao* (Kiswahili); *Omwoya Khomuluhya* (Kiluhya); *Ramogi* (Dholuo); *Thome* (Kikamba).[332]

Kikuyu News. 1908-1951. Monthly. English. Journal of the Church of Scotland Mission at Kikuyu. Printed in Scotland. Copies available at ASt. Andrew's Presbyterian Church, Nairobi.

Kilio cha Mwanyi Kazi (Workers' Cry). 1952. Kiswahili. Weekly. Editor: Bildad Kaggia.

Kimuri (The Torch). 1952-53. Nairobi. Gikuyu. Monthly. Published by Mukuria Karaba; printed by the English Press (banned: 3-1-1953, K.C.G.N. No. 20).

Kirinyaga. 1960. Nairobi. Gikuyu. Weekly. J.G. Kiano.

Kirokerwa. 1952. Gikuyu. Weekly.

◆ L ◆

The Leader. ?-1949.

Leader of British Africa, Uganda and the Lakes [name changed to *Leader of British East Africa*]. 1908-1922. Weekly up to 1910; daily from 1911. Started by the Caxton Printing and Publishing Company;

editor: Alexander Davis. Identified closely with the settler cause.

Lenga Juu. 1911-? Mombasa. Kiswahili. Church Missionary Society.

Luo Magazine. 1937. Dholuo. Editor: H.M. Owiti. Printed by Colonial Times Printing Press.

◆ M ◆

Macho ya Mfanyi Kazi (Workers' Eyes). 1952. Kiswahili. Weekly.

Maendeleo. 1947. Monthlly. Nairobi. Published by the *East African Standard*.

Mfanyi Kazi. 1956-. Nairobi. Weekly/monthly. Kiswahili, English. Kenya Federation of Labour.

Malindi Observer. 1902-1903. Malindi. Monthly, cyclostyled.

Manyani Times. Early 1950s. Oral newspaper developed by freedom fighters Manyani Detention Centre.

Matai. ?-1960? Bimonthly, Kikamba. Colonial Govrnment Printer. Circulation in 1960: 7,500.

Matemo. ?-1960? Fortnightly. Gikuyu. Colonial Government Printer. Circulation in 1960: 10,000.

Matrubhoomi (Motherland). Nairobi. Weekly.

Mau Mau High Command. 1952-57. Underground paper of the Mau Mau High Command.

Mauvoo ma Kitui. 1947-1952. Monthly. Kikamba.

Mirembe. Maragoli, Nyanza. Bi-monthly. Luhya. Other editions published in Kisii (*Amasoga*), Kalenjin (*Chamge*), Luhya (*Miremba*) and Dholuo (*Misawa*).

Misawa. Bi-monthly. Dholuo. Other editions published in Kisii (*Amasoga*), Kalenjin (*Chamge*),

and Luhya (*Miremba*).

Mombasa Diocesan Magazine. 1903-1915. Quarterly. Church Missionary Society. Printed by the Freretown Mission Press.

Mombasa Samachar (Mombasa News). 1913. Gujarati.

Mombasa Times. 1910-1965. Mombasa, daily.

Mothaereri. 195? Nyeri. Gikuyu. Monthly

Mshale. 1953?-1954. Published, edited and cyclostyled by M. E. Njeru (banned: 11-1-1954, K.C.G.N. No.103).

Mucemanio. 1948. The colonial government tried publishing its own nationality language papers to give is views to the people. The intention was to start 4 such newspapers, one each in Gikuyu, Kiswahili, Kikamba and Luhya. But only the Gikuyu one was started (*Mucemanio*) and lasted 5 months in 1948. (Kaggia, 1975, p. 85); Corfield, 1960, p.173).

Muei wa Mukamba. 1946-1948. Machakos, monthly. Kikamba. Machakos District Office.

Mugambo wa Agikuyu. 195? Nairobi. Gikuyu. Editor: J.M. Kariuki.

Mugambo wa Muembu (The Embu Voice). 1952. Kiembu. Weekly. Cyclostyled and published by G. M. Muiti; Editor: G. Mbiti. Banned: 2-12-1952, K.C.G.N. No. 1343.

Mugambo wa Ruguru (Voice of the North). 1952. Gikuyu. Bi-weekly.

Mukamba. 1945. Kikamba. Monthly.

Mukamba. 1952. Kikamba. Weekly.

Mukoma Times. Early 1950s. Oral newspaper developed by freedom fighters at Lodwar Detention Centre.

Mulina. 1952. Kiluhya. Kenya Vernacular Press. One of a range of nationality language papers started by the colonial administration after suppressing progressive Kenyan papers following the declaration of Emergency in 1952. Others included *Kihoto* (Gikuyu); *Ngao* (Kiswahili); *Omwoya Khomuluhya* (Kiluhya); *Ramogi* (Dholuo); *Thome* (Kikamba).

Mulina wa Vosi (The friend). 1948-55. Nairobi. Kiluhya. Monthly.

Mumenyereri (The Guardian). 1945-52. Nairobi. Gikuyu. Weekly. Published by Kenya African Union. Editor: Henry Mworia; printed by Colonial Printing Press; Luo Thrift and trading Cooperation; Mumenyeri Printing Press (banned: 24-10-1952, K.C.G.N. No. 1196 and 2-12-1952, K.C.G.N. No. 1543). Circulation by 1950: 10,000 copies per week.

Muramati (The Caretaker). 1950-52. Gikuyu. Weekly. Cyclostyled and published by W. K. Kihara. Banned: 24-10-1952, K.C.G.N. No.1196, and 2-12-1953, K.C.G.N. No. 11343. Kihara charged with publishing a "seditious" article on 6 September, 1952.

Mutai (Adviser). 1946. Kikamba. Fortnightly.

Mutai wa Mukamba (The Wakamba Adviser). 1952. Kikamba. Weekly.

Muthamaki (The Leader). 1950-52. Gikuyu. Weekly. Edited by Victor Wokabi (banned: 24-10-1952, K.C.G.N. No. 1196, and 2-12-1952, K.C.G.N. No. 1343). Superseded *Hindi ya Gikuyu*.

Mutongoria (The Leader). 1952. Gikuyu. Bi-weekly. Editor: Amon Gakanga. Superseded *Inoro ria Gikuyu*. Banned in 1952, Amon was arrested.

Mwalimu (The Teacher). 1945-47. Monthly/weekly. Kiswahili, English. Founded and edited by Francis Khamisi. Sponsored by the *Colonial Times*. Banned in 1952.

Mwaraniria [*Dunia*](Advisor). 1946-52. Gikuyu; Kiswahili. Published by M. Koigi, printed by Zenith Printing Works; also cyclostyled by M. Koigi at Kiburi House (banned: 24-10-1952, K.C.G.N. No. 1196); on 2-12-1952, K.C.G.N. No. 1343; and again on 15-1-1953, K.C.G.N. No. 133). Continued as *Barua*.

Mwendwoniiri (The Leader). 1952. Gikuyu. Bi-weekly.

Mwenyeji. 19?-1952. Nairobi. Editor: K.N. Gichoya. Banned on 13 May, 1953.

Mwiathia. Kikamba. Printed by Ramogi Press.

Mwigwithania [*Muigwithania wa andu na bururi wa Gikuyu*] 1927-34; 19?1945. Nairobi. Gikuyu. Irregular. Published by the Kikuyu Central Association. Editor: Jomo Kenyatta; Josaphat M. Kamau (1931). Printed by Pioneer Printing Press, River Road, Nairobi. Banned in 1945.

◆ N ◆

Nairobi News: the planters' paper. February - May 1905. Weekly (4 pages). First issue edited by W.H.Tiller, others by S.E.J. Howarth and Wilson McLellan.

Nairobi Star. 1906-1907. Nairobi. Editor: Ernst Low.

National Guardian. 1959-. Editors: Roderigues and Inde Desai who left *Daily Chronicle* when it changed policy and became conservative on changing ownership. Radical. Circulation in 1963: 3,000.

Ndimugenzi (Pilgrim). 1946. Kikamba. Fortnightly.

New Comment. 1956-1957. Nairobi. Weekly. Organ of Federal Independence Party, printed by Sun Publications, P.O.Box 150, Caxton House, Nairobi. Superceded the *Comment*; superseded by *Independent Comment*. [the African section of the

University of Nairobi Library has some issues for 1957].

New Kenya. 1958-63? Cairo. Kenya African National Union.

Ngacheti ya Wonjoria (The Trader's Magazine). 1946-48. Gikuyu. Quarterly.

Ngao (the Shield). 1952-1957. Kiswahili. Monthly. Kenya Vernacular Press. Circulation in 1954: 2,500. One of a range of nationality language papers started by the colonial administration after suppressing progressive Kenyan papers following the declaration of Emergency in 1952. Others included *Kihoto* (Gikuyu) *Mulina* (Kiluhya); *Omwoya Khomuluhya* (Kiluhya); *Ramogi* (Dholuo); *Thome* (Kikamba).

Njoki a-Gwitu (Return to origins). 1952-52. Nairobi. Gikuyu. Monthly. Published by Mbugua Book Writers, printed by the Tribune Press (banned: 3-1-1953, K.C.G.N. No. 20).

Nuru (Light). Nairobi. Kiswahili. Weekly. United Africa Press. Editor: Joram Wanjala.

Nyanza Times. 1946-. Kisumu. English; Dholuo. weekly/monthly. Started by Orinda Okun and james Omogo. Nyanza Publishers. Editor: Achieng Oneko.

Nyota ya Haki (Star of truth). 1960. Nairobi. Weekly. Kenya African Democratic Union.

Nyota ya Kenya: Cyclostyled and published by S. M. Waithaka (banned: 11-1-1954, K.C.G.N. No. 103).

Nyota ya Kirinyaga (Star of Kirinyaga). 1949; 1951. Gikuyu. Monthly. Editor: Joshua Maina.

♦ O ♦

Observer. 1923-28. Nairobi. Weekly. English, Urdu and Gujarati.Editor: I.M. Paracha. "Welcomed constitutional change and insisted upon the need for gurantees for minorities" (Carter).[333]

Omuluyia. 1945-47. Kiluhya. Monthly. Established and edited by W.W.W. Awori. Incorporated into *Radio Posta* in 1947.

Omwemeli Wabaluhya (The Baluhya Pilot). 1952. Kiluhya. Weekly.

Omwoyo kho Mluhya. 1952. Kiluhya. Kenya Vernacular Press. One of a range of nationality language papers started by the colonial administration after suppressing progressive Kenyan papers following the declaration of Emergency in 1952. Others included *Kihoto* (Gikuyu) *Mulina* (Kiluhya); *Ngao* (Kiswahili); *Ramogi* (Dholuo); *Thome* (Kikamba).

Ostafrika warte. 1938. Nairobi. Supported Nazism.

Outlaw. 1920s. Mombasa? Editors: Rene Stevenson and J.K.Robertson. Superseded by *Kenya Critic.* See: Zwannenberg (1971).

♦ P ♦

Pamoja. 1956-? Nairobi, illustrated monthly. Kiswahili. Ministry of Information. 18,000 copies were printed but went unread as the readers rejected colonial newspapers and preferred Kenyan publications. (Kaggia, 1975, p.85).

Pan Africa. 1963-67? Nairobi. Pan Africa Press, P.O. Box 8064. Fortnightly. Editor: Pio Gama Pinto. Saw the struggle for liberation in Kenya in the wider anti-imperialist struggle.

Picha (Picture). 1947. Kiswahili. Fortnightly.

Piny Owacho. Dholuo. People's Convention Party. Editor: Tom Mboya.

The Pioneer. 1908-1912. Nairobi. Weekly. (Huff, 1968, gives the years 1910-1912).

Plateau News: the voice of the settler on the Usin Gishu and Trans Nzoia. 1919. Eldoret.

◆ R ◆

Radi. 1960-63. Editor: A. Kodhek.

Radio Posta. 1947-49?. Kiswahili. Weekly, then daily. Established and edited by W.W.Awori. Printed by Luo Thrift and Trading Corporation. Circulation: 10,000 copies. Incorporated *Omuluyia.*

Ramogi (The Ancestor). 1945-62. Nairobi. Dholuo. Fortnightly, weekly. Founded by W.W.W. Awori, edited by Achieng' Oneko (1945-48). Luo Thrift and Trading Corporation. Printed by Caxton Press. Circulation in 1950: 10,000 copies weekly.
Later acquired by the Kenya Vernacular Press as one of a range of nationality language papers published by the colonial administration after suppressing progressive Kenyan papers following the declaration of Emergency in 1952. Others included *Kihoto* (Gikuyu) *Mulina* (Kiluhya); *Ngao* (Kiswahili); *Omwoya Khomuluhya* (Kiluhya); *Thome* (Kikamba).

Rongo ya Ameru (Meru Shield). 1952. Kimeru. Weekly. Editor: Bedan M,Mirito Kairo. Proscribed in 1952 under Emergency laws.

◆ S ◆

Samachar (News) 1909? Nairobi. Weekly. Gujarati."Indians frequently wrote in Samachar to present their grievances" (Scotton)[334]

Saturday Evening Paper. 1945. Gikuyu. Nairobi. Mimeographed weekly newspaper produced by students of Alliance High School. Editor: J.S. Kiano.

Sauti ya KANU. 1959-? Nairobi. Pan Africa Press. Circulation in 1960: 35,000 copies.

Sauti ya Mwafrika (*The African Voice*). 1945-49; 1951-52. Kiswahili, English. Weekly. Published by Kenya African Study Union. Editor: Fred Kubai; J.D.Kali (1952). Printed by Mumenyereri Printing Press (banned: 24-20-1952, K.C.G.N. No. 1106 and 2-12-1952, K.C.G.N. No. 1342). Editors at different times: Francis Khamisi, Tom Mbotela, W.W.W. Awori. It reflected the policies of the moderate KAU leadership.

Sekanyola [a large bird capabe of seeing a great distance]. 1920-? Nairobi. Luganda, Kiswahili, with English supplements. First editor: S.K. Sentongo. Printed by the Swift Press. Published by a group of Ugandan printers in Nairobi to support Uganda's anti-colonial struggle. Read in Kenya as well. "It criticised British colonial chiefs, their sons and heirs their land and power, merchants, mission education and even missionaries themselves". (Scotton, 1971, p. 6, 101).`

Star of East Africa. 1906-1908.

Sunday Post. 1935. weekly. Founder & Editor: Jack Rathbone. Right-wing settler paper.

◆ T ◆

Tarumbeta. (The Trumpet). 1952. Kiswahili. Monthly.

Taveta Chronicle. "The only paper in the British East African Protectorate". 1895-1901. Taveta, quarterly. Printed by Taveta Mission Press. Editor: Rev. Albert R. Steggal. *The Chronicle* contained information regarding mission stations and missionary activities in Kenya and also published articles on the history and social life of the people around the area. It sometimes contained some material in local African languages" - (Ndegwa, 1973, p.4).

Thayu wa Nduriri (National Peace). 1952-59. Gikuyu. Bi-weekly.

Thome. 1952-57. Kikamba. Kenya Vernacular Press. One of a range of nationality language papers started by the colonial administration after suppressing progressive Kenyan papers following the declaration of Emergency in 1952. Others included *Kihoto* (Gikuyu) *Mulina* (Kiluhya); *Ngao* (Kiswahili); *Omwoya Khomuluhya* (Kiluhya); *Ramogi* (Dholuo).

Times of East Africa. 1905-1907. Nairobi. Weekly. Founded by F. Watkins. Editors: Ernest Low and D.S. Garvie. "A settler paper, said to have the support of Lord Delamere, one of the leading European farmers in the Protectorate" (Ndegwa, n.d.; Scotton, 1971).

Trans Nzoia Post. 1930-1956. Kitale. Weekly. Publisher: Abdullah Mohammed, Nzoia Press. Circulation in 1956: 1,500 copies.[335]

Tribune. 1951-52. D. K. Sharda. Banned in 1952. (see Index).

◆ U ◆

Uhuru. 1959. Published by Nairobi People's Convention Party. Editor: E. Omolo Agar. Banned in 1959.

Uhuru wa Mwafrika. 19? - 1952. Published by Paul Ngai, printed by Acme Printing Press (banned: 24-10-1952, K.C.G.N. No. 1196 and 2-12-1952, K.C.G.N. No. 1343).

Urutagwo Mwiruti (Unity). 1952. Gikuyu. Weekly.

Utheri wa Kenya (the Torch of Kenya). 1952. Gikuyu. Bi-weekly.

Uzwod. Nairobi. Weekly. Konkni. Editor: Pio Gama Pinto.

◆ W ◆

Wahindi. Mombasa?/Dar es Salaam. Founded by Chatrabhy Bhat. Bhat was deported by the Sultan of Zanzibar. He went to Dar es Salaam and started publishing *Wahindi* from there.

Waigua Atia (What is the News?). 1952. Gikuyu. Monthly. Editor: Gakaara Wanjau. Published by Gakaara Book Services. Proscribed in 1952 under Emergency laws. At the time of Wanjau's detention in October, 1952, the circulation of the paper was 12,000, sold at 50 cents each.

Wasya wa Mukamba (The Voice of the Wakamba). 1951-52. Kikamba. Weekly. Cyclostyled and published by Paul Ngai (banned: 24-10-1952, K.C.G.N. No.196 and 2-12-1952, K.C.G.N. No. 1343).

Waya Times. Early 1950s. Oral newspaper developed by freedom fighters at Manyani Detention Centre.

Wathioma Mokinyu. 1915- 1983? Nyeri. Gikuyu. Consolata Catholic Mission Press.

Wendo (Unity). 1952. Gikuyu. Weekly.

Wihuge (Be Alert). 1952-53. Gikuyu. Bi-weekly. Editors: Isaac Gathanju and Kimani. Published by N. E. K. Kaman, printed by the Tribune Press (banned: 3-1-1953, K.C.G.N. No. 20).

Wiyathi (Independence). 1952. Gikuyu. bi-weekly. Editor: Chege Kabogoro. Nairobi (Kiburi House). Published by J. K. Cege, printed by the Tribune Press (banned: 2-12-1952, K.C.G N. No. 1343).

◆ Y ◆

Yetu. 1958. Nairobi. Kiswahili.

◻ PUBLISHERS ◻

Africa Press, P. O. Box 6059, Nairobi.
• *Afrika Mpya*

African Pamphleteers, Karatina.
• Has war brought equality and liberty (banned 2 May, 1954)

Cege, J. K.
- *Wiyathi*

Gakaara Book Services, P. O. Box 3632, Nairobi (and Karatina).
- Niikarire ya thikwota
- Mbere ndiremange ta thutha
- Uria tungiuma ukombo-ini
- Mwari mwru ni magambo wa kuona uteaga wa mwene
- Ihiu ni riau (parts 1-3)
- Wirute wonjoria
- Marebeta ikumi ma wendo
- Kienyu kia Ngai
- Wiathi wa Andu Airu
- Nyimbo cia *Gikuyu na Mumbi*
- Nyimbo cia kwarahura Ruiriri
- Witikio wa *Gikuyu na Mumbi*
- Kirira kia Ugikuyu
- Kenya buriri wa ngui
- Riua ritanathua kirima ngagua
- Kenya ni yakwa
- Ngwenda unjurage
- Rua ngoro mwari wa riua
- Mahoya ma *Gikuyu na Mumbi*
- Nyimbo cia ciama cia *Gikuyu na Mumbi*

Gikuyu Literature Service, P. O. Box 2122, Nairobi
- Mahoya ma *Gikuyu na Mumbi* (printed by Acme Printing Press/Punjab Printing Press).

Mbugua, Paul Evans Rua Ngoro (Regal Press / Reliance Press). Mworia, Henry
- *Mumenyereri*
- Kenyatta ni muigwithania witu (Flash Printing Works).
- Nyina witu ni tiri ithe witu ni nugi (Flash Printing Works).
- Ithe witu ni uugi (Flash Printing Works).
- Kenya Bururu wa Ngoe (Mumenyereri Printing Press)
- Ngoro ya Ugikuyu (Colonial Printing Works)

Kaggia, B.
- *Inoro ria Gikuyu*

Kahara, K.

Muramati

Kairo, B. M.

Rong'o ya Ameru.

Kaman, N. E. K. (P.O.Box 3343, Nairobi)
- *Wihuge*

Muciri, Katitwe wa Mathani ma *Gikuyu na Mumbi*. Acme Printing Press.

Kenya African Union
- *Sauti ya Mwafrika*
- Ithaka ciari Ciitu

Mugia, Kinuthia

Nyimbo cia kwarahura Agikuyu. Regal Press.

Koigi, M.

Mwaraniria

Kuria, E. N.

Wirute wonjoria. (Regal Press)

Mbugua Book Writers, P.O.Box 3632, Nairobi
- *Njokia-gwitu*
- Mathani ma *Gikuyu na Mumbi*
- Rua ngoro mwari wa riua
- Mahoya ma Waiyaki
- Uria tungumia ukombo-ini
- Mukuria Karaba, P.O.Box 3632, Nairobi
- *Kimuri*

Murage, Viktor
- *Muthamaki*

Ngei, Paul
- *Uhuru wa Mwafrika*
- *Wasya wa Mukamba*

Punjab Press
- Nyimbo cia Mutuku Maya

Tahetu, M. N.
- Kirira kia Ugikuyu (Printed by Colonial Printing Works)

U-Muchii Publications
- Marebeta Ikumi ma Wendo

Waithaka, S. M.
- *Nyota ya Kenya*

Wokabi, V. M. J.
- *Gikuyu na Mumbi* (Printed by Tribune Press)
- *Gikuyu na Mumbi* (Cyclostyled by V. M. J. Wokabi)

◻ **INFORMATION ACTIVISTS** ◻

Information activists who suffered colonial suppression, deportation, jailing and harassment and death:

Acharia, Sitaram
Ahmed, Haroon
Amer Singh
Basant Kaur
Bhatt, Chatrabh
Desai, M. A.
Dwivedi, Keshavlal
Ghadar Martyrs - three patriots sentenced to death
Gakanga, Amon
Kamau, K. C.
Murage, Victor
Patel, V. G.
Puri, Merchand
Ram, Tirath
Rawal, G. D.
Ruhinda, Francis
Ruhinda, Stephen
Savle, L. M.
Singh, Gopal
Sohan, W. L.
Temal Singh

◻ **KENYAN NEWSPAPERS** ◻

AVAILABLE IN THE BRITISH LIBRARY

Kenyan newspapers available in the British Library

British Library
Newspapers
Colindale Avenue, London
NW9 5HE

Date ranges show the earliest and latest copies held, but this does not necessarily mean that we hold all intervening copies.

Advertiser of East Africa (The)
Nairobi; Kenya
1908-1910

African Standard (The)
Nairobi; Kenya
1903-1905

Baraza
Nairobi; Kenya
1946-1973

Daily Chronicle
Nairobi; Kenya
1956-1962

Daily Nation
Nairobi; Kenya
1961 to date

East Africa and Uganda Mail
Mombasa; Kenya
1903-1904

East African Chronicle (The)
Nairobi; Kenya
1920-1920

East African Monthly Trade Journal and Commercial Record (The)
Mombasa; Kenya
1906-1906

East African Standard

Nairobi; Kenya
1995-1996

East African Standard (The)
Nairobi; Kenya
1905-1974

East African Weekly
Nairobi; Kenya
1931-1932

East African Weekly Times
Nairobi; Kenya
1932-1934

Farmers' Journal (The)
Nairobi; Kenya
1919-1922

Globe Trotter (The)
Nairobi; Kenya
1906-1908

Goan Voice (The)
Nairobi; Kenya
1958-1958

Indian Voice of British East Africa, Uganda and Zanzibar (The)
Nairobi; Kenya
1911-1913

Jicho
Nairobi; Kenya
1954-1958

Kenya Magazine (The)
Eldoret; Kenya
1948-1949

Kenya Weekly News
Nakuru; Kenya
1952-1967

Kenya Weekly News
Industrial supplement
Nakuru; Kenya
1954-1954

Leader of British East Africa (The)
Nairobi; Kenya
1908-1922

Newland, Tarlton's Monthly
(N.T.'s Monthly)
Nairobi; Kenya
1915-1919

Pioneer (The)
The British East Africa & Uganda news, etc
Nairobi; Kenya
1908-1908

Plateau News (The)
The voice of the settler on the Uasin Gishu and Trans Nzoia
Eldoret; Kenya
1919-1919

Polak w Afryce
Dwutygodnik poswiecony sprawom uchodzctwa polskiego w Afryce. Wydawany przez delegature Min. P.& O.S. w Nairobi
Nairobi; Kenya
1943-1944

Radio Times of Kenya
Nairobi; Kenya
1960-1962

Sikio
The staff newspaper of E.A.R
Nairobi; Kenya
1973-1973

Standard (The)
Nairobi; Kenya
1974-1995

Star of East Africa (The)

Nairobi; Kenya
1906-1908

Sunday Nation
Nairobi; Kenya
1967-1980

Times of East Africa (The)
Nairobi; Kenya
1905-1907

Times of East Africa (The)
Nairobi; Kenya
1930-1932
Uasin Gishu Herald
Eldoret; Kenya
1919-1920

Uasin Gishu Weekly Advertiser (The)
Eldoret; Kenya
1928-1938

Weekly Review (The)
Nairobi; Kenya
1975-1979

APPENDIX B
Banned imports. A Selected List

A. NEWSPAPERS AND MAGAZINES

African and Colonial World published by Independent Publishing Co., London. (banned: 6.11.1953).

Africa Bulletin

Awakening in Africa published by India Information Service, New Delhi. (banned: 12.2.1954).

Al Falaq (weekly) Arab Association of Zanzibar. (banned: 12.2.1954).

Contemporary Issues. (banned: 16.6.1954).

Freedom published by Freedom Associates, c/o Council on African Affairs, New York. (banned: 14.8.1953; past, present and future issues banned: 6.10.1953).

Socialist Asia-Monthly Organ of the Asian Socialist Conference. (banned: 1.10.1954).

Spotlight on Africa published by Council on African Affairs, New York. (banned: June, 1953 and 6.10.53).

B. BOOKS

Anand, Mulk Raj: The Story of India. Kutub Publishers. Bombay. (banned: 9.10.1953).

Forum. Popular Press. Bombay. (banned: 11.9.1953)

Kenya Report, 1953. London. (banned: 29.1.1954).

Kenya Under the Iron Heel. Contemporary Press, London. (banned: 19.5.1953).

Koinange, Mbiyu (1955): People of Kenya Speak for Themselves. (banned: 15.3.55).

The Mask is off. Africa Bulletin. (banned: 1.12.1954).

Pankhurst, Richard K.: Kenya; History of Two Nations. (banned: 15.7.1954).

Rawcliffe, D. H.: The Struggle for Kenya. (banned: 15.4.1954).

Stop the Slaughter in Kenya. (banned: 18.9.1954).

Slater, Montague: The trial of Jomo Kenyatta. (banned: 13.6.1955).

C. GRAMOPHONE RECORDS AND FILMS

These were mostly progressive, anti-colonial songs recorded by Kenyan artists inside and outside Kenya. The banning orders covered either importation or sale of locally-produced ones. This reveals the extensive international connections that the freedom movement had with colleagues in different countries, including India and Britain. Some examples of import bans:[336]

En Ang'o ma ni e Chunyi Piny (What is in the Middle of the World) on both sides. (Record No. S.R. 140, National Gramophone Record Manufacturing Co., Bombay. (banned: 17.7.1954, Government Notice 1071).

Gikuyu Mutigeiokie/Ndire. E.A. 197, East African Records. (banned: 11.12.1954).

Iiro Kaiyaba/ Jaki ya Kabete. E.A. 225, East African Records (banned: 27.9.1954).

Iruwa. EA 194, East African Records (banned: 11.12.1954).

Jomo Kinyatta/Niui Ma (Do you know the truth). East African Records Company, Nairobi. Record No. EA. 195 (banned: 17.7.1954, Government Notice No. 1071).

Kabuku/Mugo. E.A. 334, East African Records. (banned: 27.9.1954).

Kiambiriria/Mawenge, E.A. 337, East African Records. (banned: 27.9.1954).

Kikuyu mutigecokie/Ndire

Kisongori/Nyeri. Record No. E.A. 342, East African Records Company, Nairobi. (Banned 17.7.1954, Government Notice No. 1071).

Koinange, Peter *Pitakaunange and Gachunge* (Gikuyu). Published by Columbia Gramaphone Co., London (Banned: 15-9-1954).

Machakos/Kitui Koloes. E.A. 238, East African Records. Banned 27-9-1954.

Mbiyu Maur wa Koingage/Ninyonio Gikeno. E.A. 375, East African Records. Banned 11-12-1954.

Mtoto/Mukiongoci E.A. 237, East African Records. Banned 27-9-1954.

Nilisimama River Road by John Mwale.

Pitakaunange/Gachungi. [Peter wa Koinange] by Wa Gaithani. Record No. E.O. 315, Columbia Gramophone Co., London (banned 15.9.1954, Government Notice No. 1351).

Tigwo na Uhoro/Mwega Murata.

Wanjiru Kahia/Molesi Wambui. E.A. 351, East African Records. Banned 11-12-1954.

Yawuot Omogi (Children of Ramogi) in Dholuo on one side and Nakupenda (Kenya I love you, Kiswahili) on the other. Sung by Omolo-Okero and Akoko Mboya. National Gramophone Record Manufacturing Company, Bombay. Record No. S.R. 138. (banned: 17.7.1954, Government Notice No. 1071).

Tigwo na Uhoro/Mwega Murata. E.A. 401. East African Records. (banned 27-9-1954).

D. FILMS

Among films banned were "West of Zanzibar" (banned: 20-8-54) and "Jhansi ki Rani".

INDEX

♦ A ♦

Acharia, Sitaram 42-3, 62-3, 69
Advertiser 30, 55
Africa Samachar 149-50
African Publications 44, 67, 142
African Standard 35-6
African Times 63
Afrika Mpya 149, 156, 158, 185, 201
Agikuyu, Mau Mau na Wiyathi 210
Agricultural Journal of British East Africa 31
Ahmed, Haroon 64, 141, 145, 147, 150
Akamba 128, 143
Akamba Members Association 113
Amar Singh 64
Amasonga 128
Amershi, Hassanali 75
Anderson, A. G. 36, 55
Anti-Colonial Bureau 118
Apa Pant 183, 231
Askari 61
Awori 65, 71, 143

♦ B ♦

Bangladesh 20
Baraza 57-60, 187
BBC 57, 130, 232
Beauttah, James 23, 53, 72
Bhat, Chatrabh 36
Blitz (Bombay) 117
Blundell, Michael 133-4, 180
Books for Africa 61
British Communist Party 117-8, 324

♦ C ♦

Catholic Fathers of St. Austin's Mission 32
Catholic Times of East Africa 61
Challenge, London 119
Chamge 129
Cheche, Muthee wa 175, 209
Christian Missionary Service 61
Church Missionary Society 32-3, 61
Church of Scotland in East Africa 105
Church Publications 31-2, 60
Citizen 192, 194, 196-7
Coast Guardian 38, 56
Colonial Printing Works 81, 144, 213
Colonial Times 62-3, 65, 72, 76, 141-5, 147, 150-1, 202-3
Comment 136, 224
Communication systems 46, 69, 157, 239

Corfield Report 107, 123, 146fn, 148fn, 186-7fn, 188-9

♦ D ♦

Daily Chronicle 64-5, 139, 141-2, 144-8, 150-1, 179-83, 202-4
Daily Worker, London 103, 105fn, 119, 223fn, 226-7
Dar es Salaam 36, 80, 88
de Souza, A. C. L. 64, 76
Declaration of War in Kenya 174
Democrat, The 42, 62-3, 69
Desai, Inde 150
Desai, Manilal 34, 36-8, 49, 63, 66, 208
Dholuo 70-1, 107, 128-9, 207
Dini ya Kaggia 113
Dini ya Mariam 113
Dini ya Msambwa 113, 183, 189
Dini ya Mumbo 113
Dunia (See under *Habari*)
Durrani, Nazmi 218fn
Dwivedi, Keshavlal 43

♦ E ♦

East Africa and Rhodesia 218
East African Association 37fn, 45, 47-8, 51, 68
East African Chronicle 34, 36-8, 49, 146
East African Indian National Congress 36, 145, 212
East African Kirti 82
East African Natural History Society and National Museum. *Journal* 30
East African Quarterly 30
East African Standard 30, 55-6, 58-60, 121, 123fn, 127, 137, 139, 147fn, 180, 187, 202, 232
East African Trade Union Congress 59, 145, 147, 178, 180-1, 201, 212
East African Weekly 55
Electors' Union 130-4
Emergency (Amendment) (No.10) 10, 116
Regulations, 1953 149
Emergency Regulations, 1952 114-6, 122
English-Kikuyu vocabulary 33

♦ F ♦

Fairplay 64, 76
Fascism Has Come to Kenya 215-6
For a Pan African Trade Union 118
Fort Ternan Times 30
Forward 148

♦ G ♦

Gakaara Book Service 175, 209-10, 213
Gathanju, Isaac 199, 201
General Strike, 1922 48, 51, 53, 153
General Strike, Mombasa, 1947 70, 83, 147
Ghadar 38-41, 43-4
Ghadar di Goonj 41-2
Ghadar Press 40
Gikuyu na Mumbi 49, 158, 185, 209
Giriama 23, 26, 44
Githii, George 211
Globe-Trotter 30
Goan Voice 64
Grammar of the Kikuyu language 33
Guardian, The (Cape Town) 117

♦ H ♦

Habari 65, 143-4
Habari za Dunia 62, 64, 188
Handbills 77-9, 81, 109, 157, 178, 206, 210, 212-3, 215, 217
Hardayal, Lala 40, 42, 44
Heinemann, Margo 223
Hindi ya Agikuyu 49
Hindi ya Gikuyu 64
Hindustan Ghadar Party 40
Homeguard 109, 114, 189, 211

♦ I ♦

Ilomon le Maasai 128
Indian Employees Association 75
Indian Trade Union 75
Indian Voice 38
Indian Voice of British East Africa, Uganda and Zanzibar 38
Inooro ria Gikuyu 49, 200-1
International League for the Rights of Men 105
International Press Institute 101

• J •

Jaluo 128
Jambo 61
Jeevanjee, A. M. 35-6, 55, 66
Jhansi ki Rani 108
Jicho 143-4

• K •

Kabetu, Matthew Njoroge 32
Kadhi, Joe 211
Kaggia, Bildad 49, 58-9, 113, 149, 158, 185, 199, 200-1, 203, 212
Kali, J. D. 70, 203-4
Kamau, K. C. 64
Kamuingi koyaga Ndiri 210
Kariuki, J.M. 175
Kaur, Basant 64
Kavirondo Association 45, 47, 68-9, 100
Kenda Kenda 219
Kenya African Civil Servants Association 75
Kenya African Study Union 68, 82
Kenya African Union 45, 62, 68, 70, 82, 100, 142, 145, 151, 156, 159, 212, 226
Kenya Church News 61
Kenya Church Review 61
Kenya Committee 113, 118, 121-2, 124-5, 129, 130fn, 132-4fn, 164-6, 176, 198, 216fn, 223, 224-5, 227-8, 232
Kenya Critic 56
Kenya Daily Mail 63, 141-2, 149
Kenya Empire Party 130, 134
Kenya Independent Schools 113
Kenya Indian Labour Trade Union 75
Kenya ni Yakwa 210
Kenya Notes and News 55
Kenya Parliament 188, 196-7, 223
Kenya Terror, The 223
Kenya Uganda Railway 23
Kenya Vernacular Press 127
Kenya Weekly News 55, 126fn, 130, 133fn, 138, 170fn, 180, 222
Kenya Worker 81-2
Kenya. Agriculture Department. Bulletin 31
Kenya. Agriculture Department. Leaflet 31
Kenya. Agriculture Department Meteorological Records - Reports 31
Kenyatta, Jomo 15, 37, 49, 65, 69-70, 165, 203, 205, 208-9, 212-3, 234
Khamisi, Francis 57-8, 62, 70-1
Kiambu 83, 215
Kibachia, Chege 60, 70, 83, 100, 182
Kiburi House 155-6, 182, 201
Kienyu kia Ngai na Ithaka 210
Kihoto 127
Kijabe 83
Kikuyu Association 32, 45, 47
Kikuyu Central Association 37, 45, 49

62, 69, 99, 113, 143
Kikuyu News 32
Kimaathi Dedan 174-5, 188, 192, 196-7, 210, 214, 223, 225, 235
Kimaathi Charter 111, 191-2, 194, 197
Kimani, S. R. 150, 201
Kingsway Press, Ltd 132
Kinyatti, Maina wa 23fn, 53fn, 98, 114, 122, 125fn, 136, 137fn, 148, 158fn, 160, 165fn, 173, 174, 175fn, 199, 205fn, 211fn, 215, 230, 231
Kipande 37fn, 45-6, 92, 148, 220
Kipsigis Central Association 69
Kirira kia Ugikuyu 32, 213
Kubai, Fred 70, 158, 179-82, 199, 202

• L •

Labour Monthly (London) 117
Labour Trade Union of East Africa 76fn, 80, 82, 200, 212, 214
Labour Trade Union of Kenya 75-7, 80, 211
Leader of British East Africa 37-8, 47-9, 55-6
Leader of British East Africa and Uganda Mail 30
Lemeitre, Chris 223
Lenga Juu 32
Limuru, British East Africa Brightest Gem in British Empire 30
Luo Magazine 70, 144
Luo Thrift and Trading Corporation 68, 71, 142
Lyttelton Plan 194-6

• M •

Maasai 23
Magerio Noomo Mahota 210
Mathare Valley 107, 154, 158, 160-1, 184, 188, 217
Mathu, Mohamed 175
° 113, 129, 157, 159, 162, 184, 188, 199, 216-7, 220
Mayer, F. 36, 55
Mboya, Tom 136, 145, 151, 205, 208, 212
Mbugua Book Writers 149
Mellor, Lee 71
Miikarire ya Thikwota 210
Mirembe 128
Misawa 129
Moi, Daniel arap 15, 68
Mombasa Diocesan Gazette 33
Mombasa Diocesan Magazine 33
Mombasa Dockworkers' Strike 54
Mombasa Times 35, 55-6, 137-8
Mshauri 128
Mucemanio 50
Muei wa Mukamba 128

Mugia, Kinuthia wa 175
Mugweru, Mwaniki 210
Muiguthania 49
Muigwithania 259
Mulina 128
Mumenyereri 49-50, 62, 65, 70-3, 147-8, 159-60, 177, 211, 213
Murage, Victor 64
Muramati 49, 158
Muranga Umuthi 128
Mutai 128
Muthamaki 49, 158
Muthithu 72
Mutongoria 201
Muyaka bin Haji 92
Mwalimu 58, 62, 70-1, 147
Mwandiki wa Mau Mau Ithamirio-ini 210
Mwaraniria 49, 71
Mwathanire wa Agikuyu comba utanoka 210
Mwathe Meeting 192
Mworia, Henry 49, 62, 71-4, 147, 160, 113

• N •

Nairobi Advertiser 55
Nairobi News Planter's Paper 30
Nairobi Star 70
Nandi 23, 29
Ndia Kuu Press 61
New Africa (New York) 117
Newspapers & Books Act (1906) 112
Ngao 127
Njokia-Gwitu 149
North Kavirondo Central Association 45, 68-9, 100
Nyanza Times 70-1, 128, 159, 204
Nyimbo cia Gikuyu na Mumbi 209
Nyota ya Kirinyaga 191

• O •

Observer (Malindi) 30
Odinga, Oginga 65, 71-2, 121, 142, 151fn, 187-8, 192, 203, 207-8
Off Parade 61
Omwoya Khomuluhya 127
Oneko, Achieng 62, 71, 128, 170, 203
Orature 18, 90, 175
Our Mother the Soil. Knowledge our Father 73

• P •

Pakistan 20
Pandya, J. B. 63, 149
Parklands 107
Patel, A. Z. 63
Patel, A.B. 145-6
Patel, Ambu 40, 107, 199, 206-9, 212,

218, 234
Patel, Hirabhai 150
Patel, V.G. 49, 64, 73
Patel, Zarina 30, 35, 36, 38fn
People's Age 117fn
Pereira, Eddie 151-2
Phenomenal Rise of the Rat 30
Pinto, Pio Gama 39, 66, 142, 145-6, 148, 170, 199, 201-8, 211, 231
Piny Owach 47
Plateau News 30
Printing presses 31-2, 38, 46, 61, 69, 71-2, 74, 104, 112-3, 161, 177, 210, 213, 217
Puri, Mehrchand 35

• R •

Rafiki Yetu 61
Railway African Staff Association 75
Railway Artisan Union 75
Ram, Tirath 35
Ramogi 71, 128, 144, 170
Regal Printers 49
Reveille 30
Robertson, J. K. 56-7
Rodwell, Edward 137-9
Roho ya Kiume na Bidii kwa Mwafrika 210-11
Ruhenda, Stephen 64
Ruth Mworia 72-3

• S •

Sauti ya Kanu 203, 211
Sauti ya Mwafrika 49-50, 62, 65, 70, 84, 148, 158, 201, 203-4
Sauti ya Pwani 128
Savle, L.M. 43
Settler Publications 29-30, 55, 129, 224
Shah, R. M. 76
Sheth, Pranlal 65, 145

Siku Hizi 128
Simba 129
Singh, Amar 64
Singh, Chanan 38, 63, 145, 148
Singh, Makhan 20, 35fn, 39, 45fn, 46, 47fn, 48, 51, 66, 70fn, 75, 76fn, 78-9, 80fn, 81-3, 100, 117fn, 145-6, 147fn, 148, 178, 180-2, 183fn, 189-90, 201, 208, 211-2
Sinn Fein 36
Society for Promoting Christian Knowledge 33
Sohan, W. L. 63
Somali 23, 26
Somali Youth League 68-9
Souza, See de Souza
Squatters 69, 83, 160, 210
Sri Lanka 20
St. Augustine's Mission 32
Standard, The 55, 144
Stegal, Rev. Albert 32
Struggle for Release Jomo And His Colleagues 207

• T •

Taita Hills Association 45, 68-9, 100, 113
Tanganyika 22, 76fn, 79, 124-5
Tangazo 37
Taveta Chronicle 32
Temal Singh 64
Thakur, Narayan Shrinivas 62-3, 69
Thome 127
Thuku, Harry 37-8, 45-6, 48-9, 51, 208
Tiller, W.H. 36
Times of East Africa 30
Trade Union Committee of Mombasa 75-6
Tribune (UK) 111
Tribune (Kenya) 148-9, 200-1, 204
Tungika, atia iiya witu 72
Two Months in India 207

• U •

Ukamba Members Association 45, 68-9, 100

• V •

Vidyarthi, G.L. 49, 62-5, 72, 143-4

• W •

Waigua Atia 49
Waigwa-atia 209, 211
Wakamba 23, 125, 163
Wanjau, Gakaara wa 49, 175, 209
War Council 99, 188, 202
Wathioma Mokinyu 33
We are Everywhere 219-20
Weekly News Review 61
Weekly Review 58
Wihuge 49, 149, 158, 185, 201
Witikio 175, 185, 209-10
Wiyathi 49, 157, 185, 210
Wiyathi wa Andu Airu 210
Workers Federation of British East Africa 75
Workers' Protective Society of Kenya 75
World Federation of Trade Unions 117-8
World News, London 119

• Y •

Yakub, Salim 145
Young Kavirondo Association 47
Young Kikuyu Association 45-7, 68

Vita Books / Mau Mau Research Centre
PUBLICATIONS LIST
2006

Author	Title	ISBN No.	Price
Ngugi wa Thiong'o	*Writing against Neocolonialism* 1986	ISBN: 1 869886 00 3	Out of print *
Shiraz Durrani	*Kimaathi, Mau Mau's First Prime Minister of Kenya* 1986	ISBN: 1 869886 01 1	Out of print *
Maina wa Kinyatti	*Mau Mau: A Revolution Betrayed* 1991		£4.50
Maina wa Kinyatti	*A Season of Blood: Prison Poems* 1995	ISBN: 1 869886 07 0	£6.50
Maina wa Kinyatti	*Kenya: A Prison Notebook* 1996	ISBN: 1 869886 08 9	£12.00
Maina wa Kinyatti	*Mother Kenya: Letters from Prison* 1997	ISBN: 1 869886 09 7	£17.50
	Karimi Nduthu: A life in the struggle 1998	ISBN: 1 869886 12 7	Available in Kenya
Maina wa Kinyatti	*Mau Mau; Revolution Betrayed* 2nd ed. 2000	ISBN: 1 869886 13 5	Available in Kenya
Vita Posters	*Kimaathi / Muthoni / Arms & Struggle*		Out of print *

* Out of print publications will be available in electronic form on Vita Books website when fully established

Vita Books, P.O. Box 2908, London N17 6YY, UK
www.vitabooks.info | Email: books@vitabooks.info

FORTHCOMING (2006)
Maina wa Kinyatti, *History of resistance in Kenya*, 1885-2002, ISBN 1 869886 14 3
Maina wa Kinyatti, *The pen and the gun*

Vita Books/Mau Mau Research Centre
DISTRIBUTED AND REPRESENTED IN EAST AFRICA

Zand Graphics Ltd
P.O. Box 32843 00600, Nairobi. Kenya
Tel: 0722 344900
Email: zand.graphics@gmail.com

MMRC/VITA BOOKS CONTACT IN KENYA
MMRC/Vita Books, P.O. Box 79711, Nairobi, Kenya

Distributed by
Africa Book Centre
and represented by **GBM Distributor** in Europe

Africa Book Centre/Global Book Marketing
38 KING STREET, LONDON WC2E 8JT
TEL +44 20 7836 3020; FAX +44 20 7497 0309
tz@africabookcentre.com; www.africabookcentre.com

DISTRIBUTED AND REPRESENTED IN USA
Mau Mau Research Centre / Vita Books
138-28 107th Avenue, South Richmond Hill Station, Jamaica, NY 11419 USA